Canadian Rockies Whitewater

The Central Rockies

Stuart Smith

Canadian Rockies Whitewater - The Central Rockies.
Copyright © 1996 by Stuart Smith. All rights reserved.

ISBN 0-9699618-1-2

Canadian Cataloguing in Publication Data
Smith, Stuart, 1959-
    Canadian Rockies whitewater
    Includes index.
    Contents: Bk. 1, Southern Rockies -- Bk. 2, Central Rockies.
    ISBN 0-9699618-0-4 (bk. 1) -- ISBN 0-9699618-1-2 (bk. 2)

    1. White-water canoeing--Rocky Mountains, Canadian (B.C.
and Alta.)--Guidebooks.* 2. Kayaking--Rocky Mountains,
Canadian (B.C. and Alta.)--Guidebooks.* 3. Rafting (Sports)-
-Rocky Mountains, Canadian (B.C. and Alta.)--Guidebooks.*
4. Rivers--Rocky Mountains, Canadian (B.C. and Alta.)--
Guidebooks. * I. Title.
GV788.S64 1995   797.1'22'09711   C95-910483-6

                    Headwaters Press Ltd.
                    Box 849
                    Jasper, Alberta
                    Canada   T0E 1E0

All descriptions, maps, graphs, photos, stories and layout by Stuart Smith
unless otherwise noted.

Contributing Photographers: Sandra Cassady, Michelle Taylor, Peter
Daum, Donna Sokolik, Ted Mellenthin, Brock Wilson, Keith Klapstein,
Tom Thompson, Randy Clement, Livia Stoyke, Hugh Lecky, Ben Gadd,
Robert Beaudry, Corina Ramsey, Arn Terry, Ifor Thomas, Keith Bobey,
Derek Thomas, Gilbert Wall, Peter Stummel, Rob Brown, Al Taylor, and
Jay Carton.

Story Contributions: Sandra Cassady.

Front Cover: Bob Orava at Ender Rock on the Maligne River.

Printed in Canada

This is dedicated to the memory of Bob Orava, who shared with me so many first descents and memorable river trips. You live on in our hearts.

Contents

vi

Acknowledgements

I sincerely thank those who donated their photographs and allowed me access to their valued slide collections. Without their photos, the information contained herein would be much less appealing, to say the least. Thanks to the following people for their outstanding photographs: Sandra Cassady at Chinook River Sports, Michelle Taylor, Ted Mellenthin, Brock Wilson, Peter Daum, Donna Sokolik, Derek Thomas, Keith Klapstein, Randy Clement, Tom Thompson, Livia Stoyke, Hugh Lecky, Ben Gadd, Robert Beaudry, Gilbert Wall, Corina Ramsey, Ifor Thomas, Arn Terry, Keith Bobey, Rob Brown, Al Taylor, Peter Stummel and Jay Carton. Thanks to Sandra Cassady for the tale on page 44.

Thanks to all of the advertisers, who gave me their trust and their money, often on blind faith in me alone, thereby enabling me to publish this work. In particular, I owe a debt of gratitude to Alf Skrastins and the University of Calgary Outdoor Programs Centre for their trust and support. I would like also, to acknowledge the gracious financial support of the Jasper River Runners.

The legibility of my material has been vastly improved upon by the following people. Each sacrificed their time to read my rantings and provide feedback, opinions and helpful suggestions. Thanks to: Heather Lang, Heather Wall, Doris Marychuk, Brian Young, Ben Gadd, Jeff and Andrea O'Neill, Mike Price and James Zimmerman. Special thanks to: Joanie Veitch and Annemarie van Oploo for proof reading the entire project. I would like to thank Janet Jones for reading the volumes of my material, while maintaining enough focus and energy to jot down insightful suggestions that also kept me laughing!

Special thanks to my roommate and friend, Laureen Distefano, for the patience, understanding and support throughout this entire project. Thanks also for tearing me away from my work to make sure I had fun.

To finish, I must honour the following people. Without their assistance this book would have never been more than a good idea:

- Anita and Alan Van Camp for the enthusiastic and immeasurable support and assistance.

- Ben and Cia Gadd for all the assistance transferring files, scanning maps, lent materials and the always enthusiastic advice.

- Toby Gadd for expertly tweaking the photographs, for the knowledgable assistance whenever my limited understanding of computers failed me and for the humorous enthusiasm which always helped me to drag myself back in front of my desk to keep going.

- All the people who throughout the years have shared their knowledge of little known river runs.

Author's Foreword

This whole project has become a bit of a philosophical enigma; to be honest, I dislike guidebooks! The adventure of climbing a mountain, paddling a river or hiking a pass is, to me, a quality inherent to the process, one that loses much of its appeal when someone else tells you how to do it or ad nauseam describes how it was done before. A bit of a contradiction, particularly coming from someone who has authored a series of guidebooks! Perhaps. But what I dislike even more than the lost sense of adventure, is searching unsuccessfully for a put-in, or dragging my canoe up a mountainside to exit a canyon. I can't say I much like portaging down a log choked run, or rock climbing while carrying my kayak. These experiences and epics may build character, or in retrospect seem amusing, but for the most part they are activities most of us would rather avoid. At the very least they consume our precious recreation time!

By creating this guidebook series, I attempted to enhance peoples experiences, providing the required information to select enjoyable and challenging trips that for many folks would be otherwise unavailable. I hope this guidebook series will help to illuminate dark canyons, eliminate vague rumours and enable more people to get out there! I have tried to consistently portray the character of the many splendid rivers in the Rockies, to avoid tedious and irrelevant details and to accurately describe the rivers. Much of the work has gone into attempting to clearly explain how to find the runs.

Paddlers seem to me to be a unique, although motley, group of individuals who generally give a damn about what happens to this place we inhabit. Most of the ones I know take lots of time to enjoy the outdoor activities that recharge your soul and make the rest of life somehow more bearable. As more people like that become aware of the rivers in the Canadian Rockies, I hope we can do more to prevent the overdevelopment and abuse of such a unique place. Paddling is a low-impact activity that allows us to access many magnificent areas and provides an opportunity to experience the challenges and rewards of interacting with a spectacular environment.

So don't just use the rivers. Appreciate them and do what you can to keep them as they are. I would be sad to see the places where I gained so much enjoyment somehow become unavailable to others.

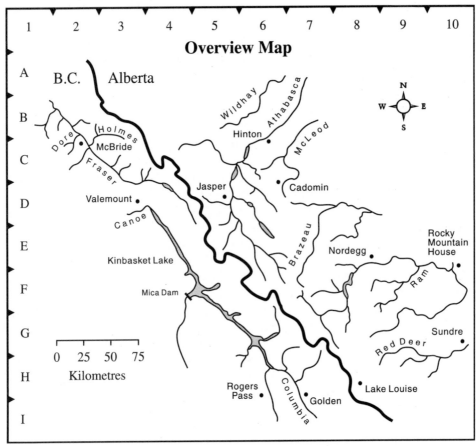

Overview Map

B.C.   Alberta

1 2 3 4 5 6 7 8 9 10

A B C D E F G H I

Dore
(Holmes
McBride
Fraser
Valemount
Canoe
Kinbasket Lake
Mica Dam

Wildhay
Athabasca
Hinton
McLeod
Jasper
Cadomin
Brazeau
Nordegg

Rocky Mountain House
Ram
Sundre
Red Deer

0   25   50   75
Kilometres

Rogers Pass
Columbia
Golden
Lake Louise

N
W   E
S

xi

Introduction

The information contained in these pages provides the background reference that enables you to explore, and enjoy, the incredible rivers in the Canadian Rockies. It allows you, the paddler, to experience the pristine environment that many of us call home. As river travellers, we each utilize these splendid streams for our own purposes. With the privilege of using the rivers there is also, I believe, a responsibility to ensure others will have the same opportunities that we have. Paddlers are the unofficial guardians of streams and rivers. We are the ones who are aware of the changes to the rivers and the developments that threaten them. We are therefore the ones who should actively seek to protect these rivers.

Our paddling community is a small, special interest group that in many ways is apathetic to issues. Too often, we turn aside, or do not present a focused effort when an issue impacts one of the elements of the paddling community. The damming of a quiet stream appears to not directly concern hairball paddlers, rafting through slalom courses appears to be a problem only for a group of racers or rafters, closing a river to rafting appears to only affect commercial rafters. Yet each of these issues concerns, and impacts, the entire paddling community. As part of the larger group of people travelling rivers, we all need to understand the needs of other river users. We also need to accept the manifold ways people enjoy rivers. River paddling in any non-powered craft is an environmentally friendly way to enjoy ourselves and to experience our surroundings.

So take this shared knowledge of these spectacular places and go out and enjoy the rivers. The same rivers provide so much to us: transportation routes, drinking water, wildlife habitat, fish habitat and varied types of recreation. With their endless motion and thundering exuberance, they remind us of our humble place in the entire ecosystem. Each of these rivers is a unique entity. Each river flooded by a hydro development, needlessly cluttered with logs, or poisoned with our waste, devalues our world and our existence.

I hope this guide allows you to enjoy the rivers, for whatever reasons you choose to use them. Please get involved in protecting them, so that in the future we may all continue to enjoy them.

Important Notice to Users of this Book

Travelling on whitewater, or any moving water, in any type of craft means you will face hazards, even at the best of times. When you choose to paddle any stretch of river, whitewater or not, you alone accept the risks which are by nature of the endeavour always involved. These risks include, but are not limited to: broaches, pins, boat entrapments, foot entrapments, serious bodily injury, drowning, damage and loss of equipment and death. Hazards on the river include: weirs, bridges, trestles, cables, fences, metal bars, trees, logs, log jams, rocks, boulders, ledges, falls, undercut rocks and cliffs, canyons and all varieties of debris, etc.. Need I say more? These hazards and risks are faced not only by experts running difficult whitewater, but by any and all persons who choose to travel on or near rivers.

This book is designed to provide the river user with a general overview of the included sections of rivers. **It is not, nor could ever be, a substitute for the knowledge, skills and experience required to attempt any stretch of river.** The decision to travel on any river is entirely yours.

Conditions on rivers are constantly changing. Landslides, floods, human activities, avalanches and fluctuating water levels are but a few of the forces which may alter the character of any river. The conditions you encounter on the river may or may not resemble, in any way, the conditions described herein.

Before attempting any section of river, consult a competent and qualified instructor to obtain the skills you will undoubtedly need on the river. All river users should have training in River Safety and Rescue procedures as well as training in First Aid and CPR. If you are unsure of your ability to handle any stretch of river, hire a competent and qualified river guide or contract someone who is familiar with the river to guide you (see the advertisers' listings for information on where to find instructors or guides). When there is any doubt about what lies ahead, stop and scout.

Access to rivers changes all the time. Often old roads are closed and new roads opened. Property may change hands. If you encounter private land or fences, ask permission prior to crossing either. The put-ins and take-outs described in the text of this book are open to the public at the time of printing unless otherwise noted. Respect all signs and any private property.

Headwaters Press Ltd., the author and the editors assume no responsibility or liability for physical harm, property damage, or any other loss or damage caused directly or indirectly by the information contained in this book. By using the information in this guidebook, you accept the statements made above and accept the responsibility for your own well being while on the river. In spite of any information contained herein, you are the ultimate judge of what rivers are safe, what runs you choose to paddle, and what actions are reasonable.

How to use this book

Information Organization

The rivers in this book are organized like the guidebook series, starting from the south. In each river basin, runs are described starting at the downstream end of the mainstem river and moving upstream. I have dealt with Alberta and British Columbia separately, because the border follows the continental divide and therefore a natural division between watersheds. The rivers in this book flow into the Atlantic, Pacific and Arctic Oceans. Rivers draining the eastern slopes in central Alberta flow into the South and North Saskatchewan rivers and eventually into the Atlantic Ocean. Further north, east-slope tributaries of the Athabasca River end up in the Arctic Ocean. Rivers draining the western slopes flow into the Columbia or Fraser and eventually the Pacific Ocean.

Each run has the basic information up front, for those who want only the bare essentials. Items such as the overall grade of the river, the class of rapids on the river, flow variations, time for the run and length are found just under the title box. Those who want only the basics can read that information, plus the character section, and come away with a pretty good feel for the run. Unless you are extremely adept at taking care of yourself, no matter what you get into, you should read the rest of the information as well.

Indexes

There is an alphabetized listing of all the runs covered in the book at the front with a reference map. All the runs are indexed by grade in the back and the best rivers are indexed if you wish to get the most out of your paddling trip in the Rockies. You will find an advertisers' listing in the back where you can find the prominent instructors, suppliers and raft companies in this part of the world. There is a listing of water gauging stations in the back of the book and information on how to obtain flow data for the rivers. Lastly, there is a list of the whitewater organizations and the major kayak and canoe clubs in the area, should you wish to connect with other paddlers.

The Grading System

To grade the runs in this book, I applied the following grading scheme, which is a modified version of the International Canoe Federation grading system. I tried to apply this system consistently throughout the book, so that once you key into it, you should not be too surprised on any run. Be sure you look it over closely. Test the ratings scale against the one you use on a section of river that is easier than the ones you usually run, or on a run you know well. For river users in western Canada, this rating system is a bit of a departure from older guides, so contain your ego when you decide to push your limits, at least until you are familiar with these grades.

Grade

Using the classification system, an overall grade is assigned to the river. The grade of the run refers to the overall stretch of river. For many rivers this is vastly different than the class of rapids on that run. To assign the overall grade, I considered the following information:
- how sustained are the rapids
- is portaging and scouting difficult or easy
- is the run committing or are there chances to bail out
- how difficult is it to negotiate the surrounding topography

By assigning a run a certain grade, I try to provide users with an idea of the overall magnitude of the undertaking. No provision is made for consequences of a swim or water temperature. The overall grade does include the norm of rapid you should expect to run, and the severity of any portages and scouting.

River Classification System

Class I   Moving water with few or no obstacles. Passages are wide open and easily seen from the river.

Class II   Rapids with small obstacles and regular features. Passages are open and obvious without scouting, but may require manoeuvring.

Class III Rapids with irregular features that require manoeuvring to negotiate. Passages can be narrow and features such as holes and irregular waves must be run to negotiate the rapid. Risk of injury.

Class IV   Rapids with highly irregular features. Complicated passages that often include vertical drops and may require scouting to find safe passages. Linked manoeuvres are required in convoluted passages. Risk of injury and possible risk to your life.

Class V   Rapids with violent and irregular features. Extremely congested passages that almost always require scouting to determine safe routes. Most class V rapids include vertical drops and require running large scale features in a complex series of manoeuvres. Definite risk of serious injury and possible risk to your life.

Class VI   The difficulties of class V taken to the extreme. Rapids with extremely violent and unpredictable features where experts require considerable advance scouting and planning to determine possible passages. All class VI rapids require the paddler(s) to negotiate vertical drops and very large features. Always a risk to your life. Generally only possible at certain water levels.

The grades and classes of whitewater are subdivided further, as follows:

I	I⁺	·II	II	II⁺	·III	III	III⁺	·IV	IV	IV⁺	·V	V	V⁺	·VI	VI	VI⁺

Class

Using the classification system, a difficulty rating is applied to individual rapids and sections of river. This is a technical rating for the degree of difficulty of the moves required to negotiate a rapid. Usually only rapids which are rated higher than the river grade are noted. If there is a long stretch of river with a grade significantly lower than the overall river grade, you will find a listing of rapids more difficult than that lower grade as well. To assign the class to a rapid, I considered the following:

- is the rapid separate and distinct from the surrounding whitewater
- are there clear and defined routes available
- is protracted manoeuvring required
- are there features which must be run to navigate the rapid
- are there places to set up safety measures on the river or on the shore

Please note: I do not include the remoteness of the rapid, water temperature, or the consequences of a swim when assigning a class to a rapid. By assigning a certain class to a rapid, I have attempted to describe the circumstances you may encounter, not the consequences of the many things that might go wrong.

Flow

Where applicable the difficulty ratings are associated with a flow level. For runs with gauges, the flow level is a specific stage reading or a specific discharge rate. However, in the many instances where there are no gauges, flow may be described in rough terms such as low, medium, or high. In many cases, users will need to take a stab at judging water levels for themselves.

Time

Under this heading you will find the normal amount of time to complete the run under reasonable conditions. High flows may shorten the time taken to complete the run or may increase the amount of scouting required. The time you spend playing river features, scouting or portaging rapids and floating along will all affect the time taken to complete the run. I have included a reasonable amount of extra time for these activities.

Length

This is the length of the run in kilometres, followed in brackets by the length of the run in miles. The listed distance is river length as measured from a map, following the path of the river in detail.

Gradient

This is the average gradient of the entire run as calculated by subtracting the elevation at the take-out from the elevation at the put-in, then dividing by the length of the run. Gradient is listed in metres (m) per kilometre (km) followed in brackets by the percent descent. Percent descent is calculated by dividing the elevation loss by the length (each in the same units) then multiplying by 100. The percent descent is the same no matter what measurement system you use. The gradient is also listed in feet (ft) per mile (mi). The gradient is for the particular run on that specific river. It does not include the gradient of any other river that the run may drain into. This gives a more accurate picture of what to expect on a particular run.

Max Gradient

This is the gradient as described by the shortest distance between two contour lines on the 1:50,000 scale topographic maps. The max gradient was estimated for the extremely steep sections which drop more than the topographic maps accurately represent. This is listed as the drop in metres (m) per kilometre (km) followed in brackets by the maximum percent descent of the river. Percent descent is calculated as described under gradient. Max gradient is also listed in feet (ft) per mile (mi). Where the max gradient differs significantly from the overall gradient, you can expect a section much steeper than the rest of the run. I have not included big waterfalls (higher than 15-20 m) in the max gradient calculation, as they are mostly unrunnable and would therefore skew the max gradient calculation.

Elevations

These are the elevations of the put-in and take-out, as taken from the 1:50,000 topographic maps. The elevations are given in metres (m) and followed below by the elevation in feet (ft). This information is useful for calculating gradients, as well as for estimating when there will be water in the river or what temperatures to expect. Lower elevation runs usually peak earlier in the season, while higher elevation runs will usually have water later in the year.

Shuttle

This is the distance via the described roads, from the put-in to the take-out in kilometres (km), followed by the equivalent distance in miles (mi) in brackets.

Season

This is a listing of the normal times of the year that the run may have reasonable water flow. In years with abnormally low or high snowfall, or in years with excess rainfall, the season may be extended beyond that listed or may be much shorter. Depending on the weather, runoff may be a steady trickle that does not peak, or may flash in a short period. When planning a big paddling trip in the central Rockies, call some of the ski areas in March and check what the snowpack is like for the season, or check with the weather offices for snowfall records. After that, you pay your money and you take your chances.

Maps

This is a listing of the 1:50,000 series topographic maps which cover the area of the run. In Canada you may also obtain the 1:250,000 series of topographic maps which are much more useful for getting an overall picture of the area, but are not as useful for examining the river itself. The 1:250,000 maps cover the same area as 16 of the 1:50,000 maps. Each drainage basin in the book has an area map to help you locate the rivers in a larger perspective. Use the drainage maps to find the river, then use the larger scale map of each run to help you find the put-in and take-out. If you need a map other than those in the book, it should only be to find the general area of the run. For remote rivers, it is useful to carry maps of the area in case you are forced to walk out.

Gauge

Under this heading you will find either a yes, if the run has an established gauge, or no, if there is no gauge. In many cases gauging stations exist, but there is no external way to relay this information to river users. Detailed information on how to check river flows can be found in the Flow Information section.

Craft

This is a listing of the types of craft suitable for use on the described run and is a reasonable estimation of what is possible for each craft. This does not mean that individuals who are willing to portage under arduous conditions or paddle at the edge of what is considered reasonable could not complete the run in any type of craft. In an attempt to keep pace with the paddlers everywhere who are pushing the limits of whitewater sports, I have been liberal in my assessment of what can be done in each craft. Note however, this does not mean any variation of the type of craft listed is suitable, but that the run can be done by certain varieties of the craft listed. Look in the character section to find out what type of features to expect. You should be able to figure out what variety of each craft type is suitable.

Notes

This is a catch-all category for any relevant information that does not fit into the other categories. For example, if the run you are paddling ends with a paddle out on another river, this is where you will find that information.

Character

Under this heading you will find a brief synopsis of the overall run. This includes a description of the type of rapids, riverbed, volume and any other outstanding features such as falls, log jams, or portages. Some of my own personal feelings about the run often show up here.

Flow Information

Under this heading you will find a description of where and how to check the river flow. Often this may include informal descriptions of natural stage markers where "real" gauges are absent. In Alberta there is a well-established water gauging information network in place. In British Columbia flow information is available, but with a 3 month delay. Some rivers have monitored gauges and flow information is available by phone. If a run has phone access to flow information, this will be listed in the run's flow information section. You will find the phone numbers and a listing of gauging stations at the back of the book.

Travel

This section is a general description of the roads you must travel when you attempt to drive to the river. The type of road surface will be listed here, as well as any special recommendations for four wheel drives, or other pertinent information about road closures, etc..

Description

Under this heading you will find descriptions of the major rapids, where to portage, novel attractions and other pieces of wisdom. You will not find any blow-by-blow blueprint on how to run any rapid in this or any other section. The techniques you have mastered may be much different than those I use and I will be the last person to tell anyone how to paddle a particular rapid. I do describe the rapids so you know what to expect, though I cannot possibly have paddled all the runs at all the water levels, so the conditions you find may or may not resemble the descriptions I provide.

Getting There

This is a broad scale description of the location of the run, which includes directions from the nearest town or highway.

Take-out

Under this heading you will find a physical description of how to get to the area where you exit the river after your run.

Put-in

Under this heading you will find a physical description of how to get to the area where you start the run. These descriptions start at the take-out point. There may be shorter routes on less reliable or rougher roads, but these routes are not described here. This will help ensure that in the future, reliable access will still be there, despite weather conditions or closure of small roads.

Camping

This section contains a brief description of camping near the run. As paddlers are notoriously stingy, I try to mention undeveloped (low cost) sites. I distinguish informal camping as places where you can pull over and crash for the night, while undeveloped sites are those where you might find an outhouse, fire pit and picnic tables. Camping for a fee is an example of a developed site.

River Profiles and Flow Hydrographs

The left axis has the elevation in feet and the line with the solid dots is the gradient profile. This information is taken from the topographic maps and may be modified based on my knowledge of the run. Each horizontal line on the graph is a 100 foot contour interval (except on low gradient runs). Our maps still have elevations in feet, but in keeping with the metric system I have used kilometres for distance. An unusual marriage of systems, but one of necessity.

The right axis has the flow in cubic metres per second (cms) and the line with the open dots shows the discharge of the river (check the conversions section in the back to reference to other units). This is the mean instantaneous discharge of the river for each month as calculated over a period of years. I tried to use the same years of information for all the rivers, however, some of the information is historical, since gauges are removed and not replaced. If the information is historical, this is indicated, with the years of the recorded data. The bottom axis lists the length of the run in kilometres plus the months (3-10) of the year for the hydrograph. The month with the highest flow is listed on the graph plus the drainage and historical peak flow, if this information is available.

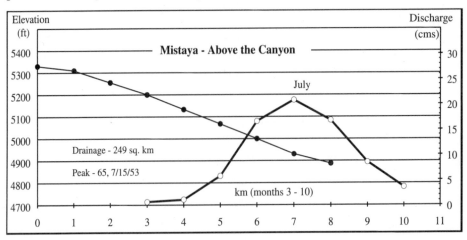

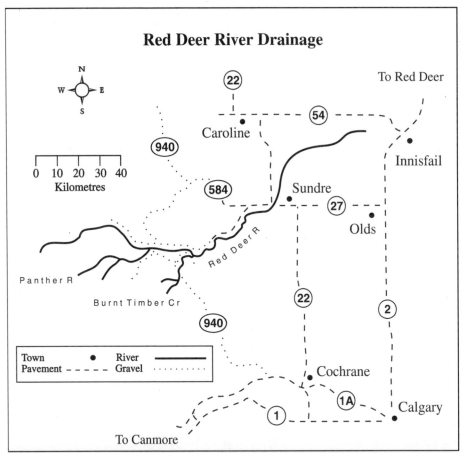

Red Deer River Drainage

To Red Deer

Caroline

Innisfail

Sundre

Olds

Red Deer R

Panther R

Burnt Timber Cr

| Town | ● | River | ——— |
| Pavement | – – – – | Gravel | ·········· |

Cochrane

Calgary

To Canmore

Rafting on the Red Deer–an ever popular activity. Photo: Sandra Cassady.

GRADE	CLASS	FLOW	TIME	LENGTH
II	II–III	Low	1–2 hours	9 km (5.6 mi)
III	II–IV	High		

Gradient 6.1 m/km (.6%)
              32 ft/mi

Max gradient 30 m in 5 km (.6%)
                  100 ft in 31 mi

Put-in elevation 1251 m
                   4105 ft

Take-out elevation 1196 m
                     3925 ft

Shuttle 8 km (5 mi) one way

Season May–September

Maps 82O10

Gauge Yes

Craft Canoes, kayaks and rafts

CHARACTER A medium to large-volume run through an open valley with a long calm stretch at the start, some good rapids in the middle and an easier section before the final few ledges.

FLOW INFORMATION The river is uncontrolled and fed by snowmelt and some glacial runoff. The run is on Alberta Environmental Protection's River Report recording. Use the flow below Burnt Timber Creek; low flow is about 30 to 70 cms and high flow is around 110 to 160 cms.

TRAVEL The shuttle is on a gravel road.

DESCRIPTION The first 4–5 kilometres of the run are open, with a few small rapids until you reach the class III–IV Double Ledge. A rock outcrop produces the first ledge, with a chute on the right. The second drop has a powerful reversal that is particularly tight on the left side. Below the Double Ledge, the rapids are more frequent, with small ledges, eddies and good surfing waves. Watch for Adrenaline, a ledge across most of the river, about 1 km below the Double Ledge. This is followed by a 1-km stretch of easier water that leads to the class II–III Coal Camp ledge at the take-out.

GETTING THERE At the four-way stop in Sundre (the 584/22 junction), go west on Highway 584 for 8 km. Turn south (left) at the sign to Mountain Aire Lodge and follow the road for 13.6 km to the campground on the south (left) side of the road.

TAKE-OUT The campground at Coal Camp is a good spot to access the river. Alternatively you can park just upstream of Coal Camp ledge, along the south (left) side of the road. The ledge is easily visible from the road about 800 m downstream of the campground.

PUT-IN Go west from the campground for 7.2 km where the river is close to the road. If you go too far, you will reach a small bridge over Williams Creek. If you wish to paddle only the section with the best rapids, put in at the Double Ledge. There is an access on the south (left) side of the road, 2 km west of the campground. Look for a small dirt pull-off on the south (left) side and follow the steep trail down to the river.

CAMPING There is developed camping at the take-out.

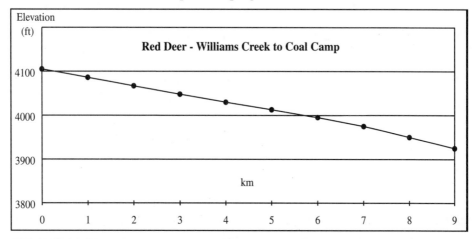

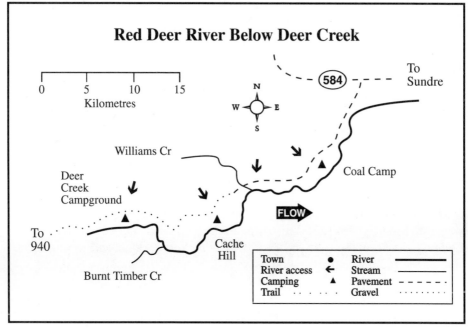

GRADE	CLASS	FLOW	TIME	LENGTH
I⁺	II	Low	1–2 hours	8.3 km (5.2 mi)
II	II⁺	High		

Gradient 5 m/km (.5%)
26 ft/mi

Max gradient 30 m in 5.4 km (.6%)
100 ft in 3.4 mi

Put-in elevation 1292 m
4240 ft

Take-out elevation 1251 m
4105 ft

Shuttle 7.5 km (4.6 mi) one way

Season May–September

Maps 82O11 and 82O10

Gauge Yes

Craft Canoes, kayaks and rafts

CHARACTER A medium to large-volume run in a scenic valley, with few major rapids. Most of the challenges consist of corners and a few split channels.

FLOW INFORMATION The river is uncontrolled and fed by snowmelt and some glacial runoff. The run is on Alberta Environmental Protection's River Report recording. Use the flow below Burnt Timber Creek; low flow is about 30 to 70 cms and high flow is around 110 to 160 cms.

TRAVEL The shuttle is on a gravel road.

DESCRIPTION There is a small ledge directly below the put-in, at a sharp right turn. This can be run easily by keeping to the right. Following this, the river runs in an open channel with a few sets of waves and easy rapids where the river drops off gravel shoals. Expect a couple of tighter channels where the river flows around islands, as well as some boulder gardens and small ledges. There are good views of the surrounding foothills.

GETTING THERE At the four-way stop in Sundre (the 584/22 junction), go west on Highway 584 for 8 km. Turn south (left) at the sign to Mountain Aire Lodge and follow the road for 13.6 km to the campground on the south (left) side of the road. See the map on page 3.

TAKE-OUT Go west from the campground for 7.2 km to where the river is close to the road. If you go too far, you will reach a small bridge over Williams Creek. Mark the take-out at the river and park well off the road.

PUT-IN Go west for a few hundred metres to a small bridge on Williams Creek. From there, continue west for 6.6 km to a small trail on the left (south) side of the road. The road goes up a large, steep hill, drops down on a left turn, then turns right at the bottom. Watch for the trail just past the right turn at the bottom. Follow the trail across the meadow to near the river.

CAMPING There is undeveloped camping at the put-in.

**Kevin Gallant and crew dropping into the Double Ledge at high flow.
Photo: Sandra Cassady.**

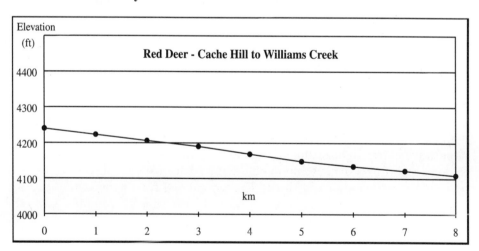

GRADE	CLASS	FLOW	TIME	LENGTH
II	II	Low	1–2 hours	11.5 km (7 mi)
II$^+$	II–III	High		

Gradient   4.9 m/km (.5%)
            26 ft/mi

Max gradient   30 m in 6 km (.5%)
               100 ft in 3.7 mi

Put-in elevation   1349 m
                4425 ft

Take-out elevation   1292 m
                     4240 ft

Shuttle   8.6 km (5.3 mi) one way

Season   May–September

Maps   82O11

Gauge   Yes

Craft   Canoes, kayaks and rafts

CHARACTER   A medium to large-volume run in a scenic valley, with rapids scattered throughout. The biggest rapids are in the last few kilometres of the run. At medium to high flows expect some great surf spots.

FLOW INFORMATION   The river is uncontrolled and fed by snowmelt and some glacial runoff. The run is on Alberta Environmental Protection's River Report recording. Use the flow below Burnt Timber Creek; low flow is about 30 to 70 cms and high flow is around 110 to 160 cms.

TRAVEL   Access to the run is primarily on a paved road and the shuttle is on a good gravel road.

DESCRIPTION   The river flows in an open channel at the put-in. The first rapid is encountered about 1 km downstream, at the class II Boulder Gardens. The difficulty then eases until about 1 km below the confluence with Burnt Timber Creek, which enters from the right. Here you encounter a diagonal class II ledge at the Sauna Hole. The river opens up until you reach a left turn, with an island not far below. The left channel contains a couple of holes and large waves. The right channel is very rocky at low flows, but is the easier route in high flows. About 500 m below the island, you encounter a series of four ledges, which are class II–III. The second and final ledges are the most difficult. The final excitement is the class II–II$^+$ Cache Hill Rapids, beneath the steep cliff on river right, just above the take-out.

GETTING THERE   At the four-way stop in Sundre (the 584/22 junction), go west on Highway 584 for 8 km to the turn-off to Mountain Aire Lodge, which is on the south (left) side of the road. See the map on page 3.

TAKE-OUT At the turn-off to Mountain Aire Lodge, turn left and follow the road for 28 km to a small trail on the south (left) side of the road. The road goes up a large, steep hill, drops down on a left turn, then turns right at the bottom. Watch for the trail just past the right turn at the bottom. Follow the trail across the meadow to near the river.

PUT-IN Go 8.5 km west on the gravel road to the Deer Creek Recreation Area, which is on the south (left) side of the road.

CAMPING There is undeveloped camping in the meadows at the take-out, or developed camping at the put-in.

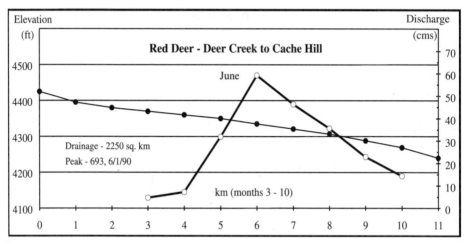

GRADE	CLASS	FLOW	TIME	LENGTH
II⁺	II⁺–III	Low	1–2 hours	4 km (2.5 mi)
III	III–III⁺	High		

Gradient 6.5 m/km (.7%)
34 ft/mi

Max gradient 26 m in 4.5 km (.7%)
85 ft in 2.8 mi

Put-in elevation 1375 m
4510 ft

Take-out elevation 1349 m
4425 ft

Shuttle 4 km (2.5 mi) one way

Season May–September

Maps 82O11

Gauge Yes

Craft Canoes, kayaks and rafts

CHARACTER A medium to large-volume run through an open valley where bedrock ledges produce distinct pool-and-drop style rapids. Many of the ledges form sharp drops with powerful reversals.

FLOW INFORMATION The river is uncontrolled and fed by snowmelt and some glacial runoff. The river is on Alberta Environmental Protection's River Report recording. Use the flow below Burnt Timber Creek; low flow is about 30 to 70 cms and high flow is around 110 to 160 cms.

TRAVEL The shuttle and the access to the run are on a solid gravel road.

DESCRIPTION The action begins immediately at a couple of small ledges. These drops are just above Gooseberry Ledge, a class III diagonal rock outcrop, where the river drops 1 m through a series of slots into a recirculation. Just downstream is Jimbo's Staircase, a 100-m-long series of small, class II–III ledges, with broken slots on the right side. This is followed by a fast chute through a set of bedrock outcrops where the river is constricted by rock walls. The river opens up for about 800 m, then you reach a right turn where at high water an island splits the channel. This is the S-Bend, a class II–III rapid with a series of low-angled ledges that produce excellent surfing and hole-riding, depending on the water level. Stay left to avoid most of the excitement. The road comes close to the river at a pipeline crossing, then the river swings away into the class II⁺–III Nationals Site. This is a 200-m-long rapid composed of broken, low-angled ledges. At low flows the rapid is technical, with scattered holes, while at high flows the water piles up to create large standing waves and much bigger recirculations behind the ledges. The take-out is just below the end of the Nationals Site.

GETTING THERE At the four-way stop in Sundre (the 584/22 junction), go 8 km west on Highway 584. Turn south (left) at the sign to Mountain Aire

Lodge and go 37 km to the Deer Creek Recreation Area. See the map on page 14.

TAKE-OUT The Deer Creek Recreation Area is on the south (left) side of the road. There is a 400-metre carry from the river to your vehicle, so mark the take-out at the river's edge.

PUT-IN Go 4 km west to a small trail on the south (left) side of the road. Follow the trail a couple of hundred metres to near the river.

CAMPING There is camping for a fee at the take-out or undeveloped camping at the put-in.

Mark Taylor experimenting with upstream lean in the playholes at the S-Bend. Photo: Michelle Taylor.

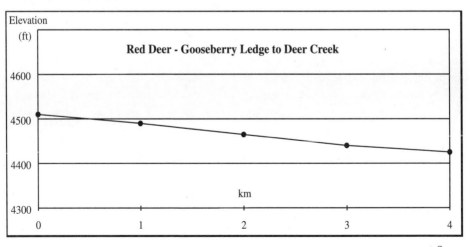

The Times They Are A Changing

It was August of 1983 at the Provincial Open Canoe Championships. The place was the S-Bend and an enthusiastic turnout had the place buzzing. In 1983 open canoeing in Alberta was a bit different than it is today. The boats were mostly composite, with fibreglass roving the most prominent material. There was one ABS boat, a Mad River ME, that was at least one if not several orders of magnitude beyond the other boats in terms of performance. Our boat was at the other end of the scale; an 18-foot fibreglass Tripper. We called that chopper-gun sprayed wonder "Big Red". It took every ounce of my strength and youthful exuberance just to get the thing on or off the car. Big Red was on semipermanent loan from my sister Anita and her husband Alan. Although it was huge and heavy, we had learned to manoeuvre it with aplomb down the most technical rivers. However, when it came time for the slalom event, we were wishing for something a bit sportier. So when our friends Pam and Glen offered the use of their 16-foot Cruiser, we leapt at the opportunity. The Cruiser was like the baby brother of Big Red; a scaled down version that was shorter, a little easier to spin and a bit narrower, which also meant a bit tippier.

My partner Donna and I had been paddling for only a couple of years and the pressure of a "Provincial Championships" had us both a little nervous. We were used to our own boat and feeling a little off as we made our practice run. Then came the real thing, and even more pressure, with all our friends rooting for us. Well, the bottom line is that we ended up in the drink. In 1983 River Rescue Fever was sweeping the province and folks everywhere were concerned with safety. We had drilled the rules of safety into our brains, so Donna held onto the boat. When the boat was swept over one of the bedrock ledges, her hand was trapped between the boat and a hard place. It was a predictable outcome, but she held on and got the boat to shore. As for me, I was swimming down the river, awkwardly bouncing over the bedrock ledges. By the time I reached the last ledge I was finally in the proper whitewater swimming position; feet downstream, on my back and looking ahead. Like a good swimmer should, I held onto my paddle. At the last ledge, the shallow water could not overcome the friction between my backside and the rock outcrop so I was left there, stuck halfway down the drop, my butt firmly adhering to the jagged rock. The crowd's response was an immediate "Don't stand up!" That made me laugh, despite my situation. I sat there, with rock shards being driven into my buttocks as I bounced up and down, using the paddle in an attempt to dislodge myself. When I finally freed myself, a throw bag hit me and I was hauled to shore.

Donna's hand healed and though I was uncomfortable sitting for the next while, the final rock fragments came free some days later. When I look back now, it is clear that our skills were as antiquated as the equipment, but at the time we could have been enthusiastic super-heroes, sporting capes on our backs. Our skills and equipment have moved far beyond those days, but I am still learning—although most of the time my experiences are not so painful!

GRADE	CLASS	FLOW	TIME	LENGTH
II	II	Low	1–2 hours	8.5 km (5.3 mi)
II	II⁺	High		

Gradient   5 m/km (.5%)   **Max gradient**   30 m in 5.5 km (.6%)
             27 ft/mi   100 ft in 3.4 mi

Put-in elevation   1417 m   **Take-out elevation**   1375 m
                              4650 ft   4510 ft

Shuttle   7.5 km (4.7 mi) one way   **Season**   May–September

Maps   82O11   **Gauge**   Yes

Craft   Canoes, kayaks and rafts

CHARACTER   A medium to large-volume run in a foothills setting. The river flows on a gravel-bed, in a single channel, for most of the run. There are a few islands and braided sections. The major rapids are formed by bedrock outcrops.

FLOW INFORMATION   The river is uncontrolled and fed by snowmelt and some glacial runoff. The river is on Alberta Environmental Protection's River Report recording. Use the flow below Burnt Timber Creek; low flow is about 30 to 70 cms and high flow is around 110 to 160 cms.

TRAVEL   The shuttle is on a solid gravel road. Access to the run requires 24 km of driving on gravel roads.

DESCRIPTION   The river flows in a single channel for the first couple of kilometres. After a short, calm section at the start, the river has numerous small rapids at bends and constrictions and becomes braided in the middle section. The first significant rapid you encounter is a midstream rock that creates a distinct class II–II⁺ rapid. Approximately 1 km downstream, the main channel drops off a class II ledge, .5–1-m high, with a chute in the centre. After this there are some waves and partial ledges, and the river flows in braided channels until the take-out. Mark the take-out to avoid the whitewater below.

GETTING THERE   At the four-way stop in Sundre (the 584/22 junction), go west on Highway 584 for 8 km. Turn south (left) at the sign to Mountain Aire Lodge and follow the road 37 km to the Deer Creek Recreation Area, which is on the south (left) side of the road. See the map on page 14.

TAKE-OUT   From the Deer Creek Recreation Area go 4 km west to a small trail on the south (left) side of the road. Turn left and follow the trail for a couple of hundred metres to near the river. Mark the take-out at the river.

PUT-IN Continue west on the gravel road to the junction with Highway 940. Go south (left) and proceed 2.8 km to the intersection where Highway 940 leaves on the south (left) side. The put-in is 100 m south, at the bridge.

CAMPING There is camping for a fee at the Red Deer Recreation Area 700 m east of the put-in bridge, or undeveloped camping along the river.

One of the many ledges on the Red Deer. Photo: Michelle Taylor.

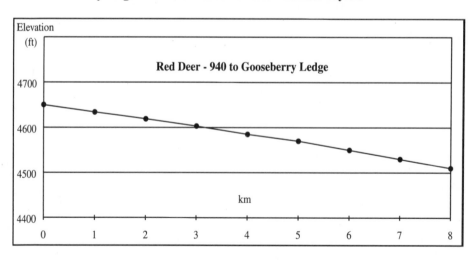

GRADE	CLASS	FLOW	TIME	LENGTH
II	I⁺–II⁺	Most Flows	5–8 hours	26 km (16 mi)

Gradient   5.6 m/km (.56%)   **Max gradient**   30 m in 4 km (.75%)
               29 ft/mi   100 ft in 2.5 mi

Put-in elevation   1562 m   **Take-out elevation**   1417 m
                         5125 ft   4650 ft

Shuttle   23 km (14 mi) one way   **Season**   May–September

Maps   82O12 and 82O11   **Gauge**   Yes

Craft   Canoes, kayaks and rafts

CHARACTER A medium-volume run through an open valley, with spectacular views of the mountains. The river flows in a braided gravel-bed for the first half of the run, then flows in a single channel in the lower part. There are a couple of small ledges in the final few kilometres.

FLOW INFORMATION The river is uncontrolled and fed by snowmelt and some glacial runoff. The river is on Alberta Environmental Protection's River Report recording. Use the flow below Burnt Timber Creek; low flow is about 30 to 70 cms and high flow is around 110 to 160 cms. At the put in you will have approximately 40 to 60 percent of that flow.

TRAVEL Access to the run is on a good gravel road as far as the take-out. The shuttle is on a rough, potholed gravel road that is in poor condition from heavy horse-trailer traffic.

DESCRIPTION The river runs in a braided gravel channel for the first 4–5 km. Braided sections continue until approximately halfway through the run, where the river flows in a single channel. Rock gardens, log jams and sweepers provide challenges in the upper class I-II section of the run. Just above Wildhorse Creek is a small class II–II⁺ ledge that can be easily run in the centre of the drop. The next couple of kilometres contain many class II rapids that are produced by channel constrictions. Near the take-out bridge is a .5-m diagonal class II–II⁺ ledge, which is followed 300–400 m below by a sharp turn at a headwall. The take-out bridge is not far below.

GETTING THERE At the four-way stop in Sundre (the 584/22 junction), go west on Highway 584 for 8 km. Turn south (left) at the sign to Mountain Aire Lodge and follow the road 45 km to the junction with Highway 940.

TAKE-OUT From the junction with Highway 940, go south (left) and proceed

2.8 km to the intersection where Highway 940 leaves on the south (left) side. The take-out bridge is 100 m south of the junction.

PUT-IN Go 100 m north of the bridge, then turn west (left) and follow the road for 22 km to the Bighorn Creek Campsite. Turn left just before the bridge on Bighorn Creek and follow the rutted trail along the fence for 900 m to the river.

CAMPING There is camping for a fee 700 m east of the take-out or at the put-in. There are informal sites along the river downstream of the take-out.

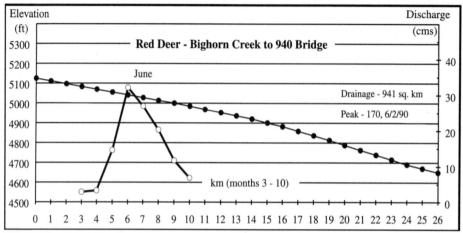

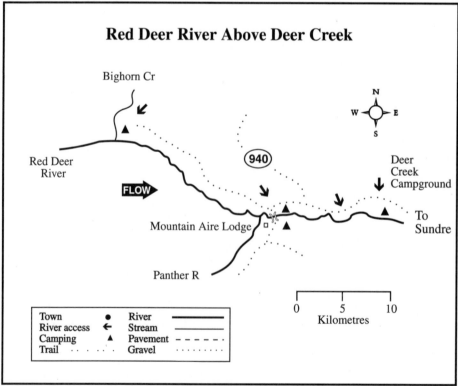

BURNT TIMBER CREEK — 940 TO ABOVE RED DEER

GRADE	CLASS	FLOW	TIME	LENGTH
II	II–II$^+$	Medium	1–2 hours	10 km (6.2 mi)
II$^+$	II–III	High		

Gradient 8.5 m/km (.85%)
45 ft/mi

Max gradient 30 m in 3 km (1%)
100 ft in 1.9 mi

Put-in elevation 1417 m
4650 ft

Take-out elevation 1332 m
4370 ft

Shuttle 11.5 km (7.1 mi) one way **Season** May–August

Maps 82O11 **Gauge** No

Craft Canoes, kayaks and small rafts

CHARACTER A small-volume run in an entrenched valley. Expect numerous sharp corners, boulder gardens and small ledges on this picturesque run.

FLOW INFORMATION Check the flow at the take-out, where the creek is spread-out. Figure on a couple of other spread-out sections during the run. The creek is fed by snowmelt and is uncontrolled.

TRAVEL Access to the run and the shuttle are both on solid gravel roads.

DESCRIPTION The run begins in a steep-sided valley on a wide and open gravel-bed. Approximately 1 km into the run is a beautiful low-walled canyon with a series of small class II–II$^+$ ledges extending off the left shore. The creek is calmer for about 300 m, then a set of small broken ledges leads to a class II–II$^+$ creekwide ledge with a chute on the left. The creek is then mellow until the rapids begin again below a powerline crossing. Downstream of the midway bridge the creek has many sharp turns at bedrock headwalls. There are also numerous short boulder gardens in low-walled canyons.

GETTING THERE The run is best accessed on Highway 584, west of Sundre. From the four-way stop in Sundre (the 584/22 junction), go west on Highway 584 for 8 km. Turn south (left) at the sign to Mountain Aire Lodge and follow the road 45 km to the junction with Highway 940. At the junction, go south (left) and proceed 2.8 km to an intersection, where Highway 940 leaves on the south (left) side. Turn left and go 100 m to a bridge on the Red Deer.

TAKE-OUT From the Red Deer bridge go south for 100 m to an intersection with the Panther River Road on the west (right) side. Stay left and go 12.5 km on the winding and narrow gravel road, to an intersection where the Stud Creek Road is on the east (left) side. The road is labelled as private and that

15

users travel at their own risk. Turn east (left) on that road and go 1.8 km to an intersection. Stay left and continue for 3.4 km, to a sharp right turn at the base of a hill, with a gas pipeline complex in front of you. Turn east (right) and proceed for 3.8 km to the bridge at the take-out.

If coming from the south on Highway 940, proceed north to the put-in bridge. About 2.4 km further is the Stud Creek Road, which is on the east (right) side. From there, follow the directions in the paragraph above to reach the take-out.

PUT-IN Return to the Stud Creek Road junction at Highway 940. Turn south (left) and proceed for 2.4 km to the put-in at the bridge.

CAMPING There is camping for a fee at the put-in or informal camping at the take-out.

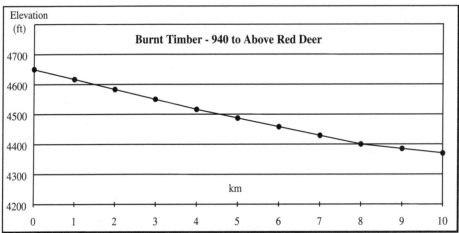

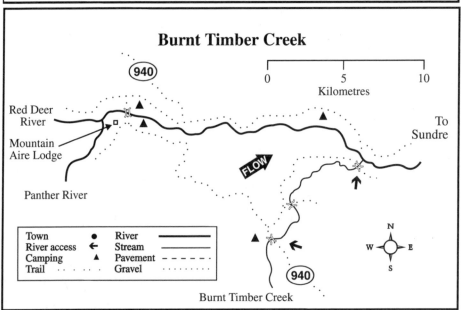

GRADE	CLASS	FLOW	TIME	LENGTH
II	II$^+$	Medium	1–2 hours	8 km (5 mi)
II$^+$	III	High		

Gradient   8.5 m/km (.85%)   **Max gradient**   30 m in 3.5 km (.86%)
45 ft/mi   100 ft in 2.2 mi

Put-in elevation   1506 m   **Take-out elevation**   1436 m
4940 ft   4710 ft

Shuttle   9.6 km (6 mi) one way   **Season**   May–August

Maps   82O11   **Gauge**   No

Craft   Canoes, kayaks and small rafts

NOTES   There is a 3-km (1.9-mi) paddle on the Red Deer to reach the take-out.

CHARACTER   A small to medium-volume run in an open valley where sharp corners produce rapids. The river has a few small rock outcrops which are covered at higher flows. Rafters will require high flows to avoid encounters with the river bottom.

FLOW INFORMATION   The only spot to estimate the flow is at the put-in. Check the Red Deer hydrograph on page 14 for an idea of the seasonal flows in the area. The river is fed by snowmelt and is uncontrolled.

TRAVEL   The shuttle is on a gravel road along the south side of the river. Accessing the run requires driving 35 km on gravel roads.

DESCRIPTION   The river runs over an open gravel and boulder channel for most of the run. Expect standing waves at most of the corners and where the river is constricted by low rock outcrops. At lower flows small bedrock ledges are encountered. Low flows also expose boulder gardens, which at high flows produce waves and holes. The most significant rapid is a small ledge, about halfway down the run. Near the finish, the river runs in an open valley.

GETTING THERE   At the four-way stop in Sundre (the 584/22 junction), go west on Highway 584 for 8 km. Turn south (left) at the sign to Mountain Aire Lodge and follow the road 45 km to the junction with Highway 940.

TAKE-OUT   At the Highway 940 junction, go south (left) and proceed 2.8 km to an intersection where Highway 940 leaves on the south (left) side. Turn south (left) and go 100 m to the bridge at the take-out.

PUT-IN Proceed south from the bridge for 100 m to the Panther River Road, which is on the west (right). Turn west (right) and follow the road for 9.5 km to where the river is close to the road, just before a sharp left turn and a hill.

CAMPING There is informal camping on the south side of the river between the take-out and the put-in. There is also camping for a fee, on Highway 940, 900 m southeast of the 940/Panther River Road junction, at the Red Deer Recreation Area.

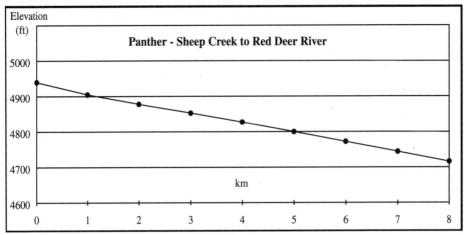

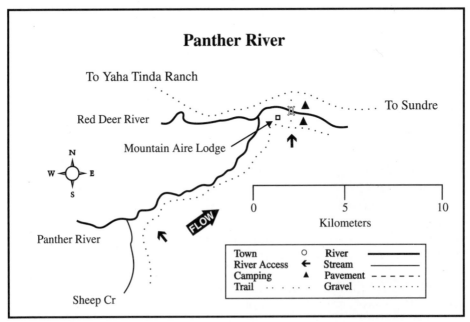

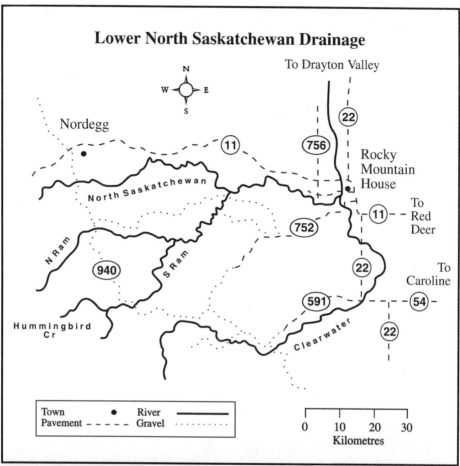

Lower North Saskatchewan Drainage

To Drayton Valley

Nordegg

North Saskatchewan

N Ram

S Ram

Hummingbird Cr

Clearwater

Rocky Mountain House

To Red Deer

To Caroline

| Town | ● | River | —— |
| Pavement | – – – – | Gravel | ········· |

0 10 20 30
Kilometres

Blaine Ritchie surfing at the Brierley's. Photo: Jay Carton.

NORTH SASKATCHEWAN RAIL BRIDGE TO BRIERLEY'S

GRADE	CLASS	FLOW	TIME	LENGTH
II	II	Low	1–2 hours	5.5 km (3.4 mi)
II	II–II⁺	High		

Gradient	2.5 m/km (.25%) 13 ft/mi	**Max gradient**	14 m in 5.5 km (.25%) 45 ft in 3.4 mi	
Put-in elevation	981 m 3220 ft	**Take-out elevation**	968 m 3175 ft	
Shuttle	4 km (2.5 mi) one way	**Season**	May–October	
Maps	83B6 and 83B7	**Gauge**	Yes	
Craft	Canoes, kayaks and rafts			

CHARACTER A short, fun run on a large-volume river that flows over a series of low-angled sandstone ledges, producing some fine surfing and hole-riding opportunities. Paddlers wishing to just surf and hole-ride often get in at the take-out parking lot and ferry across to the features at the Brierley's rapid.

FLOW INFORMATION The river is dam-controlled, fed by snowmelt and glacial runoff and subject to fluctuations dependent upon power requirements. Keep any equipment well back from the water line. The run is on Alberta Environmental Protection's River Report recording. Use the flow at Rocky Mountain House; low flow is 90 to 130 cms and high flow is 200 to 400 cms.

TRAVEL The shuttle is on a gravel road.

DESCRIPTION A large-volume run on an open gravel-bed, with short sections of rapids consisting of standing waves produced by small bedrock ledges. The first rapid starts about 400 m below the bridge, followed by 3 or 4 sets of rapids with some small ledges and good play features. You then reach the Brierley's, a class II–II⁺ set of waves and holes that extend for 200 m along the right shore of a channel to the right of a long island. The main features can easily be avoided by hugging the left shore of the channel. A 200 m carry leads to the parking lot.

GETTING THERE The run is located west of Rocky Mountain House along Highway 11. See the map on page 23.

TAKE-OUT From Rocky Mountain House, go west on Highway 11 for 9 km to a junction marked for the Rocky Mountain House National Historic Park. Turn south (left) and follow Highway 11A for 4.4 km to a junction. Cross the paved highway at the junction and continue 1.7 km south to a T intersection.

Turn east (left) and follow the road along the river for about 2 km to the parking lot at the picnic site. Approximately 800 m before you reach the parking lot is a gate, which may be closed early or late in the season.

PUT-IN Return to the T intersection and continue straight west for about 1 km to just before the railway bridge, where a dirt road on the south (left) side leads to the river.

CAMPING There is developed camping at Crimson Lake or Twin Lakes Provincial Parks, which are located north of the Highway 11 junction with Highway 756 (at the turn-off to Rocky Mountain House National Historic Park). This is 9 km north of the T intersection.

James Zimmerman surfing it up in the Brierley's.

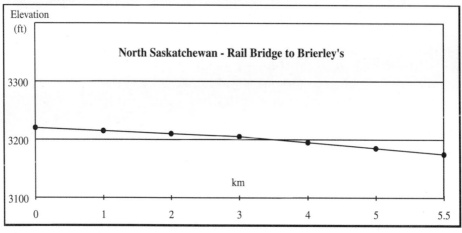

21

NORTH SASKATCHEWAN   HORBURG TO RAIL BRIDGE

GRADE	CLASS	FLOW	TIME	LENGTH
II	II	Low	3–6 hours	25 km (15.5 mi)
II	II–III	High		

Gradient 1.7 m/km (.17%)
  9 ft/mi

Max gradient 30 m in 18 km (.17%)
  100 ft in 11 mi

Put-in elevation 1024 m
  3360 ft

Take-out elevation 981 m
  3220 ft

Shuttle 32 km (20 mi) one way

Season May–October

Maps 83B6

Gauge Yes

Craft Canoes, kayaks and rafts

CHARACTER A large-volume, wide-open run with rapids created by the numerous bedrock outcrops and constricted corners. The low-angled ledges produce lots of playing opportunities. All of the bigger features can be easily avoided.

FLOW INFORMATION The river is dam-controlled, fed by snowmelt and glacial runoff and subject to fluctuations dependent upon power requirements. Keep any equipment well back from the water line. The run is on Alberta Environmental Protection's River Report recording. Use the flow at Rocky Mountain House; low flow is 90 to 130 cms and high flow is 200 to 400 cms.

TRAVEL The shuttle is on pavement, except for a short gravel section.

DESCRIPTION The river flows in a single channel below the put-in and has few rapids for approximately 4 km. A sharp right turn leads to the class II–II⁺ Devil's Elbow, a series of waves produced by bedrock ledges. These can be avoided on the inside of the turn. There are a couple of distinct class II rapids in the next 15 km, as well as numerous small rapids at corners. After a left turn, watch for a pipeline crossing, below which are the Fisher's Rapids and, 600 m further, the Little Fisher's Rapids. Both are class II rapids where you can avoid the biggest stuff on one side or the other. A few small rapids are encountered before the take-out is reached.

GETTING THERE The run is located west of Rocky Mountain House along Highway 11.

TAKE-OUT From Rocky Mountain House, go west on Highway 11 for 9 km to a junction marked for the Rocky Mountain House National Historic Park. Turn south (left) and follow Highway 11A for 4.4 km to a junction. Cross the

22

paved highway at the junction and continue 1.7 km south to a T intersection. Turn west (right) and go to just before the railroad bridge. Turn south (left) and follow the dirt road to the river.

PUT-IN Return to Highway 11, turn west (left) and proceed for 18 km to the Horburg river access, which is on the south (left) side of the road. Turn left and follow the road for 1 km to a junction. Go right and continue 3.2 km to a fork. Stay left and go 1.5 km to the river.

CAMPING There is developed camping at Crimson Lake or Twin Lakes Provincial Parks, which are located north of the Highway 11 junction with Highway 756 (at the turn-off to Rocky Mountain House National Historic Park). This is 9 km north of the T intersection.

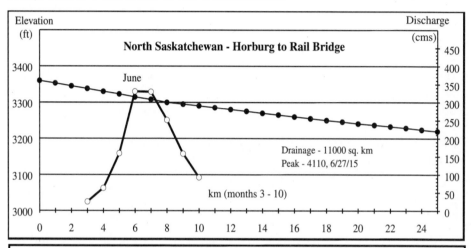

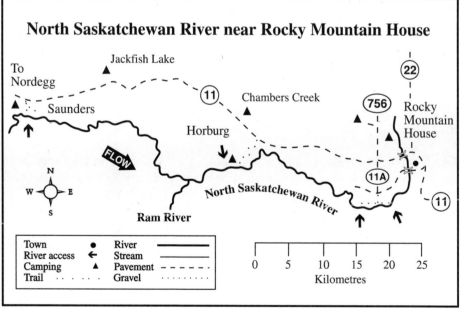

GRADE	CLASS	FLOW	TIME	LENGTH
II	I⁺–II	Most Flows	5–8 hours	41 km (26 mi)

Gradient   2.4 m/km (.24%)   **Max gradient**   30 m in 10 km (.3%)
                13 ft/mi   100 ft in 6.2 mi

Put-in elevation   1122 m   **Take-out elevation**   1024 m
                          3681 ft   3360 ft

Shuttle   51 km (32 mi) one way   **Season**   May–October

Maps   83B5 and 83B6   **Gauge**   Yes

Craft   Canoes, kayaks and rafts

CHARACTER   A large-volume run on an open riverbed, with standing waves and compression features produced by corners, constrictions and a few bedrock ledges. The river runs through a quiet and peaceful foothills setting.

FLOW INFORMATION   The river is dam-controlled, fed by snowmelt and glacial runoff and subject to fluctuations dependent upon power requirements. Keep any equipment well back from the water line. The run is on Alberta Environmental Protection's River Report recording. Use the flow at the Bighorn Plant; low flow is 50 to 80 cms and high flow is 150 to 200 cms.

TRAVEL   The shuttle is on pavement except for an 11-km gravel section.

DESCRIPTION   The river flows in a single channel through a low-walled valley for most of the run. Rapids are formed by corners and by the infrequent bedrock outcrops. All of the rapids can easily be avoided on one side of the river or the other. The river runs through the scenic foothills in a quiet valley.

GETTING THERE   The run is located west of Rocky Mountain House along Highway 11. See the map on page 23.

TAKE-OUT   From Rocky Mountain House, go 9 km west on Highway 11 to the junction with Highway 756 on the north (right). Continue west on Highway 11 for 18 km to the Horburg river access, which is on the south (left) side of the highway. Turn left and follow the road for 1 km to a junction. Turn right and go 3.2 km to a fork where you stay left and reach the river in 1.5 km. If you are approaching the run from the west, the Horburg river access is 62 km east of Nordegg.

PUT-IN Return to Highway 11, turn left (west) and go 38 km to the Saunders river access, which is on the south (left) side of the road. Turn left and follow the road for 400 m to a junction. Stay left and continue for 3 km to a junction at the base of a hill. Stay right and go another 3 km to a picnic site at the river.

CAMPING There is undeveloped camping along the river, or developed camping at the take-out and the put-in.

Relaxing at lunchtime. Photo: Ted Mellenthin.

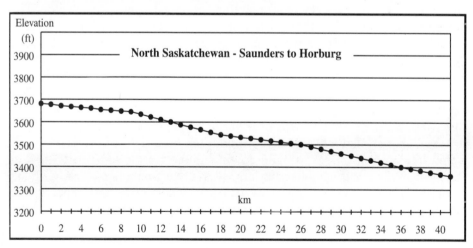

25

Getting Hooked

It was somewhere around 1980, and being athletic young men, Chris, Roger and I decided to try whitewater canoeing. My sister Anita and her husband Alan were always coming back with wild tales of whitewater adventure, so I borrowed their guidebook and we looked for a run. We didn't want to suffer through any of that beginner stuff, so we picked a grade II river that had some class III rapids. The run was less than halfway up the grading scale, which seemed reasonable to me. Hey, we were jocks and sure we could handle it. We had access to one kayak and one canoe. Since Chris had paddled a kayak a couple of times, he would use the kayak. After loading the cars with all the stuff we would need, we headed out. It was quite apparent, even then, that we had no idea what we were doing, but it certainly promised to be exciting.

We set out totally unaware that we were embarking on a river that would reach peak flow during our trip. Our first clue that something was amuck was that we were miles into the trip and had yet to encounter any of the rapids described in the guidebook. All the rapids were washed out! When we finally did reach a set of waves along the bank, we did the only reasonable thing. We headed straight for them! The river was fast and once we committed to a line we had little chance of altering course (especially given our rudimentary skills). So when Roger, who was in the bow, started yelling at me to go back while he clutched the gunnels in fear, I felt a bit helpless to say the least! As we broke through the first waves we were yelling at each other, until I spotted the "white stuff" below. I may have been a neophyte, but I knew right then that the only way to save our butts was to hit the power and blow through that thing.

Despite my threats of death and destruction if he didn't paddle, we hit that hole with Roger hanging on and screaming, while I stroked like a demon. The canoe rose up and smacked the white wall of the reversal as if it were concrete. But it got worse. As the boat started backsliding, we capsized and I was plucked from the stern and tumbled in the foam like a piece of cork. I had no idea what was happening, but I kept circulating around in the foam, unable to swim, break free or get a decent breath. Just when I thought it was curtains, I washed out wild-eyed and gasping. Roger had the canoe on the shore far below, and Chris was dragging his boat full of water onto the gravel as I finally crawled ashore. There ensued a heated debate about who was going to steer and who would ride with whom. We finally continued, but for the most part stuck to the inside of the bends, avoiding the large waves that would immediately fill the canoe. After one of the numerous swampings we wrapped the boat in polythene, forming a makeshift spraycover which was secured with ropes run around the hull. Using duct tape, we then affixed ourselves to the plastic sheet (which made Roger even more nervous). The trip was a brusque introduction to the power and allure of the river. It sparked (in me at least) the desire for further education and experience. I knew I was hooked!

GRADE	CLASS	FLOW	TIME	LENGTH
II	I–II	Most flows	4–6 hours	28 km (17 mi)

Gradient 2.4 m/km (.24%)
13 ft/mi

Max gradient 30 m in 11 km (.27%)
100 ft in 6.8 mi

Put-in elevation 1190 m
3904 ft

Take-out elevation 1122 m
3681 ft

Shuttle 43 km (26 mi) one way

Season May–October

Maps 83C8 and 83B5

Gauge Yes

Craft Canoes, kayaks and rafts

CHARACTER A medium to large-volume run through a scenic and open valley, with a few rapids in the lower part of the run. Most of the rapids consist of standing waves created by constrictions and corners.

FLOW INFORMATION The river is dam-controlled, fed by snowmelt and glacial runoff and subject to fluctuations dependent upon power requirements. Keep any equipment well back from the water line. The run is on Alberta Environmental Protection's River Report recording. Use the flow at the Bighorn Plant; low flow is 50 to 80 cms and high flow is 150 to 200 cms.

TRAVEL The shuttle is on pavement, except for a short gravel section.

DESCRIPTION For the first 6–8 km the river flows in a wide-open, braided and gravel-bottomed channel. The valley then closes in and the river enters a more defined channel. As the river cuts through the Brazeau Range, there are small rapids at most bends. In the last 9 km of the run, small bedrock ledges extend into the river channel, but most of these ledges can be easily avoided on one side or the other. The last kilometre contains some of the better rapids.

GETTING THERE The run is located west of Rocky Mountain House along Highway 11, near the town of Nordegg.

TAKE-OUT From Rocky Mountain House, go west on Highway 11 for 9 km to the junction with Highway 756 on the north (right). Continue west on Highway 11 for 56 km to the Saunders river access which is on the south (left) side of the highway. Turn left and follow the road for 400 m to a junction. Stay left and continue for 3 km to a junction at the base of a hill. Stay right and go another 3 km to a picnic site at the river. If you are approaching the run from the west, the Saunders river access is 23 km east of the town of Nordegg.

PUT-IN Return to Highway 11 and go west (left) for 25 km to the Highway 940 junction. Turn south (left) and follow the gravel road for 11 km to the bridge.

CAMPING There is undeveloped camping at the put-in, or developed camping at the take-out.

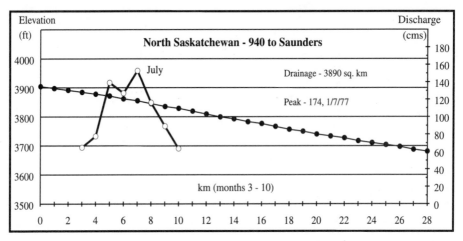

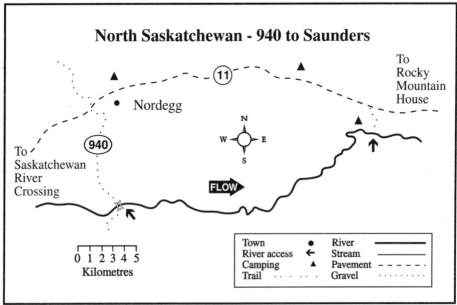

GRADE	CLASS	FLOW	TIME	LENGTH
I⁺	II	Low	5–7 hours	31 km (19 mi)
II	II	High		

Gradient   3.1 m/km (.31%)   **Max gradient** 30 m in 8 km (.38%)
                17 ft/mi   100 ft in 5 mi

Put-in elevation   1076 m   **Take-out elevation**   978 m
                        3530 ft   3210 ft

Shuttle   18 km (11 mi) one way   **Season**   June–August

Maps   83B2 and 83B7   **Gauge**   Yes

Craft   Canoes, kayaks and rafts

CHARACTER   A small to medium-volume run in a wide and open valley, with a few small rapids at corners. There are many sweepers and a couple of riverwide log jams.

FLOW INFORMATION   The river is uncontrolled and fed by snowmelt and glacial runoff. The river is on Alberta Environmental Protection's River Report recording. Use the flow at Rocky Mountain House. Low flow is 20 to 40 cms and high flow is 100 to 180 cms.

TRAVEL   The shuttle is on a paved highway.

DESCRIPTION   The river passes through an open valley in farmland and rolling hills. There are no major rapids, but sweepers are found on many of the tight corners. Beware of log jams, two of which were riverwide in 1991. Skill in reading water and knowing how to avoid obstacles is vital. The rest of the river offers little challenge other than a few tight bends.

GETTING THERE   The run is located west of Caroline, near the junction of Highways 22 and 54.

TAKE-OUT   At the 22/54/591 junction west of Caroline, go 18 km north on Highway 22 to the bridge. If you are coming from the north, the take-out bridge is 7 km south of the Highway 11/22 junction, just east of Rocky Mountain House.

PUT-IN   Go south on Highway 22 to the 22/54/591 junction west of Caroline. Directly south of the junction, a small dirt road leads 300 m across the meadow and through the trees to the river.

CAMPING   There is undeveloped camping at the put-in or at the take-out.

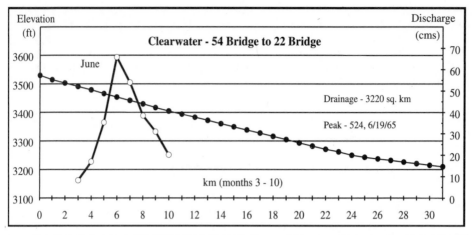

Clearwater - 54 Bridge to 22 Bridge

Elevation (ft) / Discharge (cms)

June

Drainage - 3220 sq. km

Peak - 524, 6/19/65

km (months 3 - 10)

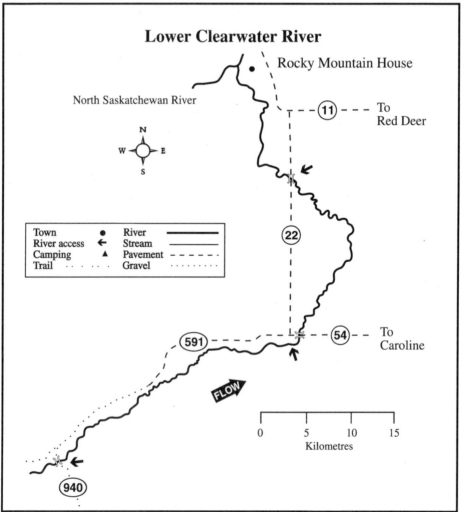

Lower Clearwater River

Rocky Mountain House

North Saskatchewan River

(11) - - - To Red Deer

N
W — E
S

Town ● River ——————
River access ← Stream ————
Camping ▲ Pavement - - - - -
Trail · · · · · Gravel · · · · · · ·

(22)

(591)

(54) - - To Caroline

FLOW

0   5   10   15
Kilometres

(940)

GRADE	CLASS	FLOW	TIME	LENGTH
I+–II	I+–II	Low	6–8 hours	37 km (23 mi)
II	II	High		

Gradient   4.8 m/km (.48%)   **Max gradient**   30 m in 5 km (.6%)
     25 ft/mi   100 ft in 3.1 mi

Put-in elevation   1253 m   **Take-out elevation**   1076 m
        4110 ft   3530 ft

Shuttle   33 km (21 mi) one way **Season**   June–August

Maps   82O14, 83B3 and 83B2 **Gauge**   Yes

Craft   Canoes, kayaks and rafts

CHARACTER   A small to medium-volume run which twists through an open valley, with numerous log jams and sweepers. This is not one of my favourites. Rafters will find the portages very trying.

FLOW INFORMATION   The river is uncontrolled and fed by snowmelt and glacial runoff. The river is on Alberta Environmental Protection's River Report recording. Use the flow at Rocky Mountain House; low flow is 20 to 40 cms and high flow is 100 to 180 cms.

TRAVEL   The shuttle is on gravel roads.

DESCRIPTION   Just below the bridge, the river leaves the mountains and begins to meander in the open valley. There are few rapids, but obstacles are created by innumerable log jams and sweepers in the twisting channel. The large amount of wood in the river makes the journey arduous and unsuitable for novices. There are good views and good fishing, but little whitewater.

GETTING THERE   The run is located west of Caroline, near the junction of Highways 22 and 54. See the map on page 30.

TAKE-OUT   From the 22/54/591 junction west of Caroline, go south on the small dirt road that leads across a meadow and through the trees to the river.

PUT-IN   Go west (left) on Highway 591 and proceed for 31 km to the junction with Highway 940. Turn south (left) and go 1.8 km to the bridge.

CAMPING   There is undeveloped camping at the take-out.

31

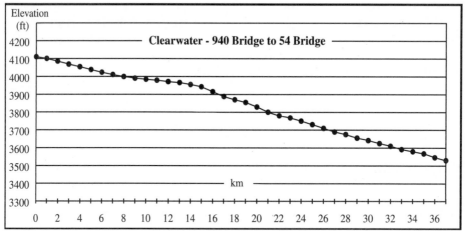

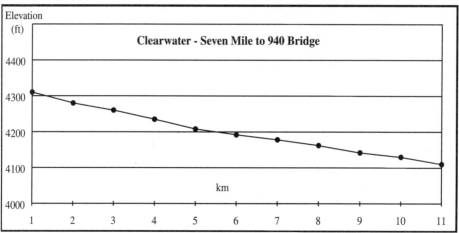

CLEARWATER — SEVEN MILE TO 940 BRIDGE

GRADE	CLASS	FLOW	TIME	LENGTH
II	I–II	Low	2–3 hours	11 km (6.8 mi)
II	II–II⁺	High		

Gradient 5.5 m/km (.55%) 29 ft/mi

Max gradient 30 m in 5.5 km (.55%) 100 ft in 3.4 mi

Put-in elevation 1314 m 4310 ft

Take-out elevation 1253 m 4110 ft

Shuttle 14 km (8.7 mi) one way

Season June–August

Maps 82O14

Gauge Yes

Craft Canoes, kayaks and rafts

CHARACTER A small to medium-volume run in an open valley, with great views and a few rapids.

FLOW INFORMATION The river is uncontrolled and fed by snowmelt and glacial runoff. The river is on Alberta Environmental Protection's River Report recording. Use the flow at Rocky Mountain House; low flow is 20 to 40 cms and high flow is 100 to 180 cms.

TRAVEL The shuttle is on gravel roads.

DESCRIPTION At the put-in, the river flows in a wandering single channel with great views of Corkscrew Mountain. The river in this section is swift, but has few major rapids. The rapids you do encounter are class II, consisting of small broken ledges and sharp corners where sweepers and log jams may occur. Approximately halfway down the run, the river braids and meanders in an open gravel channel. The gradient profile is on page 32.

GETTING THERE The run is located west of Caroline, near the junction of Highways 22 and 54. See the map on page 35.

TAKE-OUT From the 22/54/591 junction west of Caroline, proceed west on Highway 591 for 31 km to the junction with Highway 940. Turn south (left) and go 1.8 km to the bridge.

PUT-IN Go 1.8 km north to the 591/940 junction, then turn west (left) and proceed for 12 km to the Seven Mile Campground, which is on the south (left) side of the road. Turn left and go through the campground to the river.

CAMPING There is developed camping at the put-in.

GRADE	CLASS	FLOW	TIME	LENGTH
II	I–II	Low	1–2 hours	8 km (5 mi)
II	II–II⁺	High		

Gradient 4.4 m/km (.44%)   **Max gradient** 30 m in 6.5 km (.46%)
23 ft/mi   100 ft in 4 mi

Put-in elevation   1349 m   **Take-out elevation**   1314 m
4425 ft   4310 ft

Shuttle   6.3 km (4 mi) one way   **Season**   June–August

Maps   82O14   **Gauge**   Yes

Craft   Canoes, kayaks and rafts

CHARACTER A small to medium-volume run in an open valley, with some great views. Rapids are created at tight corners and small bedrock ledges.

FLOW INFORMATION The river is uncontrolled and fed by snowmelt and glacial runoff. The river is on Alberta Environmental Protection's River Report recording. Use the flow at Rocky Mountain House; low flow is 20 to 40 cms and high flow is 100 to 180 cms.

TRAVEL The shuttle is on gravel roads.

DESCRIPTION The river flows in a single channel below the bridge. The first obstacle you encounter is a class II boulder garden. This is followed not far below by a small class II–II⁺ ledge, with more boulder-garden rapids just downstream. The rapids ease and the river flows in a more open channel for a couple of kilometres until you reach a broken class II ledge. At certain water levels there is some easy surfing and hole-playing on the features formed by the bedrock outcrops. Below this there are occasional small waves and midstream boulders until you reach the take-out.

GETTING THERE The run is located west of Caroline, near the junction of Highways 22 and 54.

TAKE-OUT From the 22/54/591 junction west of Caroline, proceed west on Highway 591 for 31 km, to the junction with Highway 940. Go west (right) and proceed for 12 km to the Seven Mile Campground, which is on the south (left) side of the road. Follow the campground road to loop number 4, where the river is nearby.

PUT-IN Return to Highway 940, then turn west (left) and go 1.8 km to a junction with the road to the Cutoff Creek Equestrian Staging Area on the west (left) side. Turn left and follow the road 4.5 km to the bridge.

CAMPING There is undeveloped camping at the put-in or developed camping at the take-out.

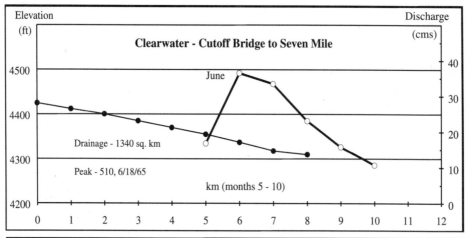

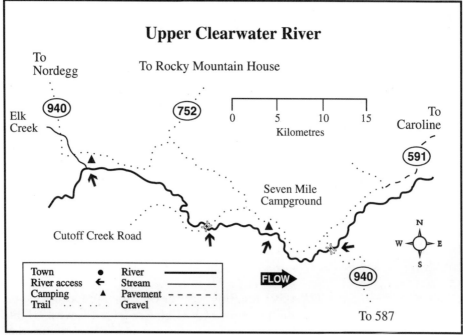

GRADE	CLASS	FLOW	TIME	LENGTH
II	II	Low	4–6 hours	21 km (13 mi)
II	II+	High		

Gradient   5.5 m/km (.55%)
          29 ft/mi

Max gradient   30 m in 4.5 km (.7%)
          100 ft in 2.8 mi

Put-in elevation   1465 m
          4806 ft

Take-out elevation   1349 m
          4425 ft

Shuttle   31 km (19 mi) one way

Season   June–August

Maps   83B4, 83B3 and 82O14

Gauge   Yes

Craft   Canoes, kayaks and rafts

CHARACTER   A small to medium-volume run on an open gravel-bed in a scenic valley. The obstacles include braided channels, log jams and sweepers.

FLOW INFORMATION   The river is uncontrolled and fed by snowmelt and glacial runoff. The river is on Alberta Environmental Protection's River Report recording. Use the flow at Rocky Mountain House; low flow is 20 to 40 cms and high flow is 100 to 180 cms.

TRAVEL   The shuttle is on gravel roads.

DESCRIPTION   The run is nearly uniform in character, as the river flows over an open gravel-bed through frequently braided channels. There are numerous tight corners and small rapids. Beware of the many log jams and sweepers. In the last part of the run, the river assumes a single channel and there are a more small rapids where the valley walls close in and bedrock outcrops occur. Enjoy the excellent foothills scenery.

GETTING THERE   The run is located west of Caroline, near the junction of Highways 22 and 54. See the map on page 35.

TAKE-OUT   From the 22/54/591 junction west of Caroline, proceed west on Highway 591 for 31 km to the junction with Highway 940. Go west (right) and proceed for 14 km to a junction with the road to Cutoff Creek Equestrian Staging Area on the west (left) side. Turn left and follow the road for 4.5 km to the bridge.

PUT-IN   Return to Highway 940, turn north (left), and proceed for 13 km to a junction with Highway 752 on the east (right). Continue north on Highway 940 for 13 km to the Elk Creek Recreation Area. About 400 m before you reach the recreation area, there is a small gravel road on the west (left) side. Turn left and follow the road, which leads along the fence for 300 m, to an open boggy area. The river is about 500 m beyond the boggy area.

CAMPING   There is developed camping at the put-in or undeveloped camping at the take-out.

Remote foothills scenery on the upper Clearwater.

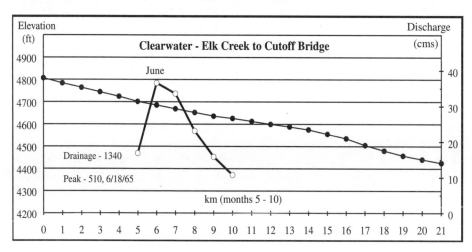

GRADE	CLASS	FLOW	TIME	LENGTH
II–III	II–VI$^+$	Low	2–4 days	54 km (34 mi)
III–IV	III–VI$^+$	High		

Gradient 7.9 m/km (.79%) **Max gradient** 30 m in 3 km (1%)
42 ft/mi   100 ft in 1.9 mi

Put-in elevation 1540 m **Take-out elevation** 1116 m
5052 ft   3660 ft

Shuttle 81 km (50 mi) to lower take-out - one way
75 km (46 mi) to upper take-out - one way

Maps 83B4, 83B5 and 83B6 **Season** June–September

Craft Canoes, kayaks and rafts **Gauge** Yes

CHARACTER A medium-volume run in a spectacular series of magnificent canyons, with numerous waterfalls, portages and plenty of grand wilderness scenery. There is no better extended overnight adventure in the area!

FLOW INFORMATION The river is uncontrolled and fed by snowmelt and glacial runoff. Use Alberta Environmental Protection's River Report recording at the mouth of the Ram. Low flow is 15 to 30 cms and high flow is 80 to 150 cms.

TRAVEL The shuttle is on gravel roads.

DESCRIPTION The put-in gives a clue as to what the entire run holds: lots of rugged terrain and the need for a good attitude and adventurous spirit to navigate the obstacles. Once you get your boat to the river, there are a few small drops in the first kilometres. You then reach a ragged class III–IV drop at a constricted broken ledge. Below this the river runs for many kilometres with a few minor rapids. The next set of good rapids consists of three class III–IV ledges, the final ledge being the largest. You then reach Tapestry Falls, a 24–28-m waterfall that occurs just below a bend to the left. Portage on river right by exiting on the sloping rock ledges and carrying your boat to the edge of the fall. The best way around is to lower your boats off the cliff to the ledge along the pool below. You must then climb up and around on the steep slope, to reach a gully that leads down below the fall. The scrambling is steep and a bit exposed. Below the fall, the river runs in a deeper canyon through rapids formed by fallen debris. Watch for a 200-m-long, constricted class III–III$^+$ boulder garden that leads to a sharp left turn, followed by a sharp right turn into a narrow canyon. This is the start of the class IV–V Powerslide, a 10–12-m drop that runs along a low-angled rock slab into a flat and powerful recirculation. You can scout things from the right shore.

Looking upstream from the put-in at Ram Falls. Photo: Sandra Cassady.

Feast Or Famine

When we arrived at the put-in the river was quite low, but we figured we would do it anyway. We planned to reach the big fall that first day, but stopped well short of our goal to set up camp. It was a beautiful evening, and we lay around the fire discussing the rapids below. Not long after we turned in, it began to rain. Not your regular type of rain; this stuff was hammering down. In my tiny ultralight tent we huddled together, trying to stay away from the dripping walls. Somehow Bob got the upper side, and for most of the night I was curled in a ball to avoid the pool of water on my side. Morning brought no relief and we packed up in the downpour. The river was no longer low or even medium. It was a seething brown serpent, twisting through the canyon.

At the final canyon we got out to scout the back-to-back waterfalls. I elected to run the second, and Bob decided to get in just below that, so we lowered his boat into the canyon. After I ran the fall, I eddied out where Bob had his boat. It was no real eddy, but rather a swirling pool that recirculated into the drop above. Just below us, the river swept through a narrow crack and around the corner to a pourover ledge. Bob had spent a lot of time waiting for me, and I could see he was having doubts, but he slid into his boat while I held it stable. Then in a sudden lurch, the boat skidded free just as he was inside, and we began to circulate in the swirling pool. That was it; Bob lost it, and in a crazed anxiety attack grabbed me. We were pulled toward the drop, Bob with his deck off, and me with two paddles across my bow, as we clutched each other. He was screaming at me and I was yelling back. We were sucked into the drop and side-surfed it for a bit, then flushed out for another go-round. Miraculously his boat was only partly filled, but now we had more momentum for our second cycle. We were heading for the worst of it, so I hauled off and smacked him, full force, right in the side of his helmet. He went wild eyed, focused slightly, then smacked me back. Locking eyes through the grapple, we spontaneously burst into outrageous laughter. Working together we got his deck on, narrowly avoiding side-by-side backenders in the hole. At the ledge below, I dropped into the hole and was violently ejected from my kayak after a merciless windowshade. I flushed out against the right bank and clambered up to see Bob in the eddy above. I was waving him on, indicating a clean line while yelling that my boat was floating away. He just looked at me and twisted his head back and forth. Nope, not this time.

So I ran down to where my boat was shooting through the narrow slot below, jumped into the river and swam after my boat. Later we met up on the shore. We finished the trip in a violent thunderstorm that left us grovelling along the bank, praying that our aluminum-shafted paddles would not attract a lightning strike. The river was chock full of water, and the banks erupted with brown frothing masses every couple of hundred metres, sending us flailing out into the exposed middle of the river, where our hair crackled with static electricity. The trip was a strange mixture of too much and not enough.

The next big drop is the 12–15-m high Table Rock Falls, which is situated on a sharp left turn, where a large flat-topped boulder sits in the river just above the fall. The rock ledges are downsloping into the river above the drop, so be aware. Although Table Rock has been run, the scenario for most folks is similar to the one for the big fall: lower your boats off the river right lip, then walk up and around to a downstream gully leading back to the river. Below Table Rock Falls the river is easier, with short class II–III rapids at small ledges. This continues for a few kilometres, until the confluence with the North Ram. Not far below the confluence, things pick up when the river enters a deep canyon. The entrance rapid is a broken bedrock ledge on a left turn, below which the river enters a long vertical-walled canyon. Near the bottom of the canyon the river drops off a class III⁺–IV⁺ diagonal ledge that at high flows has a horrendous recirculation and at low flows is a 3–4-m fall. At most flows you can stop on the right just above the drop and scramble out on the ledges to scout or portage; however, this becomes tricky at high flows. The river then makes a sharp left turn and enters a narrow boulder-strewn class III–III⁺ rapid, where slide debris makes for some tight manoeuvring.

The canyon opens up, and a few hundred metres below is a large island where the right channel is funnelled into Ricochet, a narrow class IV–V slot. At higher flows some of the river flows around to the left of the big island, where cold sulphur springs produce aqua pools. The river mellows for about 200 m, then drops into the last canyon where few people choose to paddle, so look for a good take-out on the left. The action starts with a sloping 5–6-m class V⁺–VI waterfall, followed 30 m below by a second 4–5-m class V⁺–VI fall, with an upstream sloping rock slab in the middle. Both have been run, but if you choose not to paddle there is a portage route on river left. The trail climbs the bank up into the trees, then follows the steep sidehill for 500–600 m to a gully that allows descent back to the river. You can also get back in, just below the second fall, by lowering your boats down the steep cliff. If you choose this option, there are four additional drops in the canyon.

Just below the second fall the river drops 1–2 m out of a swirling bowl, then a short pool leads to a very narrow boiling slot. The river makes a left turn, then a right turn, and pours over a class IV⁺–V riverwide ledge that drops 2–3 m into a vicious recirculation. About 20 m below this the river funnels into The Chasm, a narrow class V⁺–VI slot on the left that is often full of logs. This has been run, but you can avoid The Chasm at water level by running to the right side of the rock fin that creates the slot on the left. At low water you can climb out on the rock fin then seal-launch below the slot. Running the drops below the double fall, or portaging at water level, requires precise manoeuvres and steady nerves. You then reach the pool where the portage gully descends to the river, just downstream of a narrow slot. After this the river makes a turn then drops off a small riverwide double ledge, followed by a couple of easier broken ledges. The valley opens up and the paddling is easier, with no major rapids until you reach the take-out.

GETTING THERE   The run is located west of Rocky Mountain House off the Forestry Trunk Road (Highway 940).

TAKE-OUT   From Rocky Mountain House, go south on Highway 11 until you reach the Highway 752 junction. Turn west (right) and proceed 2.5 km to a T intersection. Turn south (left) and follow the road for 21 km to the Strachan Ranger Station turn-off.

To reach the **lower take-out,** continue 2.6 km west of the Strachan Ranger Station turn-off to the junction with the North Fork Road, which is on the north (right) side. Turn right and follow the North Fork Road for 25 km to the bridge.

To reach the **upper take-out** (which eliminates 14 km of flat water), continue 10.7 km west of the Strachan Ranger Station turn-off to an unmarked gravel road on the north (right) side of Highway 752. Turn right, cross Prairie Creek in about 50 m, then go 4 km to a junction with a road on the left. Go straight through, for 2 km, to another road on the left. Continue straight and the road will come parallel to a powerline. Travel along the powerline to where you reach a 90-degree turn to the right, with a road on the left. Stay right and you will cross under the powerline, then wind around to a pipeline valve station in 2.5 km. A rough trail leads 200 m to the edge of the valley, then a smaller trail leads another 250 m steeply down to the river. Mark the take-out!

To approach the run from the north, on Highway 940 near Nordegg, follow Highway 940 south of Highway 11 for 28 km to a junction 300 m north of the bridge on the North Ram. To reach the **lower take-out,** turn east (left) and follow the road for 49 km to the bridge on the Ram River. To reach the **upper take-out,** go south from the North Ram bridge for 32 km to the South Ram bridge, then continue another 31 km south to the junction with Highway 752. Turn east (left) and go 26 km to a bridge on Prairie Creek. Continue east for 1.2 km to an unmarked gravel road on the north (left) side. Follow the directions for the upper take-out, from the turn-off on Highway 752, in the paragraph above.

PUT-IN   At the **lower take-out,** go west from the bridge along the North Fork Road and follow it for 49 km to the junction with Highway 940. Turn south (left) and go 32 km to the Ram Falls Recreation Area, which is on the east (left) side. Turn left and follow the road into the recreation site and along to the picnic shelters at the far end. Take the trail out to the viewpoint, then descend the steep 150-m high slope to the river.

From the **upper take-out** return to Highway 752, then turn west (right) and follow the road 27 km to the junction with Highway 940. Turn north (right) and go 31 km to the bridge on the South Ram. About 600 m past the bridge is the Ram Falls Recreation Area on the east (right) side. Follow the road into the recreation site and along to the picnic shelters at the far end. Take the trail out to the viewpoint, then descend the steep 150-m high slope to the river. One slip on this one and you're a goner!

CAMPING   There is developed camping at the put-in or undeveloped camping at the take-out, as well as many splendid sites along the river.

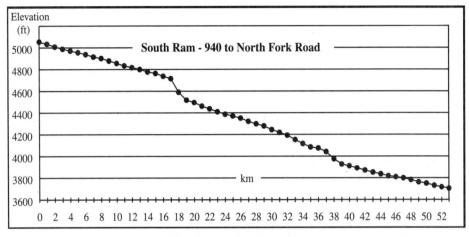

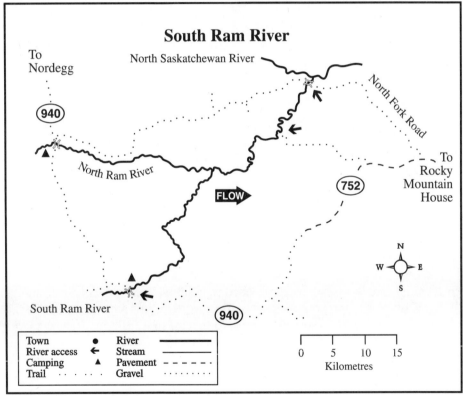

Wacky Wildlife

Over the years I've seen plenty of wildlife while travelling down the river; however, nothing quite as strange as this. It was my first trip down the Ram River, in July of 1990. There were five of us, four in the raft and Geoff Gilchrist in his kayak for safety support. Dusk was quickly approaching and we were searching the banks for a suitable campsite. We came around the bend to find a young mule deer buck, river left, on a large gravel bar. As we drifted past, it seemed complacent in our presence. I enjoy any opportunity for a wildlife photo, so we pulled in about 150 metres downstream. I was amazed that the buck did not dash for the trees. Instead he tentatively approached our group as I readied my camera.

The deer allowed a member of our party to approach within arms length, but finally his nerves got the better of him and he bolted straight through our group and into the river. He swam across, then stood on the opposite bank looking back at us, surveying the situation. Maybe he felt lonely on his own.

Whatever the reason, he jumped back in the river, making a beeline for the eddy where Geoff had been observing the action from his boat. I imagine Geoff's heart skipped a beat or two as this over-friendly deer clambered up and straddled the cockpit of his kayak. Geoff's paddle was a blur of frantic bracing as he fought to stabilize the kayak. On shore, there was shocked silence as I scrambled to photograph the event. This unusual paddling partner seemed to enjoy the view from his perch and showed absolutely no inclination to abandon ship. Finally, Geoff resorted to pushing his hairy companion unceremoniously into the river.

The deer returned to shore and proceeded to jump into our raft, sending paddles flying. Obviously our craft was not going to take him anywhere, so it was back into the river, once again swimming toward that little red kayak. Geoff was quite unwilling to take on this freeloader a second time and had to fend him off with his paddle. The deer made several attempts to get past Geoff's defence but finally gave up, swam ashore and bounded into the brush. We wished we had brought a video camera and wondered whether anyone would ever believe us, even with the photos I had taken as evidence.

Sandra Cassady

SOUTH RAM — UPPER CANYON

GRADE	CLASS	FLOW	TIME	LENGTH
II	II–II⁺	Low	1–2 hours	8 km (5 mi)
II–II⁺	II–III	High		

Gradient 8.8 m/km (.88%)
46 ft/mi

Max gradient 30 m in 2.5 km (1.2%)
100 ft in 1.6 mi

Put-in elevation 1640 m
5381 ft

Take-out elevation 1570 m
5151 ft

Shuttle 6.8 km (4.2 mi) one way

Season June–August

Maps 83B4

Gauge Yes

Craft Canoes, kayaks and rafts

CHARACTER A medium-volume run that begins on an open gravel plain, then enters a constricted canyon. The whitewater section is short, then the canyon opens up, with few rapids in the lower scenic section.

FLOW INFORMATION The river is uncontrolled and fed by snowmelt and glacial runoff. The river is on Alberta Environmental Protection's River Report recording. Use the flow at the mouth of the Ram, and expect 30 percent of that flow at the put-in. Low flow is 15 to 30 cms and high flow is 80 to 150 cms.

TRAVEL Access to the run and the shuttle are on gravel roads.

DESCRIPTION The run begins on an open gravel plain, where the river meanders across braided flats. The character changes dramatically at the canyon mouth where the river flows along a rock wall, then makes a 90-degree left turn through the bedrock slab. There is a short pool before the river drops off a broken class II–III ledge, followed by more rapids in the narrow bedrock canyon. The next 500 m contains a few easier drops, then the canyon opens up and there is some great scenery in the lower half of the run. Be sure to get out at the bridge, since the 30-m Ram Falls is only 1 kilometre downstream.

GETTING THERE The run is located west of Rocky Mountain House, off the Forestry Trunk Road (Highway 940).

TAKE-OUT From Rocky Mountain House, proceed south on Highway 11 for a couple of kilometres. At the Highway 752 junction turn west (right) and go 2.5 km to a T intersection. Go south (left) and follow the road for 58 km to the junction with Highway 940. Turn north (right) and proceed 31 km to the bridge on the South Ram. A small road just past the bridge, on the west (left) side, leads back to the river.

If you are coming from the north, the take-out bridge is approximately 64 km south of the 940/11 junction, just west of Nordegg.

PUT-IN Go north from the bridge for 3.2 km to a junction with the road to the Hummingbird Equestrian Staging Area on the west (left) side. Turn left and follow that road for 3.6 km to a small trail on the south (left) side which leads to the river.

CAMPING There is developed camping at the Ram Falls Recreation Area just north of the take-out, or undeveloped camping at the put-in.

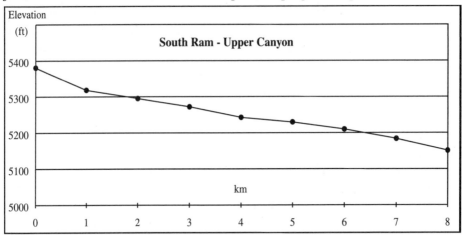

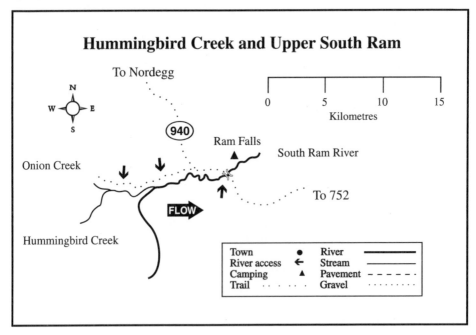

GRADE	CLASS	FLOW	TIME	LENGTH
II	II–V	Low	1–2 hours	3 km (1.9 mi)
III	II⁺–V	High		

Gradient	15 m/km (1.5%) 79 ft/mi	**Max gradient**	30 m in 1.3 km (2.3%) 100 ft in .8 mi
Put-in elevation	1685 m 5528 ft	**Take-out elevation**	1640 m 5381 ft
Shuttle	4 km (2.5 mi) one way	**Season**	June–August
Maps	83B4	**Gauge**	No
Craft	Canoes and kayaks		

NOTES The run finishes with a 1.5-km (.9-mi) run on the South Ram.

CHARACTER A small-volume run through a scenic steep-walled valley, with a couple of small ledge drops and great views of the waterfall at the put-in.

FLOW INFORMATION You have to assess the flow at the put-in. Check the North Ram hydrograph on page 48 for an idea of the seasonal flow.

TRAVEL The shuttle is on gravel roads.

DESCRIPTION The run starts downstream of the gorge and waterfall, then flows in a deep steep-sided valley. The main features in the first part are a series of small sloping ledges and a couple of narrow spots where the walls constrict the flow. A long left turn leads to a 2–4-m diagonal class IV⁺–V fall. The left side drops through a jagged slot, while the right side is a sloping drop into a shallow pool. About 100 m below is a narrow class IV–IV⁺ slot around a huge boulder. Below this there are a few minor rapids until you reach the Ram and then easy paddling to the take-out.

GETTING THERE The run is located west of Rocky Mountain House, off the Forestry Trunk Road (Highway 940). See the map on page 46.

TAKE-OUT From Rocky Mountain House proceed south on Highway 11 for a couple of kilometres. At the Highway 752 junction turn west (right) and go 2.5 km to a T intersection. Go south (left) and follow the road for 58 km to the junction with Highway 940. Turn north (right) and proceed 31 km to the bridge on the South Ram. Continue north for 3.2 km to a junction with the turn-off to the Hummingbird Equestrian Staging Area on the west (left). Turn left and follow the road for 3.5 km to a small trail on the left that leads down to the South Ram.

If you are coming from the north, the turn-off to the Hummingbird Equestrian Staging Area is 60 km south of the 940/11 junction just west of Nordegg.

PUT-IN Go about 4 km west on the road to the Hummingbird Equestrian Staging Area. The road makes a right turn, then leads up a hill to a switchback at a creek crossing. Park well off the road and descend the steep gully to the creek.

CAMPING There is undeveloped camping at the take-out. For developed camping try Ram Falls Recreation Area, on Highway 940 just north of the take-out.

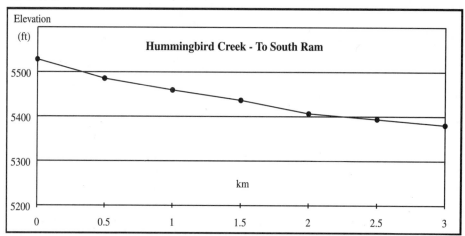

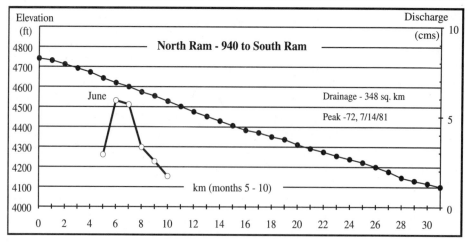

GRADE	CLASS	FLOW	TIME	LENGTH
II	II	Low	4–6 hours	31 km (19 mi)
II⁺	II⁺	High		

Gradient   6.3 m/km (.63%)
          33 ft/mi

Max gradient   30 m in 4 km (.75%)
             100 ft in 2.5 mi

Put-in elevation   1445 m
               4741 ft

Take-out elevation   1250 m
                 4101 ft

Shuttle   50 km (31 mi) one way   **Season**   June–August

Maps   83B5 and 83B4   **Gauge**   Yes

Craft   Canoes, kayaks and rafts

NOTES   The run finishes with a 19-km paddle on the Ram River. There is an upper take-out for the run which eliminates 14 km of flatwater paddling. Check the South Ram description on page 38 for details.

CHARACTER   A medium-volume run over an open gravel-bed in a scenic valley. The rapids are created by corners, bedrock outcrops and small ledges.

FLOW INFORMATION   The river is uncontrolled and fed by snowmelt and glacial runoff. Check Alberta Environmental Protection's River Report recording and use the flow at the mouth of the Ram. Low flow is 15 to 30 cms and high flow is 80 to 150 cms. Expect about one-quarter of that flow at the put-in.

TRAVEL   The shuttle is on gravel roads.

DESCRIPTION   At the put-in, the river flows in an open gravel-bottomed valley and remains that way for most of the run. A few kilometres into the run the river winds back and forth across the valley with tighter corners but no major rapids. As you approach the confluence with the South Ram small ledges appear in the river channel and there are interesting rock formations as the valley walls close in. There are a couple of class II rapids in the last few kilometres above the confluence with the South Ram. The gradient profile is on page 48. The whitewater downstream of the confluence is significantly harder than the run described here. See the description on page 38 for details of the run below the confluence.

GETTING THERE   The run is located west of Rocky Mountain House, off the Forestry Trunk Road (Highway 940).

49

TAKE-OUT From Rocky Mountain House go south on Highway 11, 1.8 km past the railroad bridge, to the Highway 752 junction. Turn west (right) and go 2.5 km to a T intersection. Turn south (left) and follow the road for 21 km to the Strachan Ranger Station turn-off. Continue 2.6 km west of the Strachan Ranger Station turn-off to the junction with the North Fork Road, which is on the north (right) side. Turn right and follow the North Fork Road for 25 km to the bridge.

If approaching the run from the north, on Highway 940 near Nordegg, follow Highway 940 32 km south of Highway 11 to a junction 300 m north of the bridge on the North Ram. Turn east (left) and follow the road for 49 km to the bridge on the Ram River.

PUT-IN Go west from the bridge, along the North Fork Road, and follow it for 49 km to the junction with Highway 940. Turn south (left) and go 300 m to the bridge.

CAMPING There is developed camping at the put-in, or undeveloped camping at the take-out.

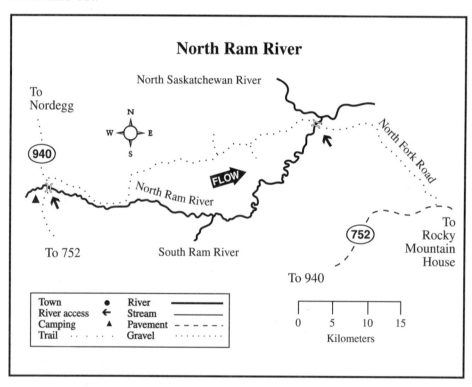

50

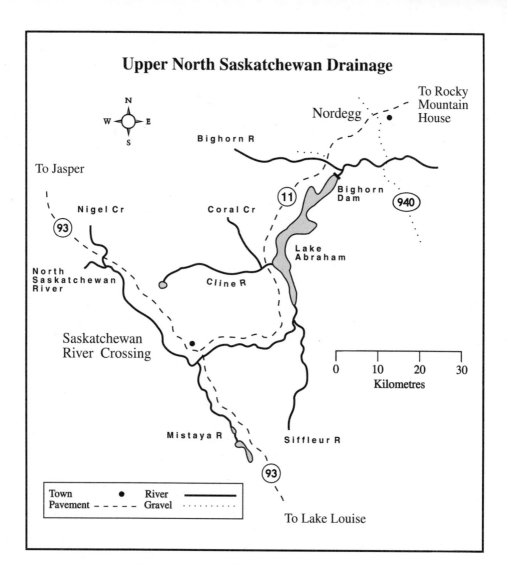

Upper North Saskatchewan Drainage

GRADE	CLASS	FLOW	TIME	LENGTH
I–II	II	Most Flows	4–7 hours	31 km (19 mi)

Gradient   1.6 m/km (.16%)   **Max gradient**   30 m in 19 km (.16%)
              8 ft/mi   100 ft in 12 mi

Put-in elevation   1393 m   **Take-out elevation**   1344 m
                             4570 ft   4410 ft

Shuttle   31 km (19 mi) one way   **Season**   May–October

Maps   82N15, 83C2 and 83C1   **Gauge**   Yes

Craft   Canoes, kayaks and rafts

CHARACTER   A medium to large-volume river that flows through an open valley. Negotiating the occasional tight corner and avoiding sweepers and log jams are the main challenges. The scenery is outstanding.

FLOW INFORMATION   The river is uncontrolled and fed by snowmelt and glacial runoff. The run is on Alberta Environmental Protection's River Report recording. Use the flow at Whirlpool Point; low flow is 40 to 70 cms and high flow is 150 to 220 cms.

TRAVEL   Both the shuttle and access to the run are on paved highways.

DESCRIPTION   The river flows over a gravel-bottomed channel that is braided for most of the run. There are a few sections where rock outcrops produce features along one shore or the other. Occasionally the river is constricted by the valley walls where the current speeds up, but for the most part the river is open and easy to negotiate.

GETTING THERE   The run is located along Highway 11 near Saskatchewan River Crossing.

TAKE-OUT   From Rocky Mountain House go 135 km west on Highway 11 to the David Thompson Resort. Continue 15 km west to the Two O'Clock Creek Campground, on the south (left) side of the road. Follow the campground loop to near the river. If you approach the run from the west, the campground is 29 km east of the Highways 93/11 junction at Saskatchewan River Crossing.

PUT-IN   Go west on Highway 11 to the junction with Highway 93. Turn south (left) and proceed 1.6 km to the bridge. There is a small dirt road on the west (right) side about 200 m south of the bridge that leads back to near the river.

CAMPING   There is developed camping at the take-out.

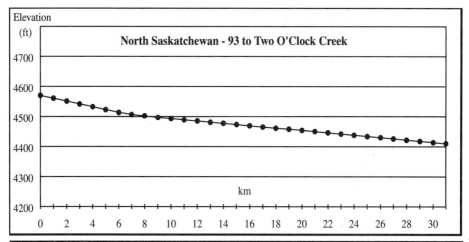

North Saskatchewan - 93 to Two O'Clock Creek

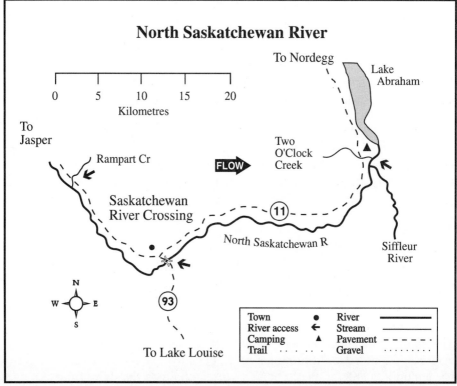

North Saskatchewan River

GRADE	CLASS	FLOW	TIME	LENGTH
II	II–V⁺	Low	2–3 hours	16 km (10 mi)
II	II–VI	High		

Gradient 2.1 m/km (.21%)
11 ft/mi

Max gradient 30 m in 12 km (.25%)
100 ft in 7.5 mi

Put-in elevation 1426 m
4680 ft

Take-out elevation 1393 m
4570 ft

Shuttle 14 km (8.7 mi) one way

Season June–September

Maps 83C2 and 82N15

Gauge No

Craft Canoes, kayaks and rafts

CHARACTER A medium-volume run through a scenic and open valley with little whitewater, except for a 1–1.5-km canyon section. For the most part, the river flows in an open gravel plain. The views below the Howes River confluence are spectacular, with a 360-degree panorama of peaks.

FLOW INFORMATION The river is uncontrolled and fed by snowmelt and glacial runoff. The river is on Alberta Environmental Protection's River Report recording. Use the flow at Whirlpool Point; low flow is 40 to 70 cms and high flow is 150 to 220 cms. You will have about 20–40 percent of that flow at the put-in. At high flows the canyon section is very pushy.

TRAVEL Both the shuttle and access to the run are on paved highways.

DESCRIPTION The river is in an open valley at the put-in and alternates between a single channel and short braided sections. About 2 km below some large islands, the channel narrows as the valley closes in. A sharp left turn, followed by a kilometre-long straight, leads to the start of the canyon section. Use caution, since the downsloping bedrock walls can make exiting tricky. The major rapids begin below a left turn, where the river drops off a class V⁺–VI diagonal 2–4-m ledge. Approximately 25 m below, the second class V–V⁺ drop has a sloping chute on the left and an insane hole on the right, followed by a series of class III standing waves in the canyon. The whitewater can be easily portaged or scouted along the trail on the left shore. Approximately 300 m below the end of the canyon is a small class II–III diagonal ledge. Then a rock outcrop on the right, at the bridge for the Glacier Lake Trail, produces the final bit of class III whitewater. Below the confluence with the Howes River, the river flows in a braided gravel plain to the take-out.

GETTING THERE The run is located near Saskatchewan River Crossing, along Highway 93. See the map on page 53.

TAKE-OUT From the junction of Highways 11/93 at Saskatchewan River Crossing, go south for 1.6 km to the bridge. There is a small dirt road on the west (right) side, about 200 m south of the bridge, that leads back to near the river.

PUT-IN Go north to the junction of Highways 93 and 11, then continue 12 km north on Highway 93 to the Rampart Creek Campground, which is on the west (left) side. Follow the campground road to near the river.

CAMPING There is developed camping at the put-in.

Looking upstream at the canyon rapids.

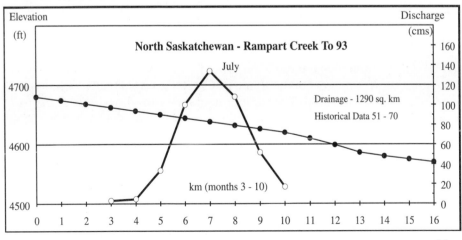

GRADE	CLASS	FLOW	TIME	LENGTH
II	I–II	Most Flows	1–2 hours	13 km (8 mi)

Gradient   4.9 m/km (.49%)   **Max gradient**   30 m in 6 km (.5%)
                26 ft/mi   100 ft in 3.7 mi

Put-in elevation   1490 m   **Take-out elevation**   1426 m
                        4890 ft   4680 ft

Shuttle   11 km (6.8 mi) one way   **Season**   June–September

Maps   83C2   **Gauge**   No

Craft   Canoes, kayaks and rafts

CHARACTER   A small to medium-volume run in an open gravel-bottomed valley with spectacular views of the surrounding mountains. The river is mostly braided, with a short constricted section.

FLOW INFORMATION   The river is uncontrolled and fed by snowmelt and glacial runoff. Assess the flow at the take-out.

TRAVEL   Access to the run and the shuttle are on paved roads.

DESCRIPTION   The river flows in a single channel at the start, but has braided sections on the open gravel plain. About 2–3 km into the run the river is constricted by steep valley walls and standing waves are formed in the narrow channel. This lasts for roughly 1 km, then the river opens up to a very braided section which extends below the confluence with Arctomys Creek. Mark the take-out at the river. The gradient profile is on the opposite page.

GETTING THERE   The run is located north of Saskatchewan River Crossing along Highway 93.

TAKE-OUT   From the junction of Highways 11 and 93 at Saskatchewan River Crossing, go 12 km north to the Rampart Creek Campground, which is on the west (left) side of the road. The campground road runs down to near the river. If you approach the run from the north, the campground is 38 km south of the Columbia Icefields Centre.

PUT-IN   Go north for 11 km to a an unnamed picnic site on the west (left) side of the highway.

CAMPING   There is developed camping at the take-out.

56

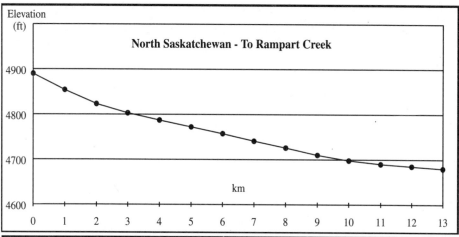

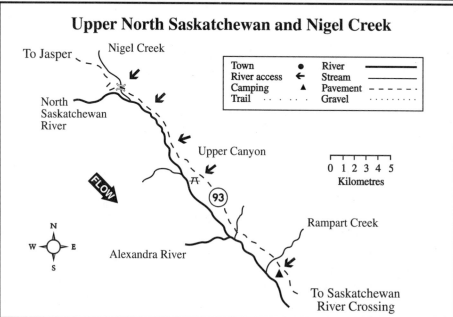

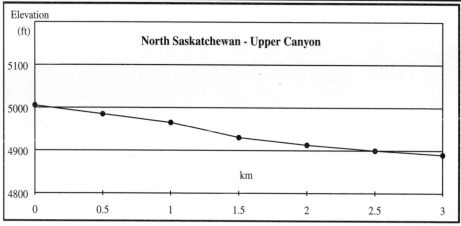

GRADE	CLASS	FLOW	TIME	LENGTH
II⁺	III–VI	Low	1–2 hours	3 km (1.9 mi)
III⁺	III–VI	High		

Gradient 12 m/km (1.2%)   **Max gradient** 30 m in 2.4 km (1.3%)
           62 ft/mi   100 ft in 1.5 mi

Put-in elevation 1526 m   **Take-out elevation** 1490 m
                  5005 ft   4890 ft

Shuttle 3 km (1.9 mi) one way   **Season** June–September

Maps 83C2   **Gauge** No

Craft Canoes and kayaks

CHARACTER A short, but exciting run on a medium-volume river, with spectacular vistas and some fine rapids. The portage around the fall is a bush thrash that presents a definite problem, particularly for canoeists.

FLOW INFORMATION The river is uncontrolled and fed by snowmelt and glacial runoff. Assess the flow at the take-out.

TRAVEL Access to the run and the shuttle are on paved roads.

DESCRIPTION There is a short section of calm water before you reach a 200-m-long class II⁺–III rapid. A second calm section leads to a class III–IV boulder garden with a log jam at the bottom on the right. Below this, a third calm section ends in a left turn where rock walls flank the river. Take out on the left and portage the 8–10 m fall by carrying along the canyon rim. Thrash through the dense undergrowth along the steep sideslope for about 200 m to a small gully. Descend the gully to a rock outcrop where you can seal-launch back into the river. There are some standing waves in the canyon below the fall, then the river eases to the take-out. The gradient profile is on page 57.

GETTING THERE The run is located north of Saskatchewan River Crossing along Highway 93. See the map on page 57.

TAKE-OUT From the junction of Highways 11 and 93 at Saskatchewan River Crossing, proceed north for 23 km to an unnamed picnic site on the west (left) side of the road. The picnic site is 27 km south of the Columbia Icefields Centre.

PUT-IN The put-in is 2.8 km north where the highway is close to the river.

CAMPING There is developed camping about 11 km south of the take-out, at Rampart Creek.

GRADE	CLASS	FLOW	TIME	LENGTH
II	I–II	Most Flows	1–2 hours	5.2 km (3.2 mi)

Gradient　4 m/km (.4%)
　　　　　　22 ft/mi

Max gradient　21 m in 5 km (.4%)
　　　　　　　　69 ft in 3 mi

Put-in elevation　1547 m
　　　　　　　　　5075 ft

Take-out elevation　1526 m
　　　　　　　　　　5005 ft

Shuttle　4.5 km (2.8 mi) one way

Season　June–September

Maps　83C3 and 83C2

Gauge　No

Craft　Canoes, kayaks and rafts

CHARACTER　A scenic medium-volume run, with spectacular peaks towering over the river. The whitewater challenges are few, as the river flows in an open gravel plain for most of the run.

FLOW INFORMATION　The river is uncontrolled and fed by snowmelt and glacial runoff. Assess the flow at the take-out. Higher flows produce fast water and standing waves in the short, constricted section.

TRAVEL　Access to the run and the shuttle are on paved roads.

DESCRIPTION　The river at the put-in is typical of the entire run, where finding your way to deep water in the braided channels will be the biggest problem. The trip is mostly a scenic float with little real whitewater, although there are a couple of tight corners and the odd sweeper. The highway is close to the river for most of the run.

GETTING THERE　The run is located north of Saskatchewan River Crossing along Highway 93. See the map on page 57.

TAKE-OUT　From the junction of Highways 11 and 93 at Saskatchewan River Crossing, proceed north for 23 km to an unnamed picnic site on the west (left) side of the road. From there continue north for 2.8 km where the river is close to the road at a wide gravel flat. If coming from the north, watch for the "Big Bend" on Highway 93, about 120 km south of Jasper. The highway descends a steep hill, makes a looping bend to the left and goes up another hill. As you go up the hill after the loop, you cross a bridge on Nigel Creek. The take-out is 6.6 km south of the bridge. If you are unsure of where to take out, go south to the picnic site, then return 2.8 km north. Park well off the road.

PUT-IN　Go north on Highway 93 for 4.5 km to just before the road goes up a steep hill. There is a small pull-off on the west (left) side of the road.

CAMPING There is developed camping 21 km north of the take-out, at Wilcox Creek, or 14 km south of the take-out, at Rampart Creek.

Some of the spectacular scenery on the upper North Saskatchewan.

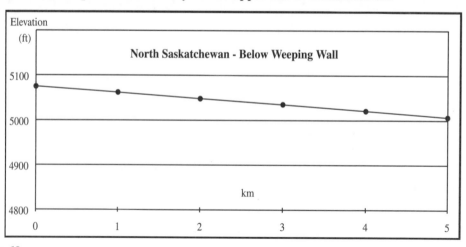

GRADE	CLASS	FLOW	TIME	LENGTH
III	II–IV	Low	1 hour	2.4 km (1.5 mi)
III⁺	II–IV	High		

Gradient   22 m/km (2.2%)
117 ft/mi

Max gradient   30 m in .8 km (3.8%)
100 ft in .5 mi

Put-in elevation   1600 m
5250 ft

Take-out elevation   1547 m
5075 ft

Shuttle   2.3 km (1.4 mi) one way

Season   June–August

Maps   83C3

Gauge   No

Craft   Kayaks and canoes

CHARACTER   A short, small-volume creek run that rips over a boulder-bed in a shallow channel. The put-in carry is demanding and the run is short, but the amazing views on the North Saskatchewan are rewarding.

FLOW INFORMATION   The creek is uncontrolled and fed by snowmelt and glacial runoff. Assess the flow at the put-in.

TRAVEL   The shuttle is on pavement.

DESCRIPTION   From beneath the highway bridge, the creek tears down a steep class III –III⁺ boulder-strewn channel. A short pool above the old road bridge is followed by a constricted 1–1.5-m class IV drop that cuts through a bedrock outcrop. Below this the creek spreads out somewhat in a alder-lined channel, then descends steeply to the North Saskatchewan River. Below the confluence, the North Saskatchewan is open, with a couple of class II play spots and some spectacular scenery. The take-out is along the highway where the road and river meet.

GETTING THERE   The run is located north of Saskatchewan River Crossing along Highway 93. See the map on page 57.

TAKE-OUT   From the junction of Highways 11 and 93, at Saskatchewan River Crossing, go north for 23 km to an unnamed picnic site on the west (left) side of the road. From there continue north for 7 km to where the river is close to the road at a wide gravel flat just before a steep hill. If you are coming from the north, watch for the "Big Bend" on Highway 93, approximately 120 km south of Jasper. The highway descends a steep hill, makes a large looping bend to the left and goes up another hill. As you go up the hill after the loop you cross a bridge on Nigel Creek. The take-out is 2.3 km south of the bridge. Park well off the road.

PUT-IN   Go north on Highway 93 for approximately 2.3 km to a bridge, where the creek is 40 m below. Park well off the highway, just north of the bridge. On the downstream river right side of the bridge, follow the steep slope down to the creek.

CAMPING   There is developed camping 14 km north of the put-in, at the Wilcox Creek Campground.

Nigel Creek tearing over the boulders, directly below the Highway 93 bridge.

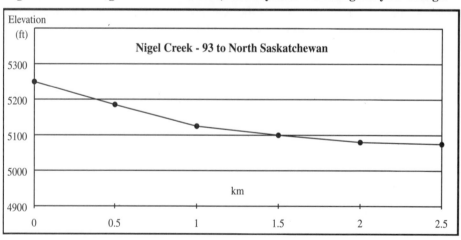

GRADE	CLASS	FLOW	TIME	LENGTH
III⁺	II–VI	Low	3–5 hours	6 km (3.7 mi)
IV	III–VI	High		

Gradient   22 m/km (2.2%)   **Max gradient**   30 m in .6 km (5%)
114 ft/mi   100 ft in .4 mi

Put-in elevation   1400 m   **Take-out elevation**   1270 m
4593 ft   4167 ft

Shuttle   8 km (5 mi) one way   **Season**   May–September

Maps   82C8   **Gauge**   No

Craft   Kayaks and canoes

CHARACTER   A small-volume run through a deep canyon with 6 waterfalls, 5 of which have been paddled. The rest of the run involves some class II–III rapids which are insignificant compared to the vertical drops. Any portages will require some scrambling and some zany cliff jumps!

FLOW INFORMATION   The river is uncontrolled and fed by snowmelt. You can check the flow at the take-out, though there is seldom insufficient water to paddle the run. Higher flows make the falls shorter, but with much more pronounced recirculations.

TRAVEL   The shuttle is on a gravel road.

DESCRIPTION   Just below the parking lot is Crescent Falls (19–21 m) which is portaged on the left, along the canyon rim. Where you descend depends on your taste in whitewater. A reasonable and well-worn trail leads down the first gully to the brink of Curtain Call, the second waterfall, which is a 9–11-m class V⁺ drop into a boiling recirculation. This is not an easy drop; the clean lines are tight and the potential for a good thrashing is very high. To avoid this drop, there are two options. The first involves the descent mentioned above, followed by a downclimb of the crack in the cliff flanking the fall (some easy climbing involved). The second option is to stay high, along the canyon rim, to well below Curtain Call, thereby avoiding the second fall completely. If you stay high along the rim you will descend a steep and open slope to the river. Once you drop down to just above Curtain Call you must climb back up to avoid the cliff descent, so choose wisely before descending!

Below the first two falls, the river has a few easy class II–III drops before you reach a sweeping left turn where the river disappears into a slot in the upsloping sedimentary layers. This is The Particle Accelerator, an 8–10-m cascading

Lidless Escapades

It was late afternoon as we hurried to the river and did the shuttle. One of my companions that day was Brock. Together he and I have survived many epic trips on innumerable rivers. He has years of experience in all types of craft and for many years has been in the top three or four in Canada in slalom and wildwater racing. On the river he is inspirational, funny and always helpful to those who are not quite sure of themselves. Generally a real solid guy, but he has this tendency. Not that it affects his paddling or makes him a liability, but at just the wrong moment he seems to be able to, well . . . misplace things. At the put-in, while lowering our boats into the canyon below Crescent Falls, Brock noticed something. He had lost his helmet! Normally that would not be a huge problem — play it safe, avoid the nasties and stay upright. However,

this was the Bighorn, where the only rapids were totally vertical ones.

But it was late and the group was slow, so we pressed on. It was cold, so Brock substituted his toque in place of a helmet. At the smaller falls he ran the drops with the flaps of that Nordic toque whipping in the breeze. We were all howling with laughter since he looked like a strange cross between Sven, the cross-country skier, and some weirdo sporting bizarre gear. At the bigger falls I would run the drop, and he would lower a rope, to which I would clip my helmet. He would then haul up my helmet, so he could run the fall with a real lid. It was another one of those experiences which, when added together, make up your relationship with someone. So far, Brock and I have had an interesting one!

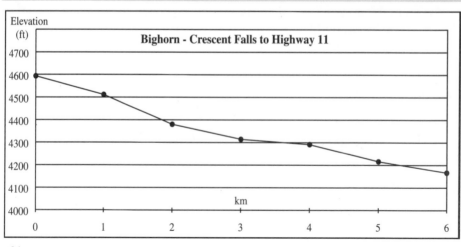

Stuart Smith in The Particle Accelerator. Photo: Brock Wilson.

class V⁺ double-drop into a narrow canyon. You can portage on the right by scampering along the downsloping ledges to the lip, tossing your boat and leaping after it. The next fall is Schoolhouse, a 2–3-m straight forward plunge off a rock ledge. About 100 m below this is Free Fall, somewhat of a misnomer, since the water drops at an 80-degree angle along the bedrock in a 6–8-m fall. Portaging this one means tossing and leaping from the left side, unless you choose the to scramble up and around on the loose rock. The last fall, Final Analysis, is a 7–9-m class V drop, with a constricted, class III boulder-garden rapid leading to the brink. The portage is another toss and leap affair, requiring that you scramble along the undercut ledges on river right and jump off the ledge at the lip of the fall.

GETTING THERE   The run is located east of Saskatchewan River Crossing or west of Rocky Mountain House, off Highway 11.

TAKE-OUT . From the junction of Highways 11/93 at Saskatchewan River Crossing, go east on Highway 11 for 70 km to where the road crosses the river. The river flows beneath the road through two huge culverts, not under a bridge. On the south (right) side, look for a small gravel road just before the road crosses the river. Turn right and follow the road south for 100 m, then turn east (left) on a small trail and follow the trail back to the river. If coming from the east, the take-out is 20 km west of Nordegg.

PUT-IN   Return to Highway 11, turn east (right), and proceed 2.2 km to the Crescent Falls road, which is on the north (left) side of the road. Follow the gravel road 4.5 km to a fork, stay left and descend the steep hill to the parking lot at the top of Crescent Falls.

CAMPING   There is developed camping at the put-in.

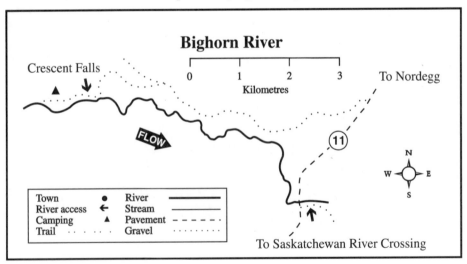

Wolfgang Haibach in Freefall.

GRADE	CLASS	FLOW	TIME	LENGTH
IV	III–IV+	Medium	4–6 hours	3.5 km (2.2 mi)
IV+	III–V	High		

Gradient   31 m/km (3%)
            161 ft/mi

Max gradient   30 m in .6 km (5%)
                   100 ft in .4 mi

Put-in elevation   1433 m
                      4700 ft

Take-out elevation   1326 m
                         4350 ft

Shuttle   A 4 km (2.5 mi) carry

Season   May–August

Maps   83C2 and 83C1

Gauge   No

Craft   Kayaks and canoes

CHARACTER   A small-volume creek run in an extremely tight gorge which then enters a medium-volume river in a deep and committing canyon. The run has several places where the rock walls are 1–1.5-m apart, and should therefore be scouted in its entirety before putting in. The confined spaces demand precise manoeuvring, and there is little room for error. A log or fallen boulder could seal off one of the many narrow passages, so do not take the run lightly! The entire run can be scouted along the river left shore on a series of small trails.

FLOW INFORMATION   Assess the flow at the take-out. Coral Creek provides about one-eighth of the flow, depending on water levels. Low flows will make Coral Creek a boulder bash! The river is uncontrolled and fed by snowmelt and glacial runoff.

TRAVEL   The shuttle is a 4.5-km carry to the put-in.

DESCRIPTION   The put-in is just below an impossible set of cataracts on Coral Creek. The creek tears along between constricting walls with sharp class IV+ drops over bedrock, followed by spread-out class IV boulder jumbles as it drops off debris in the canyon. Most of the steep gradient occurs on Coral Creek. There are spectacular overhanging cliff walls and a couple of very tight passages before you reach the confluence with the Cline River. From there the river flows calmly through a deep canyon, with a few small rapids, until you reach Desperadoes, a class V drop which tumbles off slide debris. The canyon then opens up to easier rapids before closing in at Crack in the Wall, where a class III rapid leads to a narrow gap in a rock fin. Below this, the walls close in to 1.5 m apart, with swirling and boiling whitewater in a 200-m-long gorge. The canyon opens up again and the river flows on an open gravel bottom. The final canyon is at a right bend where the river drops off the gravel shoals into a 1-m-wide crack. There are vertical walls and a couple of constricted drops as the river squeezes through the bedrock. The riverbed then opens up and the river flows to the take-out on an open gravel-bottomed channel.

GETTING THERE   The run is located east of Saskatchewan River Crossing off Highway 11.

TAKE-OUT   From the junction of Highways 11/93 at Saskatchewan River Crossing, go east for 42 km to the bridge on the Cline River. A small gravel road on the south (right) side, 400 m past the bridge, leads down to the river. If you approach the run from the east, the take-out is 48 km west of Nordegg. Watch for the road to the river on the south (left) side, just before the bridge.

PUT-IN   From the take-out, cross the highway and follow the Cline River Trail upstream along the narrow gravel path on the river left shore. In a few hundred metres the trail opens up to an old road. About 2.5 km along the road the trail heads to the right up Coral Creek, and you follow along the rim for about another 1–1.5 km to where you can descend a steep gully to the creek. You will be able to look upstream at the steep cataract.

CAMPING   There is undeveloped camping at the take-out.

Bob Orava in the heart of the Coral Creek Gorge.

69

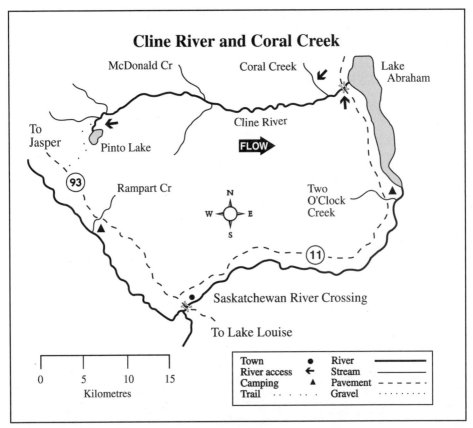

Cline River and Coral Creek

McDonald Cr

Coral Creek

Lake Abraham

Cline River

FLOW

To Jasper

Pinto Lake

93

Rampart Cr

Two O'Clock Creek

N
W   E
S

11

Saskatchewan River Crossing

To Lake Louise

Town	●	River	———
River access	←	Stream	—
Camping	▲	Pavement	- - - -
Trail	· · · · · ·	Gravel	· · · · · · · ·

0   5   10   15
Kilometres

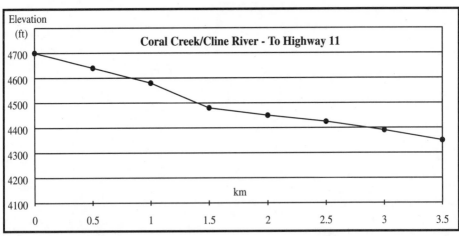

Elevation (ft)

Coral Creek/Cline River - To Highway 11

km

GRADE	**CLASS**	**FLOW**	**TIME**	**LENGTH**
III+	III–VI+	Medium	2–3 days	29 km (18 mi)
IV+	IV–VI+	High		

Gradient	13 m/km (1.3%) 68 ft/mi	**Max gradient**	30 m in 1.5 km (2%) 100 ft in .9 mi	
Put-in elevation	1753 m 5750 ft	**Take-out elevation**	1375 m 4510 ft	
Shuttle	58 km (36 mi) one way	**Season**	May–August	
Maps	82C2	**Gauge**	No	
Craft	Canoes and kayaks			

NOTES There is an extremely steep 7 km (4.3 mi) carry up to Sunset Pass, followed by an equally difficult 3 km (1.9 mi) descent to Pinto Lake. The trail is narrow and cuts across sidehills for mush of the way, so boat buggies are out. The trip finishes with the lower part of the run described on page 68.

CHARACTER A small to medium-volume remote run through very rugged wilderness with easy whitewater for most of the run, and a constricted canyon with difficult whitewater at the end. The carry over the pass is arduous, as are the portages in the lower canyon!

FLOW INFORMATION Assess the flow at the take-out. You will have only a fraction of that flow at the lake outlet. Low water trips are futile efforts! The river is uncontrolled and fed by snowmelt and glacial runoff.

TRAVEL The shuttle is on pavement.

DESCRIPTION From the trailhead you push, pull or drag your boat up a steep series of switchbacks to the pass. Follow the trail across the open meadows then down along the north side of the pass (see the story sidebar). At the outlet from Pinto Lake, the river is tiny and at medium flows is just floatable. In 2 km a creek from the left doubles the volume. A second creek from the left adds more volume in another kilometre. The next 11 km is mostly class II rapids with a couple of long sections of class II+–III whitewater where the river drops over a convoluted boulder-bed. Below the confluence with McDonald Creek (which enters from the left), the volume increases again. Short constricted sections alternate with open gravel flats until the river begins to drop toward the canyon. Expect tighter class III–IV drops in longer, but still open canyons. In the last 4 km above Coral Creek (which enters from the left), the river enters a deep canyon. The difficulty of the rapids increases to

71

That Final, Last-Gasp Trip

It was late August when he heard the message, "I've got a wicked river lined up. Call me back". He should have just hit the erase button, but instead he phoned me back. Saturday morning Brock and I were at the Norman Creek trailhead but neither of us had hiked to Pinto Lake recently, which turned out to be a bit of a miscalculation.

Hours later, we were dragging our gear-laden boats up the steep switchbacks, stopping frequently to let our rampant breathing cycles slow and to swig more water. Each time I stopped and waited, I was greeted by a slightly more worn version of the guy I had started up the trail with. At the top, we paused briefly to eat, then headed across the open meadows to the pass. On the horse-rutted trails our boats wedged in, forcing us to pull like mules. Darkness brought an end to our hideous march, and we huddled under a makeshift tarp to avoid the rain. We inhaled dinner and hit the sleeping bags, truly exhausted. The next morning, we awoke to a horrifying white sight. Snow. About 20 cm of the stuff!

Rational beings would have called it quits, but we carried on amidst a scene that would look great on any ski tour. We finally found the pass and Pinto Lake. The lake was right there, 400 m beneath our feet. It seemed that we might seal-launch and touch only air until we broke the surface. We had left the map behind and so relied on vague recollections of where the trail was. Brock swore he had found it, but 100 very steep metres later we discovered that the "trail" ended at the top of a ridiculously steep gully leading straight down to the lake. Too exhausted to go back up, we began the downclimb. I was wearing hiking boots, dragging my boat on a quick-release system, and my climbing experience left me comfortable with the heights. But Brock had on running shoes and was hardwired to his boat. One slip meant a 300-m tumble down the slope, tied to a plastic missile. The poor footing, airy heights and pending launch soon turned him into a wild-eyed, crouching savage.

Figuring two guys could better manage the 30-kg boats, Brock held the nose, I clipped my tow system to the stern, and we slowly stepped each boat down the slope. Trouble was that Brock saw the boat as something with which to stabilize himself! Halfway down, my back muscles were cramping from the weight and I bellowed at him, "Are you hanging on that damn thing?" He looked up sheepishly, then released his weight from the boat. No wonder I was sweating my way **down** the hill. We staggered back up the gully, repeated the process, then thrashed through the dense brush to the lakeshore. As we unpacked the last of our food, Brock nudged me and pointed into the bush at a dark form. "We have company." That bleary-eyed moose got one glimpse of us and promptly charged! We were frozen, arguing the merits of jumping into the boats versus cringing behind trees. Luckily, the moose broke off the charge. We downed our last bit of food, but were cold and not nearly full. Finally, we were at the put-in, but it was already 1 pm on the second day of a two-day trip. With 5–6 hours until dark, we headed across the lake to "sprint" the 34 km to the take-out. We had scouted the section below Coral Creek early Saturday morning, but I had paddled the upper part only once before, at high flows, and my memories were dim indeed. So when at dusk we reached the class V⁺ stuff, we blew it off and grovelled up the steep bank with our outrageously heavy boats on our backs. After 30 minutes of thrashing up through the trees, then back down the steep slope, we returned to the river. Finally, the wild stuff was over and we could paddle to the take-out! We floated toward the roaring blackness below, relying mightily on our recollections of the day before. It was a bit harrowing! We emerged in the calm water below, thankful that our recall was accurate. What a final sense of relief; we had only to float to the take-out.

Brock Wilson looking way down, to the put-in.

Suddenly, the walls closed in again and a loud roaring issued from the dark crack ahead. Scrambling out of our boats, we peered into the blackness. At some silent cue, we turned to gape at each other and spewed out in unison, "I don't seem to recall scouting this! Do You?" Physically exhausted and mentally defeated, we again hauled our boats up an absurdly steep cliff. At the top we thrashed along on the dark sideslope, totally spent. During the first rest stop, we decided to head straight for the trail and drag the boats to the take-out. Screw the river! After a bitter struggle through the trees, we reached the trail and dragged our boats the final couple of kilometres to the take-out in the frigid moonlight.

It was the epitome of "the" trip from hell. A 9-km carry up the insanely steep pass, horse trails with ridiculous friction, 20 cm of snow, a terrifying descent to the lake, a crazed moose, a boulder bash down most of the river, an exhausted struggle out of the canyon, a frightening paddle through a pitch black gorge, a final spent ascent of the canyon walls and a 3-km drag to the take-out. Sure, there was some good whitewater, but I only wish I could forget it!

class IV–IV+ and the walls close in. A narrow class IV–IV+ drop leads to a very narrow (1–1.5-m) dark rock gorge that ends in a calm pool. At the end of the pool the river drops into a steep rapid, with most of the water going under a huge chockstone. Portage up the steep bank on the right and along the canyon until you can descend to the river. There are two places to get back to the river, depending on your whitewater tastes. The first is above the Coral Creek confluence, where a steep gully descends to the river. The second is just below the Coral Creek confluence, where a small creek enters from the right. The first option gets you in above some class V–V+ rapids that are difficult to scout or portage. The second option gets you in below the most difficult bit. Check the run on page 68 for details on the lower part of the river.

GETTING THERE The run is located near Saskatchewan River Crossing. See the map on page 70.

TAKE-OUT From the junction of Highways 11/93 at Saskatchewan River Crossing, go 42 km east on Highway 11 to the Cline River bridge. Just east of the bridge, on the south (right) side, is a small road leading down to near the river. If you approach the run from the east, the take-out is 48 km west of Nordegg. Watch for the road to the river on the south (left) side, just before the bridge.

PUT-IN Go west on Highway 11 to the Highway 93 junction at Saskatchewan River Crossing. Turn north (right) and proceed for 16.5 km to the Sunset Pass trailhead, which is on the west (right) side of the highway. The parking area is at the bottom of a steep hill, just past a left turn.

CAMPING There is undeveloped camping at the take-out, or developed camping 4.7 km south of the Sunset Pass trailhead, at Rampart Creek. If you plan to stay in the campground at the pass during your trip, you must register and get a permit from Parks Canada.

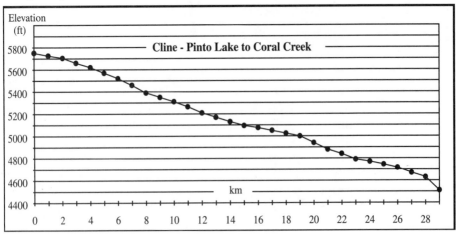

74

One of the easier rapids upstream of the confluence with Coral Creek.

GRADE	CLASS	FLOW	TIME	LENGTH
IV	III–VI⁺	Low	5–6 hours	6.3 km (3.9 mi)
V	IV–VI⁺	High		

Gradient   19 m/km (1.9%)
              100 ft/mi

Max gradient   30 m in 1.2 km (2.5%)
                  100 ft in .75 mi

Put-in elevation   1463 m
                      4800 ft

Take-out elevation   1344 m
                        4410 ft

Shuttle   A 7 km (4.3 mi) carry
             and a 1.6 km (1 mi) drive

Season   May–August

Maps   83C1

Gauge   Yes

Craft   Kayaks and canoes

NOTES   You access the run with a 7-km carry to the put-in. There is a 2–3-km flat section at the bottom of the run and a short paddle on the North Saskatchewan to reach the take-out.

CHARACTER   A small to medium-volume run through a series of canyons with an unrunnable fall in one canyon. The carry is on a root-choked trail, so buggies will be difficult to use. This is an arduous back-country adventure, with a short but intense whitewater section.

FLOW INFORMATION   You must walk 2 km to the bridge over the river to check the flow level. High water makes the lower canyon a real test. The river is uncontrolled and fed by snowmelt and glacial runoff.

TRAVEL   Access to the run is on paved roads. The 7-km carry to the put-in is on a steep and narrow trail with, for the most part, a moderate gradient.

DESCRIPTION   From the parking lot, follow the well-worn trail across the dusty valley bottom to the bridge on the river. Cross the bridge and go upstream along the river right shore. You will get a good view of the lower fall on the way, so you can scope out a place to get back into the canyon below the fall. This is no small feat and involves a certain amount of scrambling and rope work. The upper canyon has much lower walls and is more open, with a few tight class IV and V rapids and the 2–4-m class V upper fall. The river mellows on an open gravel flat before plummeting into the lower canyon at the 7–9-m lower fall. Below this are several steep class V–V⁺ drops in a constricted canyon, where scouting and portaging is difficult. In the lower part the canyon opens up to easier whitewater.

Constricted whitewater in the canyon below the lower fall.

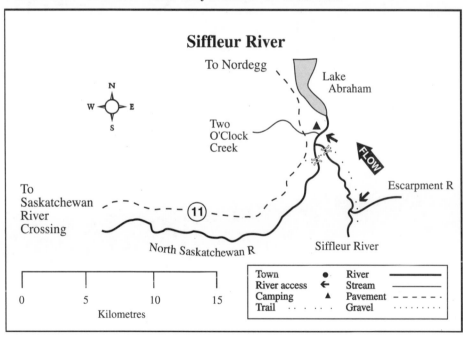

GETTING THERE The run is located east of Saskatchewan River Crossing, off Highway 11.

TAKE-OUT From the junction of Highways 11 and 93 at Saskatchewan River Crossing, proceed east on Highway 11 for 29 km to the Two O'Clock Creek campground, which is on the south (right) side of the highway. Follow the campground road to near the river. If you approach the run from the east, the campground is 61 km west of Nordegg.

PUT-IN Return to Highway 11 and go west (left) for 1.6 km to the Siffleur Falls trailhead, which is on the south (left) side of the highway. From the parking area, follow the trail upstream for about 7 km. The gradient decreases and the river valley opens up above the upper canyon. If you reach the confluence with the Escarpment River, which enters from river right 7.5 km from the trailhead, you will be above the best whitewater.

CAMPING There is developed camping at the take-out.

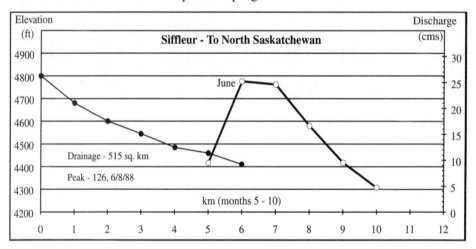

GRADE	CLASS	FLOW	TIME	LENGTH
II⁺–III	II–III	Low	2–3 hours	3.8 km (2.4 mi)
III–III⁺	II⁺–III⁺	High		

Gradient   18 m/km (1.8%)   **Max gradient** 30 m in 1.5 km (2%)
             95 ft/mi   100 ft in .9 mi

Put-in elevation   1468 m   **Take-out elevation**   1399 m
                         4815 ft   4590 ft .

Shuttle   3.1 km (1.9 mi) one way   **Season**   June–August

Maps   82N15   **Gauge**   Yes

Craft   Canoes and kayaks

NOTES There is a short float on the North Saskatchewan to reach the take out.

CHARACTER A small-volume run in a deep and tight canyon with spectacular rock formations and moderate rapids. Canoeists will find getting into the canyon a bit difficult, since the most direct entry point involves a seal-launch of 2–4 m.

FLOW INFORMATION The river is uncontrolled and fed by snowmelt and glacial runoff. Assess the flow at the put-in.

TRAVEL The shuttle is on pavement.

DESCRIPTION At the Mistaya Canyon parking lot, follow the trail to the bridge. Stay on the river right side and go downstream, along the rim of the canyon, for approximately 250–300 m to a small seep which runs down a gully to the river. On the downstream side of the seep, scramble down to a rock outcrop where you can lower your boat down to a slimy ledge, which is just upstream of a boulder garden in the canyon. Descend the gully to your boat, then seal-launch off the ledge into the canyon. The first 400–500 m consists of class II⁺–III⁺ rapids at tight corners and pinched sections with amazing rock formations on both sides. A calmer section leads through a spectacular overhung canyon before the walls open up somewhat. Open and easier rapids lead to a pool, which is backed up by a landslide. Below the pool, the river rips over boulders for a few hundred metres, then eases as the river flows out onto an open gravel plain. The scenery as you approach the confluence with the North Saskatchewan is an amazing panorama of spectacular mountain peaks.

GETTING THERE The run is located south of Saskatchewan River Crossing along Highway 93.

TAKE-OUT From the junction of Highways 11/93 at Saskatchewan River

The Circus Comes to the Mountains

It was just a short run on a once familiar river, to double-check the accuracy of my grey matter. That's how I like to remember it, but I'm sure those other folks remember our encounter in a very different way.

It was midweek and I figured the traffic would be light, but it was also a sunny day in July and I was wrong! I gunned my shuttle bike up the hill, winding it out in each gear and had topped out at 70 kph before I hit the base of the hill. The traffic whizzed by, motorhomes blowing unburned gas and foul diesel smoke in my face. I stuck to the shoulder and settled in for the ride. At the crux pitch I hammered the shifter and lurched forward in low gear, at a ridiculously humble pace. Then a motorhome pulled alongside and stayed even with me as I wound it up into second. The woman rolled down the window and asked with a smirk, "Where are you going on that thing?" I laughed and replied "Up to the canyon." She relayed the information to the driver and they proceeded. Backed up behind the motorhome was a long line of cars. As each vehicle went by, the occupants took their best shots at being funny, witty or downright rude. I sat there, revved out, wishing I had a dark face shield, a crude tattoo on my bicep or a big pistol that might dissuade the jesters.

More people slowed and honestly asked where I was going. I managed to reply, with a straight face, that I was going kayaking. A few nodded and a few looked at each other, not quite sure they understood. At Mistaya Canyon I found, to my amazement, a crowd of people. They applauded as I pulled in, obviously unsure that my tiny machine would get me up the hill. I was a bit embarrassed and quickly dragged my boat from the bushes and headed for the river! But the swarm was not put off by my abrupt exit and moved in behind me. "He really is going kayaking," they told the nonbelievers. At the canyon I made a quick right off the trail, to where I would descend. I was sure that would be the end of it. The mob hesitated, a bit unsure, then followed! I was scrambling down to the ledge below as the throng caught up. Cameras were clicking and videos were aimed at me as the inquisitive mass sought answers.

Soon I was explaining everything to the crowd, which was spread-out above me, perched on rocks, hanging from exposed roots and peering around trees. A few daredevils even crawled down to where I was lowering my boat. The boat refused to come to rest in a secure position, and every time I was tempted to toss down the rope, it started to slide. A well-meaning guy asked if he should hold the rope while I climbed down. Now they were actually participating in the adventure! He threw down the rope and I was forced to thank him. On the ledge I positioned the boat for the seal-launch and once in my boat I attached my deck and grabbed my paddle. In a final exchange with the mass above, I told them I hoped they had enjoyed the show as much as I did. Once more, I thanked the fellow for holding the rope, then shoved off. When I spouted back out of the water, I was swept into the rapid below and left the cheering horde behind. I, at least, could escape the circus.

Some of the scenery in the lower section of Mistaya Canyon.

Crossing, go south on Highway 93 for 1.6 km to the bridge on the North Saskatchewan. About 200 m south of the bridge is a dirt road on the west (right) side leading back to the river. If you approach the run from the south, look for the North Saskatchewan bridge just south of Saskatchewan River Crossing.

PUT-IN Proceed 3.1 km south on Highway 93 to the Mistaya Canyon parking area, which is on the west (right) side of the road.

CAMPING There is developed camping 10 km east of Saskatchewan River Crossing on Highway 11, at Thompson Creek. You can also try Waterfowl Lakes, which is approximately 15 km south of the put-in, on Highway 93.

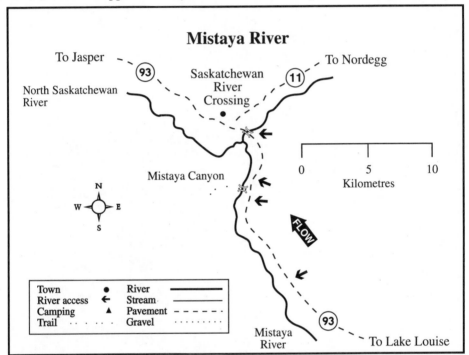

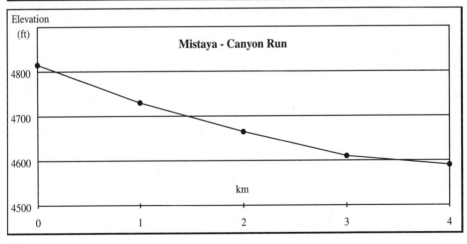

GRADE	CLASS	FLOW	TIME	LENGTH
II	II–II⁺	Low	2–3 hours	8.5 km (5.3 mi)
II–III	II⁺–III⁺	High		

Gradient 17 m/km (1.7%)
88 ft/mi

Max gradient 30 m in 1.5 km (2%)
100 ft in .9 mi

Put-in elevation 1625 m
5330 ft

Take-out elevation 1483 m
4865 ft

Shuttle 7.6 km (4.7 mi) one way

Season June–August

Maps 82N15

Gauge Yes

Craft Canoes, kayaks and small rafts

CHARACTER A small-volume run over a continuous boulder-bed in a narrow channel. The run is quite technical and requires manoeuvring in tight quarters. At higher flows, the river is bouncy and a lot more fun. Mark the take-out, since the river disappears into a narrow gorge directly below the end of the run.

FLOW INFORMATION The river is uncontrolled and fed by snowmelt and glacial runoff. Assess the flow at the take-out, where the river is constricted, to best gauge the water level. Rafters will need medium to high flows.

TRAVEL The shuttle is on pavement.

DESCRIPTION At the put-in the river is mellow but quickly picks up to some class II, then continuous class II⁺ rapids. Expect nonstop class II–III boulder-garden action once things take off. There are some steep surf waves and play spots, but the water rips downstream so fast you have to be sharp to catch them. A particularly narrow spot, approximately two-thirds of the way down the run, is probably the most difficult rapid. Paddlers must squeeze through a narrow channel created by large boulders. In this section there are some great technical boulder-garden rapids. The gradient eases, then picks up again as you approach the take-out. The exit point was marked well in advance in 1995, by a highway sign in the trees. However, do not count on that sign being there. As you approach the canyon at the take-out, a series of low ledges with increasingly large recirculations makes exiting directly above the canyon difficult. Get out well above the canyon to be safe.

GETTING THERE The run is located south of Saskatchewan River Crossing along Highway 93. See the map on page 82.

TAKE-OUT From the junction of Highways 11/93 at Saskatchewan River Crossing, go 5 km south on Highway 93 to the Mistaya Canyon parking area, which is on the west (right) side of the road. If you approach the run from the south, watch for the Mistaya Canyon pull-off on the west (left) side of the road as you descend the steep hill to Saskatchewan River Crossing. Be sure to walk down to the river to inspect and mark the take-out.

PUT-IN From the canyon parking area, go south up the hill for 7.6 km to an unnamed parking area on the west (right) side of the highway. The river is reached after a short carry through the trees.

CAMPING There is developed camping 10 km east of Saskatchewan River Crossing on Highway 11, at Thompson Creek. You can also try Waterfowl Lakes, which is approximately 7 km south of the put-in on Highway 93.

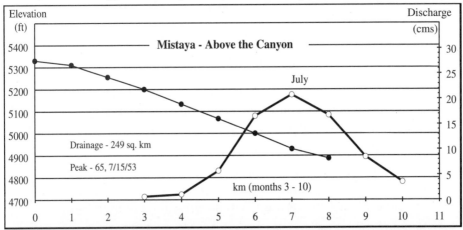

Stuart Smith playing above the canyon. Photo: Rob Brown.

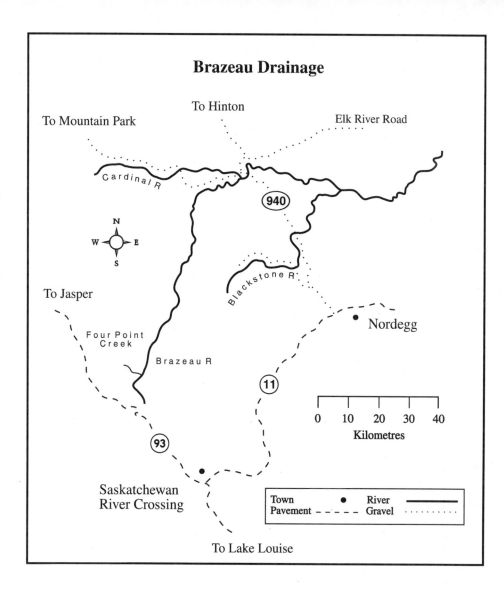

Brazeau Drainage

GRADE	CLASS	FLOW	TIME	LENGTH
II	II–II+	Low	3–6 hours	29 km (18 mi)
II+–III	II+–III	High		

Gradient 4.8 m/km (.48%)   **Max gradient** 30 m in 4 km (.75%)
25 ft/mi   100 ft in 2.5 mi

Put-in elevation   1255 m   **Take-out elevation**   1116 m
4117 ft   3660 ft

Shuttle   58 km (36 mi) one way   **Season**   May–September

Maps   83C15 and 83C16   **Gauge**   Yes

Craft   Canoes, kayaks and rafts

CHARACTER A medium to large-volume run in an open valley with rapids at constrictions and boulder gardens. The river flows over bedrock outcrops that produce standing waves.

FLOW INFORMATION The river is uncontrolled and fed by snowmelt and glacial runoff. The river is on Alberta Environmental Protection's River Report recording. Use the flow below the Cardinal River; low flow is 30 to 60 cms and high flow is 150 to 300 cms.

TRAVEL Access to the run and the shuttle are on gravel roads.

DESCRIPTION The run starts in an open valley, with some tight corners below the put-in. About 1 km below the bridge, rapids begin with numerous sets of standing waves where the river is constricted and passes over small ledges. This continues for 4–5 km with intermittent rapids that offer some great surfing at higher flows. At low flows there are a couple of small ledges about 6 km downstream of the put-in. By about kilometre 10–12, the valley opens up and the whitewater section ends. The river is smooth flowing, with few rapids, until you reach the take-out.

GETTING THERE The run is located between Hinton and Nordegg, off the Forestry Trunk Road (Highway 940).

TAKE-OUT If coming from the north, start at the set of lights on Highway 16 at the east end of Hinton. Go about 1 km south, past the hospital, to a set of lights. Turn south (right) onto the Robb Road and follow the road for 47 km to the junction with Highway 47. Turn south (right) and follow the road for another 9 km to the junction with Highway 40. Continue straight ahead onto Highway 40 (toward Nordegg) and go 43 km to a junction. Turn south (right) toward

Nordegg and go 8 km to the Brazeau bridge. Continue south for another 27 km, to the bridge on the Blackstone River. Go 1.1 km, past the bridge and up the hill, to a gravel road on the east (left) side of the road.

If coming from Nordegg, turn north onto Highway 940 off Highway 11, 2.2 km west of Nordegg. Proceed north on the gravel road for approximately 34 km to the bridge on the Blackstone River. Turn around and go 1.1 km south of the bridge (back the way you came), to a gravel road on the east (left) side.

At the gravel road 1.1 km south of the Blackstone Bridge, turn east (left) and follow the road for 17 km, past two road junctions on the right, to a fork with a gate and a gas plant on the right. Stay left and go another 1.2 km to a bridge on the Blackstone. Cross the bridge and go 2.6 km to a junction (the road will wind around to the west). Go right and continue 5.8 km to a fork with a gas plant on the right. Stay left and follow the road for 900 m to an old gravel pit, which is on the left side. Go 1.3 km further, through the far end of the gravel pit where the road becomes more of a trail, to a cutline on the right at 90 degrees to the trail. The cutline is marked at a tree on the right with an inordinate amount of orange flagging tape. This cutline leads to the river in about 1 km. Four-wheel-drives may be required to reach the river, but you should mark the take-out so you can spot it from the river.

PUT-IN Retrace your route to the 940 bridge on the Blackstone River, then continue north for 27 km to the bridge on the Brazeau, which is the put-in. A small road on the west (left) side, just before you reach the bridge, leads down to the river.

Foothills scenery near the take-out. Photo: Ted Mellenthin.

CAMPING There is developed camping at the put-in or undeveloped camping at the take-out.

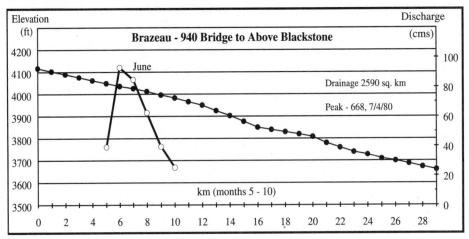

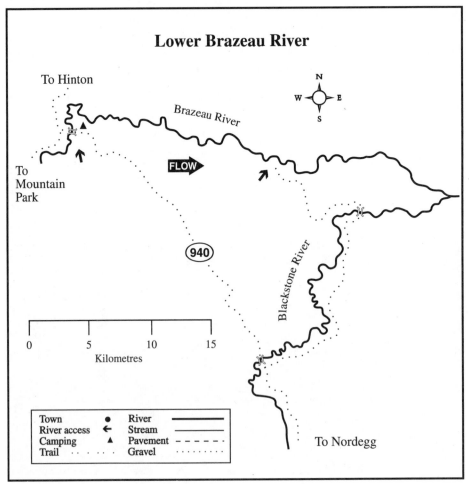

GRADE	CLASS	FLOW	TIME	LENGTH
II	II	Most Flows	1–2 hours	9 km (5.6 mi)

Gradient 4.1 m/km (.41%)
             22 ft/mi

Max gradient 30 m in 6 km (.5%)
                  100 ft in 3.7 mi

Put-in elevation 1292 m
                      4239 ft

Take-out elevation 1255 m
                        4117 ft

Shuttle 10 km (6.2 mi) one way

Season May–September

Maps 83C15

Gauge Yes

Craft Canoes, kayaks and rafts

CHARACTER A short, medium to large-volume run through pretty foothills scenery with a couple of easy rapids.

FLOW INFORMATION The river is uncontrolled and fed by snowmelt and glacial runoff. The river is on Alberta Environmental Protection's River Report recording. Use the flow below the Cardinal River; low flow is 30 to 60 cms and high flow is 150 to 300 cms.

TRAVEL Access to the run and the shuttle are on gravel roads.

DESCRIPTION At the put-in, the river is open and flows in a single channel. Watch for a few sharp corners and some constricted drops where the river accelerates through narrow spots, producing short rapids with standing waves. There are two such rapids above the confluence with the Cardinal River and a couple more below the confluence.

GETTING THERE The run is located between Hinton and Nordegg, off the Forestry Trunk Road (Highway 940).

TAKE-OUT If coming from the north, start at the set of lights on Highway 16 at the east end of Hinton. Go about 1 km south, past the hospital, to a set of lights. Turn south (right) onto the Robb Road and follow the road for 47 km to the junction with Highway 47. Turn south (right) and follow the road for another 9 km to the junction with Highway 40. Continue straight ahead onto Highway 40 (toward Nordegg) and go 43 km to a junction. Turn south (right) toward Nordegg and go 8 km south to the Brazeau bridge.

If coming from Nordegg, turn north onto Highway 940 off of Highway 11, 2.2 km west of Nordegg. Go north on the gravel road for about 61 km to the bridge on the Brazeau.

PUT-IN Go 1 km north of the bridge to the junction with the Cardinal River Road, which is on the west (left) side. Turn left and follow the Cardinal River Road for 6.6 km to a right bend in the road, with a small gravel road on the south (left) side. Turn left and follow the road for 1.5 km to near the river. The last 600 m is very steep.

CAMPING There is undeveloped camping at the put-in, or developed camping at the take-out.

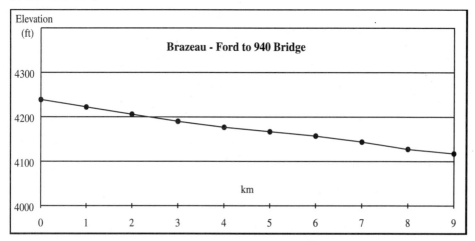

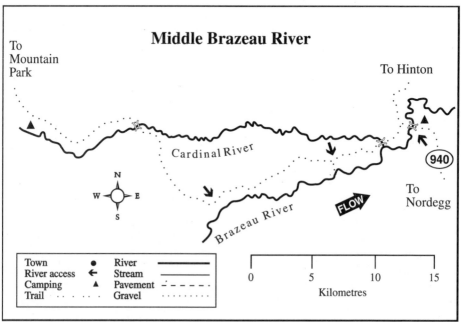

GRADE	CLASS	FLOW	TIME	LENGTH
II	II–II⁺	Low	2–3 hours	15 km (9.3 mi)
III	II–III	High		

Gradient   5.1 m/km (.51%)   **Max gradient** 30 m in 2.8 km (1%)
              27 ft/mi   100 ft in 1.7 mi

Put-in elevation   1368 m   **Take-out elevation**   1292 m
                      4488 ft   4239 ft

Shuttle   14 km (8.7 mi) one way   **Season**   May–September

Maps   83C15   **Gauge**   Yes

Craft   Canoes, kayaks and rafts

CHARACTER A scenic medium to large-volume run with numerous fun surfing opportunities. The rapids are created by small bedrock ledges and constrictions as the river cuts through a deeply incised valley. The valley is beautiful, with many interesting rock formations in the canyon sections.

FLOW INFORMATION The river is uncontrolled and fed by snowmelt and glacial runoff. The river is on Alberta Environmental Protection's River Report recording. Use the flow below the Cardinal River; low flow is 30 to 60 cms and high flow is 150 to 300 cms.

TRAVEL Access to the run and the shuttle are on gravel roads.

DESCRIPTION   The river at the put-in flows swiftly in the deep valley. There are some good surfing waves at the tight corners as the river twists between rock walls. About one-third of the way down the run, a ledge off the left shore produces a constricted class II–III chute on river right. Enjoy the excellent scenery and numerous well-defined features produced by the bedrock outcrops. There are several small ledges and tight corners in the next 3–4 km, which produce class II⁺–III rapids. About two-thirds of the way down the run, a left turn leads to a rapid with huge boulders that constrict the flow. In the lower part of the run, the gradient decreases and the rapids ease as the river valley opens up.

GETTING THERE The run is located between Hinton and Nordegg, off the Forestry Trunk Road (Highway 940). See the map on page 90.

TAKE-OUT You can approach the run from the north at Hinton, or from the south at Nordegg. If coming from the north, start at the set of lights on Highway

16 at the east end of Hinton. Go about 1 km south, past the hospital, to a set of lights. Turn south (right) onto the Robb Road and go 47 km to the junction with Highway 47. Turn south (right) and follow the road for another 9 km to the junction with Highway 40. Continue south on Highway 40 (toward Nordegg), and go 49 km to a junction. Turn south (right) toward Nordegg and go 7 km south to the Cardinal River Road, which is on the west (right) side.

If coming from Nordegg, turn north onto Highway 940 off Highway 11, 2.2 km west of Nordegg. Proceed north on the gravel road for approximately 61 km to the bridge on the Brazeau. Continue for another kilometre up the hill to the Cardinal River Road, which is on the west (left) side.

From the junction at the Cardinal River Road, turn west and go 6.6 km to a right bend in the road with a small gravel road on the south (left) side. Turn left and follow the road for 1.5 km to near the river. The last 600 m is very steep.

PUT-IN Return to the Cardinal River Road, then go west (left) and follow the road for 11 km to the Smallboy Camp administration buildings. Continue past the buildings for 1.1 km, to a cutline on the south (left) side of the road. The cutline is just before a fence that surrounds a small lagoon. Park out of the way, then follow the cutline for about 1.5 km to the steep bank, which descends to the river.

CAMPING There is undeveloped camping at the take-out or developed camping near the Highway 940 bridge on the Brazeau, 1 km south of the Cardinal Road junction.

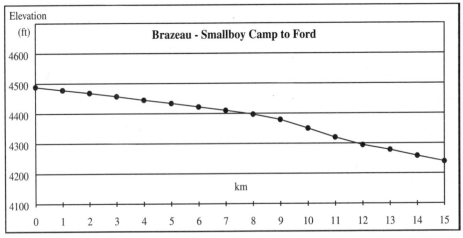

BRAZEAU NIGEL PASS TO FORD

GRADE	CLASS	FLOW	TIME	LENGTH
II–III	I–VI$^+$	Low	3–6 days	85 km (53 mi)
III–III$^+$	I–VI$^+$	High		

Gradient 6.4 m/km (.64%)
   34 ft/mi

Max gradient 30 m in 1 km (3%)
   100 ft in .6 mi

Put-in elevation 1910 m
   6266 ft

Take-out elevation 1368 m
   4488 ft

Shuttle 200 km (124 mi) one way

Season June–September

Maps 83C3, 83C6, 83C7, 83C10 and 83C15

Gauge No

Craft Canoes, kayaks and rafts

NOTES This run encompasses the 15-km (9.3-mi) stretch described on page 91. You must carry 14.5 km (9 mi) to the put-in.

CHARACTER A back-country expedition through incredibly wild and scenic mountain terrain. The run includes a long carry over a 2200 m (7200 ft) pass, grade V canyons, arduous portages and some great whitewater. You need to be a proficient paddler, hiker, map reader and lightweight camper and have good wilderness survival skills. In the case of accident or emergency, you are a long way from assistance.

FLOW INFORMATION The river is uncontrolled and fed by snowmelt and glacial runoff. The river is on Alberta Environmental Protection's River Report recording. Use the flow below the Cardinal River; low flow is 30 to 60 cms and high flow is 150 to 300 cms. At the put-in you will have a tiny fragment of the flow on the gauge. You need medium flows for the spread-out parts, but can then expect serious whitewater in the upper canyons.

TRAVEL The shuttle involves 135 km of driving on gravel roads.

DESCRIPTION The journey begins with a 7-km carry up a moderate trail to the pass. At the pass you swing right and cross a small stream (the Brazeau). Descend on the river right bank, then cross the flat to a bridge. You could put in here at higher flows, but the river descends the moraine in a small canyon not far below, where most of it disappears into the rocks. Better to cross the bridge, then continue for another 4 km to the Four Point Creek Campground. You put in on an open flat, where the river is spread-out in many fragmented channels. This continues for 4–5 km, with incredible views looking upstream at the headwall of the valley, until you reach a small bridge. Downstream of

The Good, The Bad and The Crazy

I packed extremely light and prepared myself for the carry and any portages. After hours of scheming, I had devised a rig to strap my kayak to my backpack that in theory should ease the carry. That was before I found myself on the frozen, snow covered, 50-degree scree slope. I was off the trail, on a desperate shortcut down the steep gully. Grovelling on all fours, I tried to stand up, but the top-heavy boat shoved my head down and my back threatened to explode on each attempt. But hey, anything was better than falling over backwards. The thought of rocketing down that scree slope, strapped to my kayak in a hideous reverse seal-launch, made my blood curdle. I moved very slowly and very carefully. At the river, I expected to float down, but it was so spread-out that I ended up dragging my boat, then paddling a pool, then dragging my boat . . . etc. After a strenuous day, I camped well short of my goal.

The next day, the river gathered into one channel and the rapids began. The canyon on the South Fork left me exhilarated and the next one, on the main stem, brought a portage. Then the river wound back and forth on the flats and hours later, at dusk, I was exhausted. All I had left to eat was a bit of Red River, some dried fruit and a Power Bar. That was of little concern at the time, for my stomach was full and the nearby log jam provided an immense amount of dry wood. So I lay back, warmed by my fire and enjoyed the night sky. I was up early and paddled all day, with only a few brief rests to chew on my Power Bar. Seventy km later, I reached the bridge on the Trunk Road. It was dusk and getting cold. I searched every spot near the bridge, but my van was missing. Obviously my shuttle arrangements had failed. So I headed over to some folks in a motorhome. They had a huge fire blazing and were real friendly. That is until I told them my predicament and asked them for a ride to a phone. "We have our motorhome all set up for the night and it is a little hard to move it now." I was a bit shocked and thought I must be cold, maybe even hypothermic and my brain was slightly off. Here I was, 100 km from the nearest town, out in the backwoods in the freezing dark, with no food or vehicle. This guy doesn't want to move his motorhome to give me a 15-km ride to a phone? I explained again, just in case I wasn't clear the first time, but got the same response. I smiled in disbelief, then turned and started walking.

About 6 km later, I was deep in reflection when this truck came sailing over the hill. I waved frantically amidst the flying gravel as the truck braked wildly. The driver had a cellular phone, so I called a friend to come and get me. Later I was crouched beside my fire of wet smouldering wood when a vehicle pulled up. It was the guy in the truck again, with a couple of bags of food and drink. I sat there stuffing my face and contemplating people as I waited for my ride. On that crazy trip into the wilds I met the good and the bad. Sure, there are some folks out there who you might be able to do without ever seeing again, but there are also a lot of real good people, who will be there when you need them. I think I'm lucky to have met so many of the good ones.

the bridge the river forms a single channel. About 4 km below the bridge, the river begins to drop off some small, class II–II⁺ ledges in a low-walled canyon. The river opens up, then closes in again at a small ledge that is 100 m above a class IV⁺–V slot on a right turn.

Here the river drops sharply through bedrock and enters the South Fork canyon, which is a low-volume series of waterfalls and steep drops. About 200 m of easier water follows the entry rapid, then there is a class II–II⁺ rapid 50 m above the brink of a 4–5-m, class V waterfall. If you run the first drop, you are committed to the waterfall or left with a tough climb out. The walls open up for about 250 m, then a sharp right turn leads to a class IV–IV⁺ broken-ledge rapid. The next drop is 100 m below, where a class V–V⁺ chute drops 3–4 m into a narrow canyon. The walls abate for another 250 m, then a sharp right/left turn combination leads to Wild Thing. This class V⁺–VI double fall drops 3–5 m into a pool above a rock arch, where most of the water flows out beneath the arch. At low flows you can run the first fall, then drop out through the tunnel into the lower pool. At high flow the water drops off the first fall into a bowl, with most of the water exiting under the arch and some pouring over the rock fin in a 3–4-m drop. The final drop in the upper canyon is 150 m downstream at The Shining, a 5–7-m fall into a vicious recirculation. It is difficult to portage the drops at water level, so choose intense whitewater with arduous portages, or one long portage. The entire canyon can be portaged on river left by heading up to the horse trail. Below The Shining is about 1 km of class II rapids until you reach the confluence with the North Fork of the Brazeau.

Looking downstream from Nigel Pass. Photo: Ted Mellenthin.

Looking upstream at the top section of the South Fork Canyon.

Below the confluence with the North Fork, the volume doubles and the river meanders in an open valley, with spectacular vistas of the surrounding peaks. The river is open and easy for about 8 km, where you encounter the Arete Canyon. The walls close in and the rapids increase in difficulty to class II–III until you reach a sharp left turn, at a distinct horizon line. Just below, the class V Initiation drops into a narrow chute that begins the difficult whitewater in Arete Canyon. You can scout the 2-km-long canyon on river right by climbing the steep slope to the treed ridge, then following the rim to the fall. Below Initiation, the rapids are pool-and-drop with a couple of class IV–IV+ rapids before you reach a left turn just above an immense horizon line. There is a series of small ledges, then a 3–5-m drop directly above Terminal Velocity. This thundering class VI+ fall starts as a chute that drops 15–20 m into a bedrock gorge, followed by a 4–6-m drop out of the final bowl. If you paddle to the top of Terminal Velocity, you portage on river right up the steep slope, around the rock fin creating the waterfall and back down to the pool just below the fall. If you portage from the top of the canyon, expect a 1.5-km-long carry on the open ridge, then a descent into, and steep ascent out of, a side gully. Finally, you portage to below the fall.

Downstream of Terminal Velocity are some class III–III+ ledges, then the river opens up for about 20 km in a mud-bottomed valley where there are no rapids. There are, however, incredibly spectacular views of the surrounding mountains as the river wanders back and forth across the valley. This continues until you reach Dowling Ford, where a small Parks Canada sign on the left bank indicates that no firearms are allowed in the park. Below this the rapids begin again, with 2–3 km of class II whitewater as the gradient increases. A 3–4-m drop starts a section of ledges which continues until a few kilometres above the confluence with the Southesk River, which enters from the river left. In this area the river is medium-volume and has much more power as it cuts through a trench in the surrounding bedrock. There are many low-angled ledges and some great surfing at tight corners with standing waves. The gradient eases and the river is easy and more open below the confluence with the Southesk. Then, once again, the gradient increases and the rapids become more numerous and powerful for a couple of kilometres. A right turn at the end of a short straight, with sloping ledges along the right shore, leads to Psycho Crack, a class V–V+ drop. The river funnels into a narrow slot, then drops off sharp ledges. The portage is on river right, through the old river channel, to the pool below. There are a few more small ledges in the next couple of kilometres. The gradient then eases and the rapids are more open and fun, with lots of good surfing. The rest of the run is described on page 91.

GETTING THERE The run is located between Highway 93 and the Forestry Trunk Road (Highway 940).

TAKE-OUT If coming from the north, start at the set of lights on Highway 16 at the east end of Hinton. Go about 1 km south, past the hospital, where you reach another set of lights. Turn south (right) onto the Robb Road and follow the road for 47 km to the junction with Highway 47. Turn south (right) and follow the road for another 9 km to the junction with Highway 40. Continue straight ahead onto Highway 40 (toward Nordegg), and go 43 km to a junction. Turn south (right) toward Nordegg and go 7 km to the Cardinal River Road, which is on the west (right) side.

If coming from Nordegg, turn north onto Highway 940 off Highway 11, 2.2 km west of Nordegg. Proceed north on the gravel road for approximately 61 km to the bridge on the Brazeau. Continue for another kilometre up the hill, to the Cardinal River Road, which is on the west (left) side.

From the junction at the Cardinal River Road, turn west and go 6.6 km to a right bend, where there is a small gravel road on the south (left) side. Turn left and follow the road for 1.5 km to near the river. The last 600 m is very steep.

PUT-IN   Return to the Cardinal River Road/940 junction and go 62 km south to Highway 11. Turn west (right) and proceed to the junction with Highway 93 at Saskatchewan River Crossing. Turn north (right) and go 37 km to the Nigel Pass trailhead. This is on the east (right) side of the road, on a steep ascent, a few km past the big bend in Highway 93. A gravel road leads 200 m to the trailhead. The trail branches off on your right, just past the gate.

CAMPING   There is undeveloped camping at the take-out. For developed camping try the Wilcox Creek Campground, 11 km north of the trailhead, on Highway 93. There is also developed camping at the Highway 940 bridge over the Brazeau, which is 1 km south of the Cardinal River Road/940 junction. You can camp along the river, however, the river is the boundary of Jasper National Park, so you must obtain a permit to use the designated campgrounds on river left, or else camp on river right. The park extends along the left bank until downstream of the Southesk River.

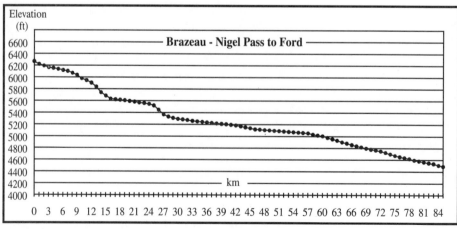

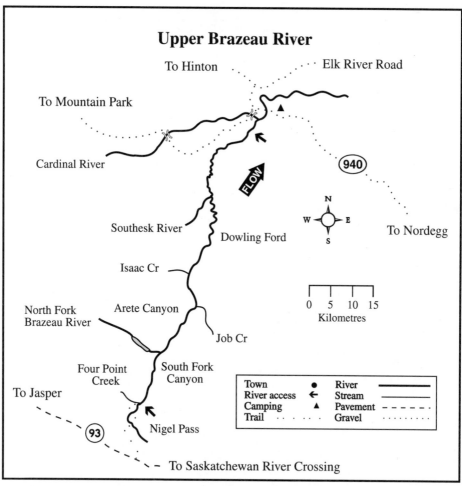

Upper Brazeau River

To Hinton

Elk River Road

To Mountain Park

Cardinal River

FLOW

940

To Nordegg

Southesk River

Dowling Ford

Isaac Cr

Arete Canyon

North Fork
Brazeau River

Job Cr

Four Point
Creek

South Fork
Canyon

To Jasper

93

Nigel Pass

N
W · E
S

0   5   10   15
Kilometres

Town	●	River	———
River access	←	Stream	———
Camping	▲	Pavement	− − −
Trail	· · · ·	Gravel	· · · · ·

To Saskatchewan River Crossing

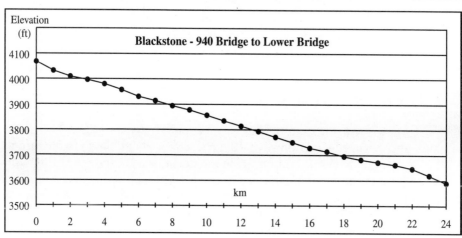

Elevation (ft)

Blackstone - 940 Bridge to Lower Bridge

km

GRADE	CLASS	FLOW	TIME	LENGTH
II	II–II+	Low	3–5 hours	24 km (15 mi)
III	II+–III	High		

Gradient 6 m/km (.6%)
32 ft/mi

Max gradient 30 m in 5 km (.6%)
100 ft in 3.1 mi

Put-in elevation 1240 m
4068 ft

Take-out elevation 1094 m
3590 ft

Shuttle 20 km (12 mi) one way

Season May–September

Maps 83C9 and 83C16

Gauge No

Craft Canoes, kayaks and rafts

CHARACTER A medium-volume run in an open, gravel-bottomed foothills valley. The rapids are formed by channel constrictions, boulder gardens and small bedrock ledges.

FLOW INFORMATION The river is uncontrolled and fed by snowmelt. Check the information on page 93 for an estimate of the water levels in the area.

TRAVEL Access to the run and the shuttle are on gravel roads.

DESCRIPTION The river flows through the open valley with a few class II rapids in the first 5–6 km, at small bedrock outcrops and tight corners. The valley for most of the run is scenic, with large gravel bars on the inside of the wide bends. This section lacks the constrictions of the upper runs, but you can expect standing waves at corners where the river drops off the gravel shoals and rock bars. About halfway down the run there is a steep-walled section, with more rapids. In the last half of the run the gradient decreases and the river has fewer rapids as the valley opens up. The gradient profile is on page 99.

GETTING THERE The run is located north of Nordegg, off Highway 940.

TAKE-OUT At the junction of Highway 11 and Highway 940, 2.2 km west of Nordegg, turn north on Highway 940. Proceed for about 34 km to the bridge on the Blackstone River. If coming from the north, start at the set of lights on Highway 16 at the east end of Hinton. Go about 1 km south, past the hospital, to a set of lights. Turn south (right) onto the Robb Road and follow the road for 47 km to the junction with Highway 47. Turn south (right) and go for another 9 km to the junction with Highway 40. Continue straight ahead onto Highway 40 (toward Nordegg) and go 43 km to a junction. Turn south (right) toward Nordegg and go 8 km south to the bridge on the Brazeau River. Continue south for another 27 km to the bridge on the Blackstone.

At the Blackstone bridge on Highway 940, go 1.1 km south to a gravel road on the east (left) side. Turn left and follow the road for 17 km, past two road junctions on the right, to a fork with a gate and a gas plant on the right. Stay left and go another 1.2 km to a bridge on the Blackstone.

PUT-IN   Return to the Blackstone bridge on Highway 940.

CAMPING   There is undeveloped camping at the take-out and put-in.

Barbara Daum in one of the boulder-garden rapids. Photo: Peter Daum.

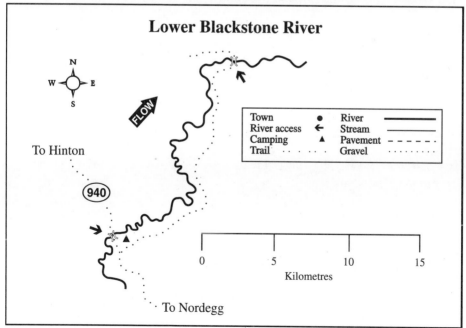

GRADE	CLASS	FLOW	TIME	LENGTH
II	II–II⁺	Low	2–4 hours	17 km (11 mi)
III	II⁺–III	High		

Gradient   5.9 m/km (.59%)   **Max gradient**   30 m in 4.7 km (.64%)
                    31 ft/mi   100 ft in 2.9 mi

Put-in elevation   1340 m   **Take-out elevation**   1240 m
                            4396 ft   4068 ft

Shuttle   36 km (22 mi) one way   **Season**   May–September

Maps   83C9   **Gauge**   No

Craft   Canoes, kayaks and rafts

CHARACTER   A scenic small to medium-volume run through an open and gravel-bottomed foothills valley. The rapids are created by small bedrock ledges and corners in the river channel.

FLOW INFORMATION   The river is uncontrolled and fed by snowmelt. At low flows there are many technical features that are fun to play in, while things flush out quite a bit at higher flows. Check the flow information on page 93 for a rough estimate of water levels in the area.

TRAVEL   Access to the run and the shuttle are on gravel roads.

DESCRIPTION   The river runs in an open gravel-bed until about 2 km below the put-in. You then encounter small class II rapids, which at low flows are ledges, but at high flows are standing waves. The river mellows, with increased braiding for 3–4 km and a few small features at bends. A second section of rapids occurs about halfway down the run, at a series of small ledges. In the last 3–4 km the river flows in a single channel. The gradient increases at a section of tight bends and the river winds back and forth just above the take-out.

GETTING THERE   The run is located north of Nordegg, off Highway 11. See the map on page 105.

TAKE-OUT   From the junction of Highway 11 and Highway 940, 2.2 km west of Nordegg, go north on Highway 940. Proceed for approximately 34 km to the bridge on the Blackstone River. If coming from the north, start at the set of lights on Highway 16 at the east end of Hinton. Go about 1 km south, past the hospital, to a set of lights. Turn south (right) onto the Robb Road and follow the road for approximately 47 km to the junction with Highway 47. Turn south (right) and follow the road for another 9 km to the junction with

Highway 40. Continue straight ahead onto Highway 40 (toward Nordegg), and go 43 km to a junction. Turn south (right) toward Nordegg and go 8 km south to the bridge on the Brazeau River. Continue south for another 27 km to the bridge on the Blackstone.

PUT-IN Go 23 km south of the take-out bridge, to a road on the west (right) side signed as Chungo Road (also with signs to the Blackstone Recreation Area). Turn right and follow the road for 13 km to the bridge on the Blackstone River.

CAMPING There is developed camping at the put-in or undeveloped camping at the take-out.

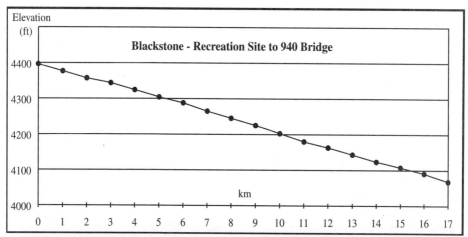

Surf time for Donna and Keith Bobey. Photo: Peter Daum.

BLACKSTONE   OLD BRIDGE TO RECREATION SITE

GRADE	CLASS	FLOW	TIME	LENGTH
II	II–II⁺	Low	1–2 hours	11 km (6.8 mi)
III	II–III	High		

Gradient 9.8 m/km (.98%)   **Max gradient** 30 m in 3 km (1%)
52 ft/mi   100 ft in 1.9 mi

Put-in elevation 1448 m   **Take-out elevation** 1340 m
4751 ft   4396 ft

Shuttle 8 km (5 mi) one way   **Season** May–August

Maps 83C9   **Gauge** No

Craft Canoes and kayaks

CHARACTER A small-volume run with tight and technical sections where the river drops over small ledges and through constricted boulder gardens.

FLOW INFORMATION The river is uncontrolled and fed by snowmelt. Check page 93 for a rough estimate of water levels in the area.

TRAVEL Access to the run and the shuttle are on gravel roads.

DESCRIPTION The river flows in an open low-walled valley, with class II–II⁺ ledges and rapids at constrictions in the river channel. In the first half of the run the river has many tight bends where rock outcrops produce distinct features in the scenic canyon. Below the confluence with Wapiabi Creek, which enters from the right, the volume increases and the creek flows in a more open valley, with a few small rapids before you reach the take-out.

GETTING THERE The run is located north of Nordegg, off Highway 11.

TAKE-OUT From the junction of Highway 11 and Highway 940, 2.2 km west of Nordegg, go north on the gravel Highway 940. In 10.5 km you reach the Chungo Road on the west (left) side (also marked for the Blackstone Recreation Area). Turn left and follow the road for 13 km to the bridge on the Blackstone River.

PUT-IN Go north, 400 m past the bridge, to a fork where you go west (left) along the Blackstone. Proceed 7.2 km upstream to another fork. Take the left fork, which leads down to the river in 500 m.

CAMPING There is undeveloped camping at the put-in or developed camping at the take-out.

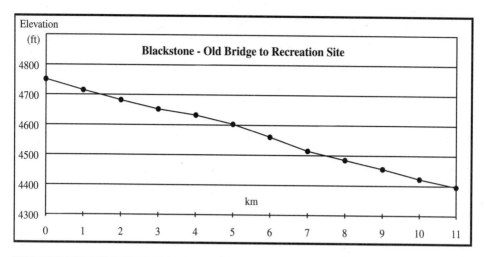

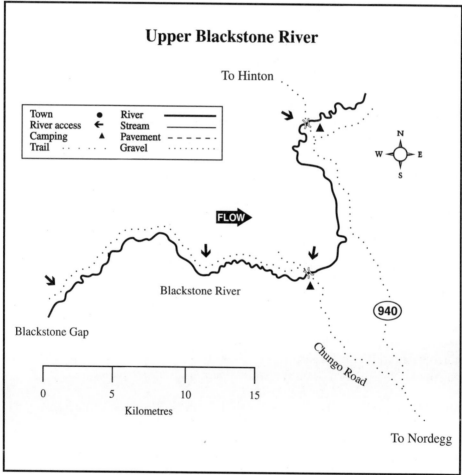

GRADE	CLASS	FLOW	TIME	LENGTH
II	II–II⁺	Low	2–4 hours	15 km (9 mi)
III	II⁺–III	High		

Gradient   10 m/km (1%)   **Max gradient**   30 m in 2.5 km (1.2%)
              53 ft/mi   100 ft in 1.6 mi

Put-in elevation   1600 m   **Take-out elevation**   1488 m
                       5249 ft   4751 ft

Shuttle   13 km (8 mi) one way   **Season**   May–August

Maps   83C10 and 83C9   **Gauge**   No

Craft   Kayaks and canoes

CHARACTER   A small-volume run through a beautiful low-walled canyon, with bedrock outcrops that produce interesting technical paddling.

FLOW INFORMATION   The river is uncontrolled and fed by snowmelt. Check the flow information on page 93 for a rough estimate of the water level.

TRAVEL   Access to the run and the shuttle are on gravel roads. The road to the put-in has a couple of extremely steep sections and a few very rutted passages. In poor weather, four-wheel-drives are recommended.

DESCRIPTION   The river is small and flows through a tight channel at the put-in. The views are spectacular looking west at the mountain range. Not far below the put-in are some class II rapids where the river drops off small ledges and flows through narrow boulder gardens. A sharp right turn at a small rapid starts a section of class II⁺–III rapids in a tight canyon. The river twists back and forth in the interesting, low-walled canyon, where small ledges provide the excitement. The largest of these is a .5-m drop. The valley opens up somewhat about halfway down the run. Watch for small class II ledges that lead to a narrow canyon with a sharp right turn at the end. The river drops through a narrow (1–1.5-m) slot, then the walls open up to easier paddling.

GETTING THERE   The run is located north of Nordegg, off Highway 11. See the map on page 105.

TAKE-OUT   From the junction of Highway 11 and Highway 940, 2.2 km west of Nordegg, go north on the gravel Highway 940. In 10.5 km, you reach the Chungo Road on the west (left) side (also marked for the Blackstone Recreation Area). Turn left and follow the road for 13 km to the bridge on the Blackstone

Just Getting There is an Adventure

Driving to the area was no big deal; it was just a little remote. But when I turned that corner and saw the hill in front of me, I knew that the impending rain could turn my escape into a nightmare. As I am often prone to do, I kept going, optimistic that things would work out. My van bogged down, huffing up the hill at just above an idle. I was narrowly defeating gravity, though my right foot was on the floor. The hill went on forever, and when I finally crested the top, the temperature gauge was climbing and I was sweating. The next kilometre brought an even steeper downhill, deep ruts that ran for hundreds of metres and threatening storm clouds. I dropped my bike for a shuttle, then completed the run below the Gap in the dark. When I pulled my bike from the bushes the rain soaked road was a mud bath. It was a major effort to stay balanced on my squirming motorcycle. Several times the front wheel kicked sideways and I was dumped into the muck. So I limped along at low speed, wrestling the bars, trying to stay atop the bike. At the van, I was plastered with mud and snow and chilled to the bone. Now all I had to do was get out of there.

Inside the van, with the heater blasting hot air, I felt a bit more secure. Then came the really steep uphill just before the long downhill, but a slippery corner prevented a good run at it. When I came to a tire-howling halt, well short of the summit, I was a bit nervous. That was before I started backing down, which was when I really got frightened! In a near-terminal slide, the front end whipped around and the back end slid toward the trench at the edge of the road. After tense moments of sliding along, brake pedal on the floor, the van came to rest with one rear wheel hanging over the void. I tried going forward but it was a futile effort. After a soggy, frantic and hopeless rage I was slumped dejectedly against the side of my van. Then I came up with a desperate plan.

I rooted out my throw bag and set a line from the back of my van, across to the other side of the road, onto a tree. Using a zillion-to-one pulley system composed of every 'biner, pulley and prussik in my gear bag, I heaved the line tight. After a moment of prayer to the polypropylene gods, I gingerly put the transmission in reverse. The first few feet were excruciating as the van moved slowly downhill, but didn't really start to come back over the road. Then the stretch in the line began to exert itself, and the backend slowly skidded around. In another metre I had the hanging wheel on the road. At the back of the van my 10-mm rope was stretched out like a thin piece of red and yellow dental floss. Even the slightest touch of the line sent off strange musical notes. After disassembling the rig, I skidded ever so slowly down to the bottom of the hill. With the foreknowledge of the hill's layout and the approaching corner, I slowly backed up for about a kilometre, then prepared myself. By the time I reached the hill, I was in a full-blown powerskid at 90 kph and was swinging the wheel back and forth, attempting to keep the headlights on the road. I crested that hill with the engine screaming and promptly skidded to a halt, got out and screeched "Yeaaaaaaaah!" So what do I remember about the upper Blackstone? Oh, the river is good fun, but buddy watch out for those roads!

River. Continue north, 400 m past the bridge, to a fork where you go west (left) along the Blackstone. Proceed upstream for 7.2 km to another fork. Take the left fork, which leads down to the river in 500 m.

PUT-IN Return 500 m to the road leading upstream along the Blackstone and go west (left) for about 13 km to where the road drops steeply down to a creek ford. The road is closed just ahead, so this is a convenient put-in.

CAMPING There is undeveloped camping at the take-out and the put-in.

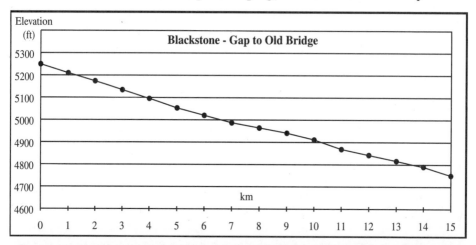

Ted Mellenthin in Squeezebox on the lower Cardinal at high flows.
Photo Al Taylor.

GRADE	CLASS	FLOW	TIME	LENGTH
II–II⁺	II–III⁺	Medium	5–6 hours	30 km (18 mi)
II⁺–III	II⁺–IV	High		

Gradient   8 m/km (.8%)   **Max gradient**   30 m in 3 km (1%)
42 ft/mi   100 ft in 1.9 mi

Put-in elevation   1510 m   **Take-out elevation**   1275 m
4954 ft   4183 ft

Shuttle   26 km (16 mi) one way   **Season**   May–August

Maps   83C15   **Gauge**   Yes

Craft   Canoes, kayaks and small rafts

CHARACTER   An interesting small to medium-volume run in a steep-sided valley, with great scenery amidst the varied rock formations. The rapids are formed by small bedrock outcrops where the river drops off ledges. Rafters will find the last 2 km difficult to run, due to the constricted channel.

FLOW INFORMATION   The river is uncontrolled and fed by snowmelt. Assess the flow at the take-out.

TRAVEL   Access to the run and the shuttle are on gravel roads.

DESCRIPTION   The river drops quickly into a steep-sided valley, just below the put-in. About 200 m below the bridge, the river is funnelled into a narrow class II⁺–III chute that drops .5–1 m on river right. The river twists and turns in the tight canyon-like valley. Watch for a sharp left turn about 1.5 km below the second creek entering from the right. The corner has low-angled sloping ledges on the right and is just above Squeezebox, a 1–2 m class III–IV drop into a narrow, low-walled canyon. Not far below is a spectacular waterfall dropping into the river from the left side. A sharp right turn then leads to a convoluted class II⁺–III boulder garden. This is followed 100 m below, by a small double-drop through broken ledges. The tight valley continues for 2-3 km, then opens up and the rapids are farther apart. The gradient decreases and the river is easy and open until about 3 km upstream of the take-out. Here the river slows and enters a lake in the valley. You paddle 800 m across the lake, with trees sticking up from the depths. The whole thing is ghostly and unusual. A huge landslide at the downstream end of the lake backed the river up to quite a height at one time, as you can see from the waterline on the dead trees. Where the river exits over the mudslide, the channel is very narrow and strewn with logs and boulders. The slide rapid is about 400–500 m of very tight class II⁺–III. Then the river opens up and the take-out is not far below.

GETTING THERE The run is located between Hinton and Nordegg, off the Forestry Trunk Road (Highway 940). You can approach the run from the north, at Hinton, or from the south at Nordegg. You can also access the run near Cadomin, on a rough gravel road that leads south of Mountain Park. See the map on page 112.

TAKE-OUT If coming from the north, start at the set of lights on Highway 16 at the east end of Hinton. Go about 1 km south, past the hospital, to a set of lights. Turn south (right) onto the Robb Road and follow the road for 47 km to the junction with Highway 47. Turn south (right) and follow the road for another 9 km to the junction with Highway 40. Continue straight ahead onto Highway 40 (toward Nordegg) and go 43 km to a junction. Turn south (right) toward Nordegg and go 7 km south to the Cardinal River Road, which is on the west (right) side.

If coming from Nordegg, turn north onto Highway 940, off Highway 11, 2.2 km west of Nordegg. Proceed north on the gravel road for approximately 61 km to the bridge on the Brazeau. Look for the Cardinal River Road, 1 km north of the bridge, on the west (left) side.

From the Cardinal River Road/940 junction, go west for 2.5 km to the bridge on the Cardinal.

If you are coming from near Cadomin, the take-out bridge is approximately 57 km south of the old townsite of Mountain Park.

PUT-IN Go west from the take-out for 26 km to the bridge on the river.

CAMPING There is undeveloped camping at the take-out.

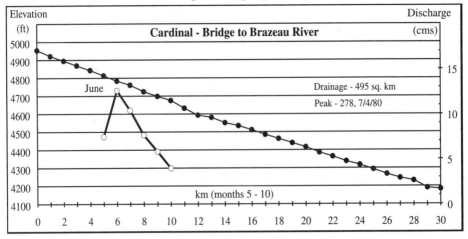

GRADE	CLASS	FLOW	TIME	LENGTH
II	II–II⁺	Low	1–2 hours	12 km (7.5 mi)
II	II–III	High		

Gradient 10 m/km (1%)
55 ft/mi

Max gradient 30 m in 3 km (1%)
100 ft in 1.9 mi

Put-in elevation 1635 m
5364 ft

Take-out elevation 1510 m
4954 ft

Shuttle 10 km (6.2 mi) one way

Season May–August

Maps 83C14 and 83C15

Gauge Yes

Craft Canoes, kayaks and small rafts

CHARACTER A scenic, small-volume run in a wide gravel-bottomed valley with a couple of short rapids.

FLOW INFORMATION The river is uncontrolled and fed by snowmelt. Assess the flow at the take-out, where the river flows in a constricted canyon.

TRAVEL Access to the run and the shuttle are on gravel roads.

DESCRIPTION The river runs in a single channel that alternates with open, braided sections. The rapids are formed by small bedrock ledges and tight corners. Near the end of the run look for a couple of class II–II⁺ rapids at bedrock outcrops, where the river has cut into the gravel plain. There are excellent views of the surrounding foothills and headwall mountains.

GETTING THERE The run is located between Hinton and Nordegg, off the Forestry Trunk Road (Highway 940). You can approach the run from the north at Hinton, or from the south at Nordegg. You can also access the run near Cadomin, on a rough gravel road that leads south of Mountain Park.

TAKE-OUT If coming from the north, start at the set of lights on Highway 16 at the east end of Hinton. Go about 1 km south, past the hospital, to a set of lights. Turn south (right) onto the Robb Road and follow the road for 47 km to the junction with Highway 47. Turn south (right) and follow the road for another 9 km to the junction with Highway 40. Continue straight ahead onto Highway 40 (toward Nordegg), and go 43 km to a junction. Turn south (right) toward Nordegg and go 7 km south to the Cardinal River Road, which is on the west (right) side.

If coming from near Nordegg, turn north onto Highway 940 off Highway 11, 2.2 km west of Nordegg. Proceed north on the gravel road for approximately 61 km to the bridge on the Brazeau. Look for the Cardinal River Road, 1 km north of the bridge, on the west (left) side.

From the Cardinal River Road/940 junction, go west for 28 km to the bridge on the Cardinal.

If you are coming from near Cadomin, the take-out bridge is approximately 31 km south of the old townsite of Mountain Park.

PUT-IN Go west (upstream) on the Cardinal River Road for 10 km to a small gravel trail on the south (left) side at an open meadow. Follow the trail for 600 m to a junction, stay left and follow the old campground loop to near the river.

CAMPING There is undeveloped camping at the put-in.

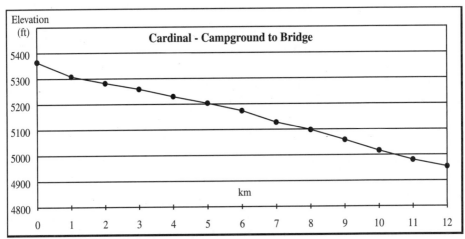

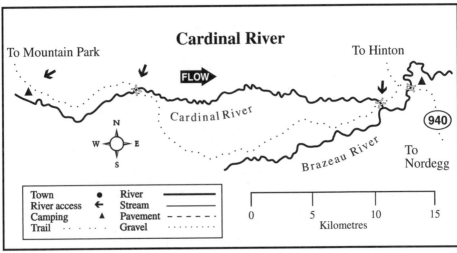

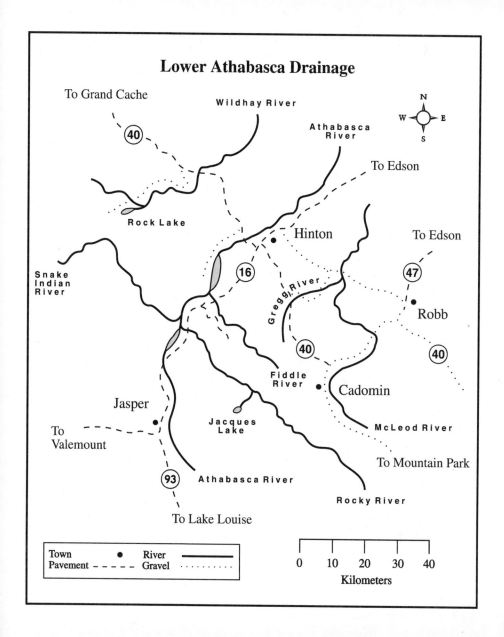

Lower Athabasca Drainage

To Grand Cache

Wildhay River

Athabasca River

To Edson

N
W E
S

40

Rock Lake

Hinton

To Edson

Snake Indian River

16

Gregg River

47

Robb

40

40

Fiddle River

Cadomin

Jasper

Jacques Lake

To Valemount

McLeod River

To Mountain Park

93

Athabasca River

Rocky River

To Lake Louise

| Town | ● | River | —— |
| Pavement | – – – | Gravel | ·········· |

0   10   20   30   40
Kilometers

ATHABASCA BRULE LAKE TO HIGHWAY 40

GRADE	CLASS	FLOW	TIME	LENGTH
I–II	II	Most Flows	1–2 hours	14 km (8.7 mi)

Gradient 1.2 m/km (.12%)
6.1 ft/mi

Max gradient 16 m in 14 km (.12%)
52 ft in 8.7 mi

Put-in elevation 984 m
3228 ft

Take-out elevation 968 m
3175 ft

Shuttle 15 km (9.3 mi) one way

Season May–September

Maps 83F5

Gauge Yes

Craft Canoes, kayaks and rafts

CHARACTER An open run on a large-volume river. There are a few short sets of standing waves at corners and where the river drops off rock bars.

FLOW INFORMATION The river is on Alberta Environmental Protection's River Report recording. Use the flow at Hinton; low flow is 200 to 300 cms and high flow is 500 to 900 cms. The river is uncontrolled and fed by snowmelt and glacial runoff.

TRAVEL Access to the run and the shuttle are on paved roads.

DESCRIPTION At the put-in, drag across the tracks to reach the lake then paddle 2 km across the lake to the outlet. From there, the river flows swiftly in a single channel. There are short sets of standing waves at the corners, although the presence and size of these waves is water level dependent. The river starts into a deep valley where the views of the open lake above are cut off. Look for your marker on the right shore, just below the Highway 40 bridge.

GETTING THERE The run is located north of Hinton, off Highway 40.

TAKE-OUT From the junction of Highway 16 and Highway 40 North, just west of Hinton, proceed north on Highway 40 for 4.2 kilometres to a gravel road on the east (right) side. The gravel road is 700 m south of the bridge. Follow the gravel road to where it is barricaded and mark the take-out at the river.

PUT-IN Return to Highway 40, then go 1 km north to a paved road on the west (left) side. Turn left, go 100 m, then turn right and follow the road for 13 km to a bridge over a small creek. Turn south (left), just past the creek, on the road signed Swan Landing. Go south 700 m, then turn right and park off to the side. Carry across the tracks to the lake.

CAMPING There is developed camping north of the take-out, off Highway 40, in William Switzer Provincial Park.

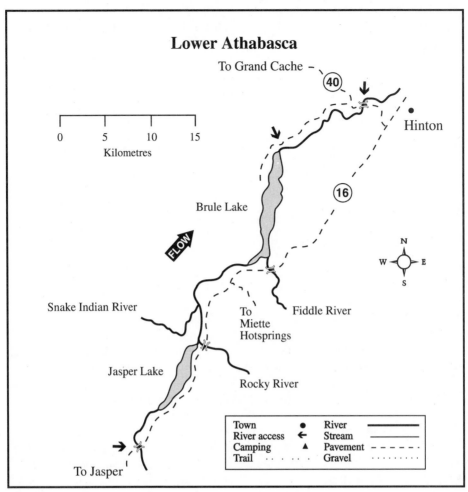

Lower Athabasca

To Grand Cache

Hinton

Brule Lake

Snake Indian River

Fiddle River

To Miette Hotsprings

Jasper Lake

Rocky River

To Jasper

Town	●	River	———
River access	←	Stream	——
Camping	▲	Pavement	- - -
Trail	· · · · ·	Gravel	· · · · · · ·

0 · 5 · 10 · 15
Kilometres

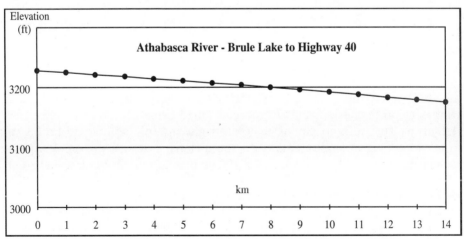

Elevation (ft)

Athabasca River - Brule Lake to Highway 40

km

GRADE	CLASS	FLOW	TIME	LENGTH
I	II	Most Flows	1–2 days	42 km (26 mi)

Gradient   .48 m/km (.05%)
              2.5 ft/mi

Max gradient 20 m in 42 km (.05%)
                 66 ft in 26 mi

Put-in elevation   1004 m
                      3294 ft

Take-out elevation   984 m
                        3228 ft

Shuttle   70 km (43 mi) one way

Season   May–September

Maps   83E1, 83F4 and 83F5

Gauge   No

Craft   Canoes, kayaks and rafts

CHARACTER   A large-volume run in an open and scenic valley. The river flows through a series of lakes, with little real whitewater.

FLOW INFORMATION   The river is on Alberta Environmental Protection's River Report recording. Use the flow at Hinton; low flow is 200 to 300 cms and high flow is 500 to 900 cms. The river is uncontrolled and fed by snowmelt and glacial runoff. Low flows turn the lakes into mud plains.

TRAVEL   Access to the run and the shuttle are on paved roads.

DESCRIPTION   At the put-in, the river flows swiftly over a gravel-bed. About 1 km downstream the river enters Jasper Lake. The ever shifting sand bars can make finding the main channel in the shallow silt-laden water somewhat difficult, but the scenery is incredible. Below Jasper Lake the river assumes a single channel for about 15 km then enters Brule Lake, which is easier to navigate than Jasper Lake. Exit at the east end of the lake on the north shore.

GETTING THERE   The run is located east of Jasper, along Highway 16. See the map on page 115.

TAKE-OUT   At the junction of Highway 16 and Highway 40 North, near Hinton, go north on Highway 40. Proceed 6 km to a small paved road on the west (left) side. Turn left, go 100 m, then turn right and follow the road for 13 km to a bridge over a small creek. Turn south (left), just past the creek, on the road labelled Swan Landing. Go south 700 m, then turn right. Mark the take-out.

PUT-IN   Return to the junction of Highways 40 and 16, then go west (right) on Highway 16. Proceed for 50 km to the bridge on the Athabasca. There is parking on the south (left) side of the highway, just before you reach the bridge.

CAMPING   There is developed camping, 8.4 km west of the put-in, at Snaring Campground.

GRADE	CLASS	FLOW	TIME	LENGTH
I+	I+–II	Low-Medium	6–8 hours	35 km (22 mi)
II	II–II+	Medium-High		

Gradient 4.9 m/km (.49%)
26 ft/mi

Max gradient 30 m in 5.5 km (.55%)
100 ft in 3.4 mi

Put-in elevation 1323 m
4340 ft

Take-out elevation 1152 m
3780 ft

Shuttle 41 km (25 mi) one way

Season May–August

Maps 83F3 and 83F6

Gauge Yes

Craft Canoes, kayaks and small rafts

CHARACTER A small to medium-volume run in an open foothills setting, with rapids created by small ledges and sharp turns. The views in the first half of the run are exceptional.

FLOW INFORMATION The river is on Alberta Environmental Protection's River Report recording. Use the flow above the Embarras River; low flow is 30 to 60 cms and high flow is 100 to 300 cms. The river is uncontrolled and fed by snowmelt.

TRAVEL Access to the run and the shuttle are on gravel roads.

DESCRIPTION The river runs on an open gravel flat for the first couple of kilometres, then you encounter small class II ledges and sharp corners. This continues for 6–7 km until you reach a .5 m class II–II+ ledge across the river. Below the ledge are numerous small ledges and boulder gardens in the narrow channel. This continues for about 10 km, with excellent views of the Rockies in this area. The river then turns away from the mountains, the gradient decreases and the rapids are less frequent. Watch for a couple of log jams in this section. Near the end of the run, the river makes a sharp left, then enters a 1-km-long section of class II–II+ whitewater that ends at the confluence with the Gregg River. The river is then easier until you reach the take-out.

GETTING THERE The run is located south of Hinton, off Highway 40.

TAKE-OUT From the set of lights on Highway 16 at the east end of Hinton, go south, past the hospital for 1 km, to another set of lights. Turn south (right) onto the Robb Road, and follow the road for 26 km to the bridge on the McLeod.

PUT-IN Go 21 km south of the bridge to the junction with Highway 47, near

Robb. Turn west (right) and follow the road for 9 km to a junction, with Highway 40 on your right. Turn west (right) and go 11 km to the bridge. If you want a short run on the best whitewater, you can also access just the final kilometre of rapids at the end of the run. Proceed 400 m south of the take-out bridge, then turn west (right) and follow the road into the meadow. Carry 150 m through the trees at the south end of the meadow to the river.

CAMPING   There is undeveloped camping at the put-in and at the take-out.

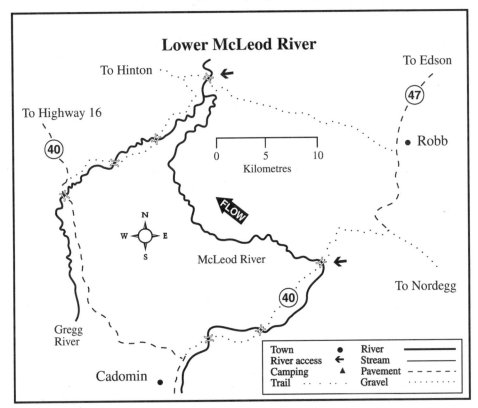

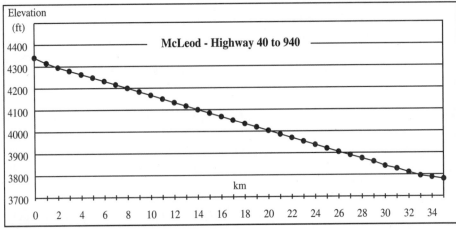

GRADE	CLASS	FLOW	TIME	LENGTH
III	II–VI	Low	1–3 hours	4 km (2.5 mi)
IV	III–VI	High		

Gradient 24 m/km (2.4%)
125 ft/mi

Max gradient 30 m in 1.2 km (2.5%)
100 ft in .75 mi

Put-in elevation 1680 m
5511 ft

Take-out elevation 1585 m
5200 ft

Shuttle 4.2 km (2.6 mi) one way

Season May–August

Maps 83C14

Gauge Yes

Craft Canoes and kayaks

CHARACTER A small-volume run in a bedrock canyon, with lots of steep drops and waterfalls. The whitewater between the drops is inconsequential compared to the major drops, which are the main attraction. All the drops can be portaged near water level. This is a class V adrenaline-seekers' type of run.

FLOW INFORMATION The river is on Alberta Environmental Protection's River Report recording and is uncontrolled and fed by snowmelt. Use the flow above the Embarras River; low flow is 30 to 60 cms and high flow is 100 to 300 cms. The flow at the put-in will be about 10 to 25 percent of that on the recording.

TRAVEL The shuttle is on gravel roads.

DESCRIPTION The river runs in an open gravel channel at the put-in, then is compressed not far below by rock walls. The first drop is a class III–IV chute that falls 1–2 m into a pool. There are a couple of small ledges in a low-walled canyon, then the river opens up until Prospect Creek, which enters from the left. Below the creek confluence there are more small ledges and tight corners. The river makes a sharp left, just above an old railroad bridge, and enters Teetering Towers, a narrow class II–III rapid under the precariously balanced bridge supports. The river then opens up for about another 1 kilometre, to where there are bedrock ledges along the right shore, just above a sharp left/right combination. This is Just Plain Crazy, a class V⁺ drop that starts as a narrow chute along the rock ledges and ends at a 90 degree turn that plunges off a 4–5-m waterfall. The left and right sides fall onto rock outcrops, so hitting the centre chute is the only way through. Scout or portage on the right by scrambling along the ledges, then descending through the brush in a gully beside the drop.

Rob Evans-Davies getting radical in Gravity Sucks.

The river opens up again for 500 m, then you reach a sharp left turn into a rock canyon. This is Pincushion, a narrow class IV–V slot that double-drops 2–3 m into a canyon. Scout on the right by getting out just above the drop. Below Pincushion the river drops into Maelstrom, a vicious class V⁺–VI boulder choke that drops 3–5 m through very constricted passages and ends in a narrow boiling chute. Scout or portage on the right. About 100 m below, the river drops off a 1-m diagonal ledge, then starts into a low-angled chute that leads to Gravity Sucks, a 6–9-m fall. The fall can be portaged on river right, by scrambling down a steep gully to the big pool. You can also walk along the tracks, high on the right shore, from Pincushion to below the Gravity Sucks.

The river then enters another canyon, with a class II$^+$–III$^+$ drop followed by an overhanging, twisting canyon. After the canyon opens up, you reach the final drop at Hammer Time, a class V$^+$–VI chute that bounces off a rock ledge then drops 2–3 m to a boiling pool against the cliff on the right. You can portage on the right by crawling down the old potholed channel, then launching immediately below the drop or by climbing up and along the rim of the canyon, then down to below the fall. The rapids are easy and open to the take-out.

GETTING THERE The run is located south of Hinton, off Highway 40.

TAKE-OUT From the junction of Highway 16 and Highway 40 South, just west of Hinton, go south on Highway 40 for 48 km to a T intersection. Turn west (right) and follow the road south for 8.2 km, through the town of Cadomin, to the bridge on Whitehorse Creek. Just south of the bridge is an old trail on the east (left) that leads 200 m to the McLeod. Mark the take-out at the river.

Paul Lauzon rising out of the foam at Pincushion.

PUT-IN Continue south of the Whitehorse Creek bridge for 4.2 km to a small road on the east (left) side that leads to near the river.

CAMPING There is undeveloped camping at the put-in or developed camping near the take-out, at the Whitehorse Recreation Area.

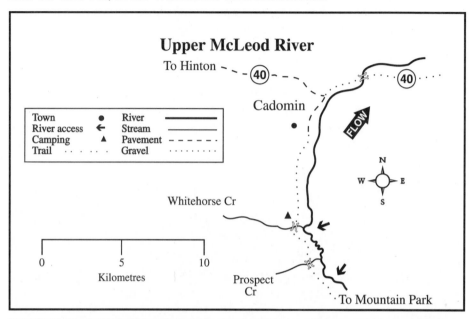

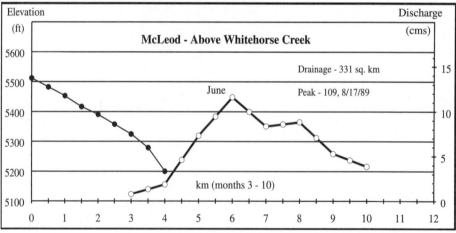

GRADE	CLASS	FLOW	TIME	LENGTH
II	I⁺–II	Low	1–2 hours	7.5 km (4.7 mi)
II	II⁺	High		

Gradient   8.3 m/km (.83%)
44 ft/mi

Max gradient   30 m in 3.5 km (.86%)
100 ft in 2.2 mi

Put-in elevation   1221 m
4005 ft

Take-out elevation   1158 m
3800 ft

Shuttle   4.3 km (2.7 mi) one way   **Season**   May–August

Maps   83F6   **Gauge**   Yes

Craft   Canoes, kayaks and small rafts

CHARACTER   A small-volume run in an open valley, with a few rapids at sharp corners and small ledges.

FLOW INFORMATION   Check the flow for the McLeod River on Alberta Environmental Protection's River Report recording. Use the flow above the Embarras River; low flow is 30 to 60 cms and high flow is 100 to 300 cms. Expect the Gregg to have 15–20 percent of that flow. The river is fed by snowmelt and is uncontrolled.

TRAVEL   Access to the run and the shuttle are on gravel roads.

DESCRIPTION   At the put-in the river runs in a single channel on an open gravel-bed. The rapids you encounter are caused by tight corners, small ledges and the occasional boulder garden. Watch for sweepers and log jams in the narrow channel. There are a couple of play spots about halfway down the run and some class II rapids near the end.

GETTING THERE   The run is located south of Hinton, off Highway 40.

TAKE-OUT   From the set of lights on Highway 16 at the east end of Hinton, go south, past the hospital, for 1 km to another set of lights. Turn south (right) onto the Robb Road and follow the road for 25 km to a fork, with the Gregg River Road on the right. Go west (right) and follow the road for 2.7 km to a small trail in a meadow on the south (left) side of the road.

PUT-IN   Continue west along the Gregg River Road for 4.3 km, to the bridge.

CAMPING   There is undeveloped camping at the take-out.

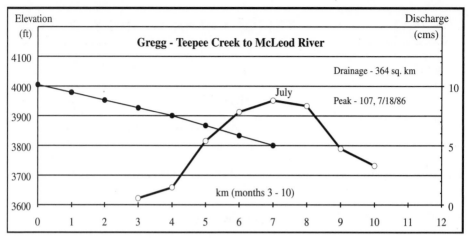

Gregg - Teepee Creek to McLeod River

Elevation (ft) / Discharge (cms)

Drainage - 364 sq. km

July

Peak - 107, 7/18/86

km (months 3 - 10)

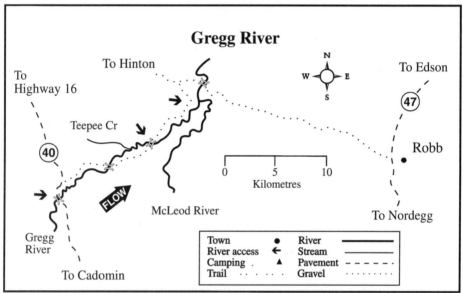

Gregg River

To Hinton

To Highway 16

To Edson

47

Robb

Teepee Cr

40

Kilometres
0   5   10

FLOW

McLeod River

To Nordegg

Gregg River

To Cadomin

Town	●	River	━━━
River access	←	Stream	——
Camping	▲	Pavement	– – –
Trail	· · · · ·	Gravel	··········

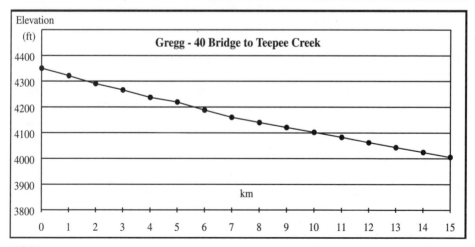

Gregg - 40 Bridge to Teepee Creek

Elevation (ft)

km

GRADE	CLASS	FLOW	TIME	LENGTH
II	I⁺–II	Low	2–3 hours	14.5 km (9 mi)
II	II	High		

Gradient   7.3 m/km (.73%)   **Max gradient** 30 m in 3.5 km (.86%)
             38 ft/mi   100 ft in 2.2 mi

Put-in elevation   1326 m   **Take-out elevation**   1221 m
                      4350 ft   4005 ft

Shuttle   12 km (7.5 mi) one way   **Season**   May–August

Maps   83F3 and 83F6   **Gauge**   Yes

Craft   Canoes and kayaks

CHARACTER   A small-volume run in an open valley, with rapids created by small rock outcrops and tight corners.

FLOW INFORMATION   Check the flow for the McLeod River on Alberta Environmental Protection's River Report recording. Use the flow above the Embarras River; low flow is 30 to 60 cms and high flow is 100 to 300 cms. The Gregg will have 15–20 percent of that flow. There is a hydrograph for the river, which is uncontrolled and fed by snowmelt, on page 124.

TRAVEL   Access to the run and the shuttle are on gravel roads.

DESCRIPTION   At the put-in, the river flows in a wandering channel in the open valley. There are easy class II rapids at sharp corners and at small ledges. There may be a couple of log jams in the middle of the run. At higher flows the river flushes through a narrow channel, and log debris on the shore and at islands becomes hazardous. The gradient profile is on page 124.

GETTING THERE   The run is located south of Hinton, off Highway 40. See the map on page 124.

TAKE-OUT   From the set of lights on Highway 16 at the east end of Hinton, go south, past the hospital, for 1 km to another set of lights. Turn south (right) onto the Robb Road and follow the road for 25 km to a fork, with the Gregg River Road on the right. Go west (right) and follow the road for 7 km to the bridge.

PUT-IN   Continue 11 km west along the Gregg River Road, to the junction with Highway 40. Turn south (left) and go 300 m to the put-in.

CAMPING   There is undeveloped camping all along the Gregg River Road.

GRADE	CLASS	FLOW	TIME	LENGTH
II	I⁺–II	Low	1–2 hours	5 km (3 mi)
II	II	High		

Gradient 5.5 m/km (.55%)
29 ft/mi

Max gradient 27 m in 5 km (.55%)
89 ft in 3 mi

Put-in elevation 1248 m
4095 ft

Take-out elevation 1221 m
4005 ft

Shuttle 12 km (7.4 mi) one way

Season May–August

Maps 83F12

Gauge Yes

Craft Canoes, kayaks and rafts

CHARACTER A small to medium-volume run in an open valley, with a few isolated rapids and play spots.

FLOW INFORMATION The river is on Alberta Environmental Protection's River Report recording. Use the flow near Hinton; low flow is 8 to 15 cms and high flow is 40 to 60 cms. The river is uncontrolled and fed by snowmelt.

TRAVEL The shuttle is on gravel roads.

DESCRIPTION At the put-in, the river flows in an open gravel-bed where rapids are formed at tight corners and boulder gardens. The valley is open, with some good views. There are a couple of play spots where small ledges create holes. The river lacks the well-defined character of the upper run.

GETTING THERE The run is located north of Hinton, off Highway 40.

TAKE-OUT At the junction of Highway 16 and Highway 40 North, just west of Hinton, go 36 km north on Highway 40 to the bridge. If coming from the north, the bridge is about 102 km south of Grande Cache. There is a small road on river left, just downstream of the bridge, that leads to the river.

PUT-IN Go north from the bridge for 4.1 km to the Rock Lake Road, which is on the west (left) side of the road. Turn left and follow the road for 2.2 km to a T intersection. Turn south (left) and go 4.1 km to another junction, with a road on your right. Go straight down the hill to an old bridge site. The old bridge site is just past a road on the right, which leads to the group camp.

CAMPING The developed camping at the group campground can be booked by calling (403) 865-2400, or there is undeveloped camping at the take-out.

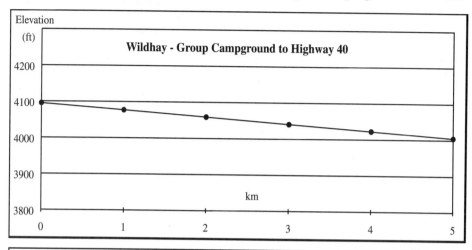

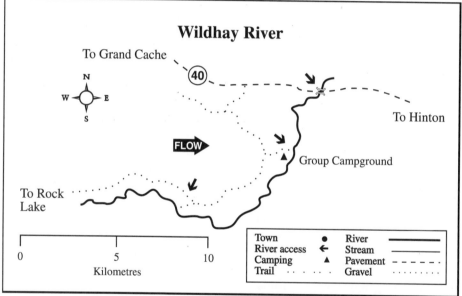

GRADE	CLASS	FLOW	TIME	LENGTH
II	I–II	Low	2–3 hours	10 km (6.2 mi)
II	II⁺	High		

Gradient 5.2 m/km (.52%)
27 ft/mi

Max gradient 30 m in 5.5 km (.55%)
100 ft in 3.4 mi

Put-in elevation 1300 m
4265 ft

Take-out elevation 1248 m
4095 ft

Shuttle 6 km (3.7 mi) one way

Season May–August

Maps 83E8, 83E9 and 83F12

Gauge Yes

Craft Canoes, kayaks and rafts

CHARACTER A low to medium-volume run through scenic foothills, with lots of excellent practice spots and well-defined features. This makes the run perfect for beginner to novice paddlers.

FLOW INFORMATION The river is on Alberta Environmental Protection's River Report recording. Use the flow near Hinton; low flow is 8 to 15 cms and high flow is 40 to 60 cms. The river is uncontrolled and fed by snowmelt.

TRAVEL The shuttle is on gravel roads.

DESCRIPTION At the put-in, the river flows in a single, winding channel containing numerous easy boulder-garden rapids. This continues for 2–3 km with a few good play spots on small surf waves. The river encounters bedrock outcrops that produce well-defined eddies at sharp turns. There are two class II sharp left turns at undercut rock headwalls. The second of these is known as Jaws, where you stay left to avoid the jagged rock face. The river then flows in an open channel with boulder-garden-style rapids. Below a small surf wave, watch for an island just downstream of a distinct eddy at a rock outcrop from the left. The right channel is often clogged with logs. It is difficult to see the whole channel from above, and once you start down there is little chance to stop. Scout from the island to be sure. Near the end of the run there are some easy play waves and a couple of small holes. Watch for the gauging station cable car, which is not far above the take-out.

GETTING THERE The run is located north of Hinton, off Highway 40. See the map on page 127.

TAKE-OUT From the junction of Highway 16 and Highway 40 North, just west of Hinton, go 36 km north on Highway 40 to a bridge on the river. If coming from the north, the bridge is about 102 km south of Grande Cache. Proceed 4.1 km north from the bridge to the Rock Lake Road, which is on the west (left) side of the road. Turn left and go 2.2 km to a T intersection. Turn south (left) and go 4.1 km to another junction, with a road on your right. Go straight down the hill to an old bridge site. The old bridge site is just before a road on the right, which leads to the group camp.

PUT-IN Return 500 m up the hill to the junction. Go west (left) and follow the road upstream for 5 km to a fork. Take the smaller left fork and go 400 m to the site of an old bridge, which is the put-in.

CAMPING There is undeveloped camping at the put-in or developed camping at the group campground, which can be booked by calling (403) 865-2400.

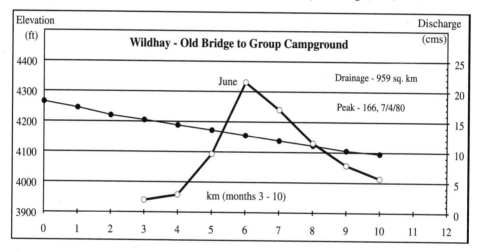

GRADE	CLASS	FLOW	TIME	LENGTH
IV–V	II–V⁺	Low	4–6 hours	6.5 km (4 mi)
V–V⁺	II–VI	Medium		

Gradient   21 m/km (2%)   **Max gradient**   30 m in 1 km (3%)
               109 ft/mi   100 ft in .6 mi

Put-in elevation   1146 m   **Take-out elevation**   1012 m
                       3760 ft   3320 ft

Shuttle   17 km (10.6 mi) one way   **Season**   May–September

Maps   83F4   **Gauge**   No

Craft   Kayaks

CHARACTER   An insane descent into the bowels of the earth. The river runs
on bedrock over a series of falls and ledges into one of the narrowest and deepest
gorges I have seen. Slight water level changes at the put-in produce wild changes
in the gorge. After one attempt and a rainstorm, I returned to find a new log
jam hanging 20 m above the water. It is essential to scout the entire gorge on foot
before you get in. Climbing skills, short boats and steady nerves are required.

FLOW INFORMATION   Assess the flow at the take-out and the put-in, to
get a feel for the water level. Ridiculously low flows are mandatory for success.
The river is uncontrolled and fed by snowmelt.

TRAVEL   Access to the run and the shuttle are on paved roads.

DESCRIPTION   The run starts in an open channel, with a couple of class III
drops at bedrock ledges, then the river flows on gravel until about 1 km below
the road viewpoint. From there the river flows around increasingly higher
rock outcrops, with constricted rapids at low-angled ledges and tight corners.
A sharp right turn at a small ledge leads to a tight canyon which contains a 1–2-m
class IV⁺–V double-drop into a hole. This is followed by a fast chute through
a narrow gap. Below this the river flows over a spectacular bedrock display of
finely layered sedimentary rocks, then opens up for a bit. There are a couple
of small boulder gardens and ledges until you begin to descend to the gorge.

The gorge starts with a 2–3-m drop into the 1–1.5-m wide slot, then is followed
by 100 m of calmer water in the deep canyon. The river then drops 2–3 m at
Blinders, a steep class V–V⁺ chute that is difficult to scout. The river drops
into a narrow gap created by a fallen chockstone which constricts the flow.
The gorge walls at this point are 35 m in height and vertical or overhung.
Below this drop is 100 m of calmer water that leads to two smaller drops. The
river then reaches a 90-degree right turn at Do It In The Dark, a narrow class

Fiddle Friday

In the mid-1980's, I worked four days a week as a raft guide and explored the rivers near Jasper on my days off. But I had one other project which officially occupied at least one day of my week. The first day of my weekend became known as Fiddle Friday. The Fiddle is a tiny-volume river that tumbles along bedrock in a narrow valley, with incredible limestone walls and a wicked gorge at the bottom. The first descent was a "get in and see what happens" event that ended at the gorge with a carry back upstream to the road. A second attempt at lower flows met with the same fate. Then things got serious. Armed with climbing ropes, pitons and rock gear, we went for it. That day, the river was 6–8 cm higher than I had seen it. Hardly cause for concern, or so I thought.

While descending to the gorge our plans ran amuck when Fred dropped into a hole and did a flying backender after taking his lumps in the hole. Somewhat routine, as far as holes go, but when Fred erupted out of the water there was a problem. His boat had split along the seamline and he looked like a giant banana rising from the depths, with the boat peeled back exposing the contents. Well that was it for him, and the event so impressed my nephew James that he also packed it in. Robert and I continued to the gorge, where that 6–8 cm of extra water squeezed into the narrow slot and piled up on itself. The water level was about 1 metre higher than before and the river was boiling and erupting through the narrow passages, which had previously been calm.

We decided to try to get around the wild bits and paddle as much as we could. Hours later we were high on the cliffs, climbing bald faces, with numerous ropes strung together, hanging off our PFD tow systems. After scaling to rope's end, we would haul our boats up the cliff, then repeat the process. At one downclimb we lowered our boats off a cliff into the trees below. It is always a tense moment when you wiggle the rope, testing to see if your boat is stable, before you toss the rope and climb down. Robert lowered his boat, tossed his rope and I lowered mine. After a couple of test tugs, I turfed the rope. Then I heard the sound: the sound of hollow plastic on rock. The noise got louder, and there was a wild bashing, banging and skidding below. I ran back to the edge in time to see a red kayak rocketing down the slope, porpoising above the tree tops before disappearing, only to emerge once again far below, throw rope trailing. My boat was history. At least I wouldn't have to carry the damn thing any more! After the downclimb I found Robert sitting, head in his hands, cursing repeatedly. I had knocked his boat loose! After much searching we found it pinned up to the footrests in the forest floor, at the lip of a sheer rock dihedral that led straight down into the gorge. When we finally descended to the river, we bathed in a feeble attempt to remove the sap, sweat and memory of the epic. It was a couple of years later when I returned, still intrigued, but after the rumours of that trip no one would attempt the gorge with me. So in a final salute to the Fiddle, I paddled solo through the gorge on a sunny Friday!

James Van Camp in one of the tight drops just above the lower Fiddle gorge.

V–V$^+$ drop off a 2–4-m fall into a swirling bowl. You have almost no chance to scout this drop from the river. This is followed by a long calm pool in a narrow chasm that leads to a sharp class IV–IV$^+$, 1–2-m drop through a constricted boulder mess. Then the river opens up and drops off a small ledge into another boulder garden. This is followed by a narrow slot through bedrock, with a small drop at the end. Finally, the walls open up and the gradient decreases. There is about 1.5 km of easier paddling on the open gravel channel until you reach the bridge.

GETTING THERE The run is located in Jasper National Park, east of Jasper, off Highway 16.

Looking down into the Fiddle Gorge.

TAKE-OUT From Jasper, proceed east on Highway 16 for 41 km to the Miette Hot Springs Road. From there continue east for 5.6 km to the bridge over the Fiddle. If coming from Hinton, go west on Highway 16 to the junction with Highway 40 North. Continue west for 22 km to the bridge on the Fiddle.

PUT-IN Go 5.6 km west to the Miette Hot Springs Road, then turn south (left) and follow the road up the hill for about 9 km, to a viewpoint on the east (left) side of the road. Continue past the viewpoint for about 2.5 km to where the road is close to the river near Villeneuve Creek.

CAMPING There is developed camping 31 km west of the Miette Hotsprings road at the Snaring River Campground.

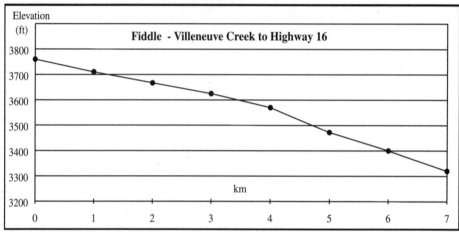

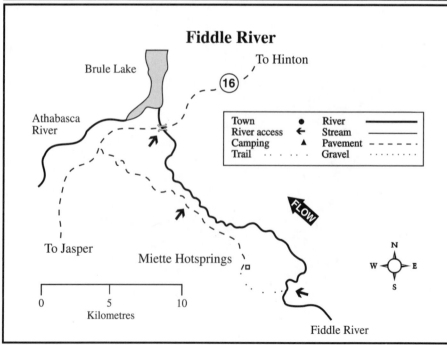

GRADE	CLASS	FLOW	TIME	LENGTH
II⁺	II⁺–IV⁺	Low	4–6 hours	12 km (7.5 mi)
III	II⁺–V	High		

Gradient 16 m/km (1.6%) 86 ft/mi

Max gradient 30 m in 1 km (3%) 100 ft in .6 mi

Put-in elevation 1341 m 4400 ft

Take-out elevation 1146 m 3760 ft

Shuttle 6 km (3.7 mi) one way

Season May–August

Maps 83F4

Gauge No

Craft Canoes and kayaks

NOTES There is a 3.5-km (2.2-mi) carry to the put-in.

CHARACTER A scenic small-volume river that runs over an open boulder-bed in the upper part and in a bedrock canyon in the lower part.

FLOW INFORMATION Assess the flow at the take-out. High flows make the run much more interesting. The river is uncontrolled and fed by snowmelt.

TRAVEL Access to the run and the shuttle are on paved roads.

DESCRIPTION The run starts in a open gravel-bed, with boulder gardens that build in difficulty to class III–IV. In a few kilometres you reach a canyon that is open at water level, with small bedrock ledges and class II–III rapids. Near the lower part of the canyon is Switchback, a two-part class IV⁺–V drop through bedrock at a right turn where sloping ledges enter the river from the right. The river drops 1–2 m to a short pool, then drops another 1–2 m in a narrow crack. You can easily scout from the right shore. Below this are more small drops at bedrock ledges, some as difficult as class III–III⁺. Near the take-out, the canyon opens up, although there are still a couple of drops.

GETTING THERE The run is located in Jasper National Park, east of Jasper, off Highway 16. See the map on page 134.

TAKE-OUT At the eastern Highway 16 exit to the town of Jasper, go east on Highway 16 for 41 km to the Miette Hot Springs Road, which is on the south (right) side. If coming from Hinton, go west on Highway 16 to the junction with Highway 40 North. Continue west for 27 km to the Miette Hot Springs Road which is on the south (left) side. Turn south and go about 9 km up the Hot Springs road to a viewpoint on the east (left) side. Continue 2.5 km past the viewpoint to where the road is close to the river near Villeneuve Creek. Mark the take-out.

PUT-IN Go upstream to the Hot Springs parking area. From the southwest end of the parking lot, carry your boat up the hill on the trail to Mystery Lake and the Sulphur Skyline. About 1.5 km along the trail you stay left at a junction where the Sulphur Skyline trail goes right. The trail climbs another 1.5 km to the pass, then descends to the river.

CAMPING There is developed camping 31 km west of the Miette Hotsprings road at the Snaring River Campground.

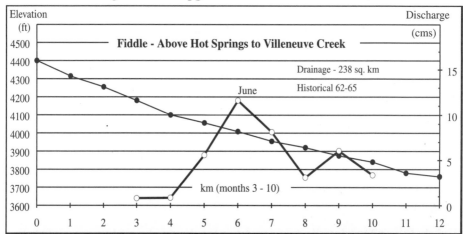

One of the constricted boulder gardens above the Hotsprings.

GRADE	CLASS	FLOW	TIME	LENGTH
II	II–VI⁺	Low	2–3 days	39 km (24 mi)
III	II⁺–VI⁺	High		

Gradient 8.2 m/km (.82%)
43 ft/mi

Max gradient 30 m in 2.5 km (1.2%)
100 ft in 1.6 mi

Put-in elevation 1341 m
4400 ft

Take-out elevation 1021 m
3350 ft

Shuttle 160 km (99 mi) one way

Season June–August

Maps 83E8 and 83E1

Gauge Yes

Craft Canoes, kayaks and rafts

NOTES There is a 14.5-km (9-mi) carry from the trailhead to the river.

CHARACTER A remote wilderness adventure on a medium-volume river that flows in a steep-sided valley, with a couple of canyons and one big waterfall. At medium to high flows there are numerous excellent play spots.

FLOW INFORMATION The river is uncontrolled and fed by snowmelt and glacial runoff. Use the flow information on page 114 to estimate flows in the area.

TRAVEL Approximately half of the shuttle is on gravel roads.

DESCRIPTION At the put-in, the river flows smoothly in a wide channel through an open valley. The river stays this way for about 3–4 km to where the valley walls close in. There are a few easy rapids and small sets of standing waves at corners. Look for a sharp left turn, followed 150 m below by a sharp right turn that is about 150 m above Snake Indian Falls. The 22–25-m fall is difficult to spot from above, so be aware. Portage the fall on river left, up to the old fire road, then along to where you can descend to the river. There is a gully that leads down to above the short canyon below the fall. If you choose this option, you will be shot through the narrow class III–IV slot just below the fall. If you do not like this drop, then carry down to below the canyon and descend through the trees to the river.

Below the fall, the river runs in an open channel with easy class II rapids for about 4–5 km. The river then begins to drop faster, with numerous boulder gardens and midstream rocks that make for technical class II–III paddling. The scenery is great, with lots of interesting rock formations at the cliffs that extend into the water. Watch for where the river runs along sloping rock ledges on river right, then makes a sharp right turn off a class III–IV ledge into a narrow canyon. The canyon offers amazing views of the overhanging rock walls and opens up not far below the ledge. The whitewater is class II–II⁺ until you reach the fire road bridge. There is a steep carry up to the road, then a 400–500-m carry to your vehicle.

GETTING THERE The run is located west of Hinton.

TAKE-OUT If coming from Jasper, proceed to the east Highway 16 exit to Jasper. Go 9.4 km east on Highway 16 to the Snaring River Campground turn-off, which is on the north (left) side. If coming from Hinton, proceed west on Highway 16 to the junction with Highway 40 North. Go 50 km west on Highway 16 to the bridge on the Athabasca. Continue for 8.4 km to the campground turn-off, which is on the north (right) side.

Turn north on the paved road to the campground and follow it under the railroad bridge, then for another 28 km to the end of the road. The road becomes gravel just past the Snaring River bridge. Beyond that, the road is rough and narrow as it winds along the north side of the Athabasca valley. The road has specific time intervals for travel in and travel out that are in effect from May to November. Travel in is restricted to the following hours: 8:00–9:00, 11:00–12:00, 2:00–3:00 and 5:00–6:00. Travel out is restricted to the following hours: 9:30–10:30, 12:30–1:30, 3:30–4:30 and 6:30–7:30.

PUT-IN Return to the campground turn-off at Highway 16. Proceed 58 km east on Highway 16 to the junction with Highway 40 North, just west of Hinton. Turn north (left) on Highway 40 and proceed for 36 km to a bridge over the Wildhay River. Continue for another 4 km to the Rock Lake Road, which is on the west (left) side. Turn left and follow the gravel road for 2.2 km to a T intersection. Turn south (left) and go 4 km to another junction with a road on the right. Turn west (right) and follow the main road for 17 km to the Rock Lake Recreation Area. There is a map on the right side of the road, about 150 past the North Fork Wildhay bridge, just before you reach the recreation area. Check that map to find your way to the trailhead if you are unsure of the directions below.

From the first junction in the recreation area, turn right and go 500 m to another junction, stay left and continue for 300 m to yet another junction. Stay right and follow the road for 1 km to a fork. Stay right to Willmore Wilderness Park and you will reach another fork in about 300 m. Again, stay right to Willmore Wilderness Park and you will reach the trailhead in 2.2 km. Grab your boat and hike for about 2 km to where a branch of the trail on the south (left) side leads toward Willow Creek. Take the Willow Creek trail and go about 10 km south to a warden cabin. The trail forks and you take the left trail downstream along Willow Creek. Do not go west to the upper Snake Indian. The trail comes alongside the river in 2.5 km.

CAMPING There is developed camping at the trailhead or near the take-out, at Snaring River Campground. There is undeveloped camping along the road

138

up to the trailhead. If you plan to camp along the river, you must obtain a back-country overnight permit from Parks Canada in Jasper.

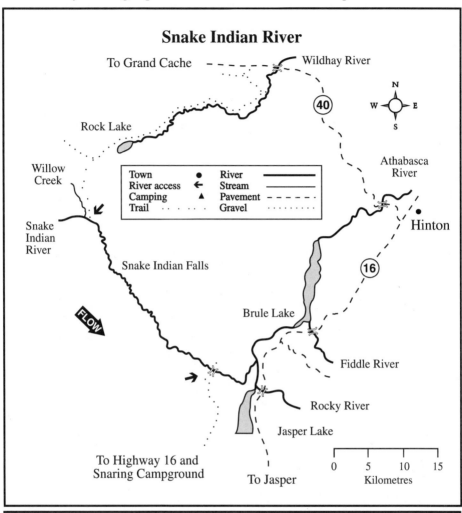

Snake Indian River

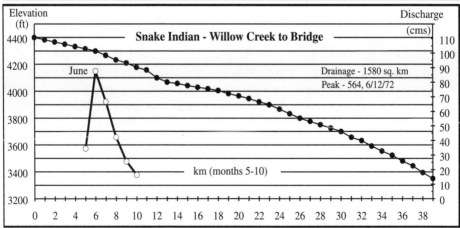

Elevation (ft) — Snake Indian - Willow Creek to Bridge — Discharge (cms)

Drainage - 1580 sq. km
Peak - 564, 6/12/72

km (months 5-10)

GRADE	CLASS	FLOW	TIME	LENGTH
III–III⁺	III⁺–V	Low	2–3 days	32 km (20 mi)
III–IV	III⁺–V	High		

Gradient   9.7 m/km (.97%)   **Max gradient** 30 m in 1.2 km (2.5%)
51 ft/mi   100 ft in .75 mi

Put-in elevation   1307 m   **Take-out elevation**   998 m
4288 ft   3275 ft

Shuttle   58 km (36 mi) one way   **Season**   June–August

Maps   83C13 and 83F4   **Gauge**   No

Craft   Canoes and kayaks

NOTES   Access to the run is via a 13-km (8.1-mi) carry, then a 9-km (5.6-mi) paddle down Jacques Creek to the river. At low flows paddling sections of Jacques Creek is not possible and you will have to carry some of the distance. See the description for Jacques Creek on page 147 for details.

CHARACTER   A remote whitewater adventure in a spectacular setting. The river is medium-volume and flows in a tight canyon in the lower part.

FLOW INFORMATION   Assess the flow at the take-out. Low flows expose narrow and technical drops in the tight canyons. High flows produce much more powerful features. The uncontrolled river is fed by snowmelt and glacial runoff. Use the flow information on page 114 to roughly estimate flows in the area.

TRAVEL   Access to the run and the shuttle are on paved roads.

DESCRIPTION   From the Jacques Creek confluence, the river flows in an open channel with few features. Watch for a long straight along rock ledges on the left shore, which ends in a sharp left turn. Directly below the left turn is Overture, a 2–3-m, class IV⁺–V drop into a sharp recirculation. Scout on river left from the rock outcrop creating the drop. Below this the river runs in a short canyon, then opens up again. There are great views of hoodoos as you approach the canyon. At the entrance the river drops over a series of small ledges, then enters a narrow, low-walled canyon that gets deeper the further downstream you go. The river twists and turns through beautiful overhanging rock walls with class IV–V whitewater sections alternating with calmer sections. At Crap Shoot you reach an eddy above a narrow slot, with whitewater leading to a midstream rock in the narrow gap. The river splits to either side, then makes a tight blind corner. It is difficult to get out once you are in the eddy above the drop, so be wary about descending too far. Not far below, the river reaches The Trap, a class V drop with no good exit point above it. There is a narrow

140

crack on river left, just above the drop, where you can get out, but at higher water levels this is difficult. Scout and portage the drop on the left by scrambling over the rockfall debris to where you can seal-launch just above a narrow slot. Just downstream is another slot, that at low flows is very narrow and undercut. Below this the canyon is deeper, but much more open. There are many tight corners, with bedrock ledges that create rapids. Near the end of the canyon you are in a 100-m-deep slot through sedimentary rocks that are layered all the way to the rim of the canyon. The entire canyon section is 7–8 km long. The river then flows out onto a wide and open gravel plain that runs for 6 km to the take-out.

Keith Klapstein entering Overture.

GETTING THERE The run is located east of Jasper, off Highway 16. See the map on page 145.

TAKE-OUT From Jasper, proceed 32 km east on Highway 16 to the bridge on the Rocky. If coming from Hinton, proceed west on Highway 16 toward Jasper. There are two bridges on the Rocky; the first you reach going west from Hinton is not the correct one; continue to the second bridge, which is below the open gravel flats, 8.5 km west of the Miette Hot Springs Road.

PUT-IN Go 30 km west on Highway 16 to the Maligne Lake Road, which is on the south (left) side of the highway. Turn south (left) and go 200 m to a fork. Stay left and follow the road for 27 km to the Jacques Lake trailhead, which is on the east (left) side of the road, just past a sharp turn to the left.

CAMPING There is developed camping 23 km west of the take-out, at the Snaring River Campground.

Back-country Bullshit

We arrived at the trailhead hours late, as the last minute details had delayed us. We were to paddle down Jacques Creek to the Rocky River, where we would bivouac for the night. Back-country bivouacs are a bit of an anomaly in National Park's policy. Historically, the policy allowed climbers to overnight at the base of long climbs, where camping is not normally allowed. We checked with a warden prior to departure and were assured we could bivy at the Rocky, within the regulations, without obtaining a camping permit. By 6 p.m. we had reached Jacques Lake. The rain had turned to snow just above our elevation and it was another 9 km to the river, so I headed to the warden cabin to see if we might stay the night. I found it empty and turned back to the campsite. I was 80 m from the creek when I saw a horse and rider halfway across the narrow bridge. The horse started, and the rider reined in hard. This caused the horse to side-step and nearly lose its rear foot off the bridge. The now unbalanced rider promptly heaved on the reins again and the horse sidestepped once more. The horse, complete with rider, broke through the pole railing and plunged into the creek. The rider erupted from the water sputtering and gasping for breath. He turned to me, still 70 m away, and hollered, "Stay where you are! You've done enough damage already!" He then drug his dripping wet personage ashore, and was joined by another rider who calmly crossed the bridge.

When everyone was safely ashore, I continued, while struggling to contain my laughter. On closer inspection, I found that the drenched tenderfoot was the warden! He was cussing me up and down for putting him in the drink! I was taken aback and came close to telling him what I thought he was full of. He continued ranting about us not having a camping permit. I tried to explain that we were planning to continue to the Rocky, but he interrupted. "You can't stay here, you can't go back and if you try to keep going, I'll call in a helicopter and have you flown out at your expense!" With that tirade he stormed off, yelling that when the group arrived we had better get over to his cabin. I returned to discuss the "options" with the rest of the group.

Two guys went immediately to speak with the warden. An hour later they returned with the details. The warden was upset because I caused him to fall into the creek! Furthermore, he wanted me to get a permit for the group and to miss the trip as punishment! That seemed a bit absurd, so we came up with a plan. The Maligne Lake staff drove up early in the morning, passing by the trailhead. If we met the van, and convinced them to get us a permit, we could return in time to paddle the creek. We thought we could still reach the take-out without another night out. Given the other "options", that sounded very appealing. So at 5:30 a.m. the next morning, I started running to the highway. At one sharp corner, I came face to face with a black bear that was running down the hill! Leaping off the trail, I tumbled head-over-heels down the slope. Once I ceased my panicked slide, a few steps were all it took to confirm that my knee was injured. Not to be put off, I straight-legged it up the trail, holding the injured leg stiff. At 7:30 a.m. I reached the highway, somewhat exhausted. Moments later the van came around the corner and I leapt up to flag it down. It was early afternoon when I limped back into the campsite. The warden had never shown his face, but I wanted to go over there, and with my good leg, kick his sorry butt. But, I packed my gear, and we headed off.

After the trip we all sent letters to Parks Canada. They sent Ifor and I back a warning ticket. They supported the warden's actions and said if Ifor or I were ever apprehended for this sort of thing again, they would take away our guide's licences! I heaved that letter in the trash years ago, but sometimes I wish I had framed it. The important thing is the memories, good and bad, of those three days. I never saw that warden again and I'm sure that's a good thing.

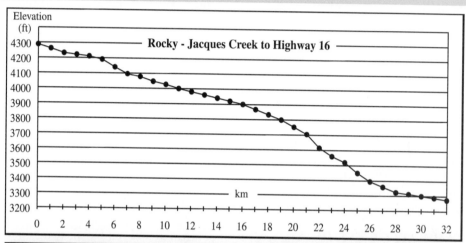

Ifor Thomas in The Trap at medium flow.

GRADE	CLASS	FLOW	TIME	LENGTH
II–III	II–VI+	Most Flows	2–3 days	30 km (18 mi)

Gradient 9.3 m/km (.93%)
49 ft/mi

Max gradient 30 m in 1.2 km (2.5%)
100 ft in .75 mi

Put-in elevation 1580 m
5184 ft

Take-out elevation 1307 m
4288 ft

Shuttle 110 km (68 mi) one way

Season June–August

Maps 83C14 and 83C13

Gauge No

Craft Canoes, kayaks and rafts

NOTES There is a 10-km (6.2-mi) carry to reach the put-in. The trip finishes with the 32-km (20-mi) run described on page 140.

CHARACTER A back-country tour with incredible scenery, portages around falls and some short, but extreme, whitewater sections. Do not go for the whitewater, but for the whole back-country experience. The whitewater sections are short and extremely difficult. The whitewater in the lower canyon is best accessed via the Jacques Lake trail.

FLOW INFORMATION The river is uncontrolled and fed by snowmelt and glacial runoff. Estimate the flows in the area as described on page 140.

TRAVEL Most of the shuttle is on gravel roads.

DESCRIPTION The trail over the pass is easy for the first 2 km, then goes down to a creek drainage, crosses the drainage and ascends a steep shoulder on the other side. At 6 km from the trailhead you reach the pass, then descend to the Medicine Tent River at kilometre 10. You can paddle/scramble/drag along the Medicine Tent River, which flows in an open gravel-bottomed valley for most of the way to the Rocky. It is 8.5 km down the Medicine Tent to the confluence with the Rocky. At the confluence the Rocky is about three-quarters of its size at the take-out.

The first 4 km on the Rocky are open and easy as the river cuts across the gravel plain. You then reach a sharp left turn, after which the river cuts back sharply to the right. About 100 m below, the river starts into a series of rapids at bedrock outcrops with broken bedrock ledges. This continues for about 1 km, with very difficult rapids as the river tumbles over exposed rock. The class IV+–V+ rapids alternate with calm stretches. The rapids then ease for 1–2 km. About 1 km below a tributary creek entering from the right, the river swings left and plummets of Rocky Falls. This is a chaotic assortment of drops off

144

bedrock outcrops. The drops pound onto bedrock for the most part, and offer little attraction to most paddlers. Portage along the right shore. Below the fall, the river is calm for about another 1 km, until it turns right and drops off broken bedrock drops in a much narrower canyon. Portage on the right shore. You then paddle on the open and easy riverbed until Jacques Creek. Check the description on page 140 for details of the run below Jacques Creek.

GETTING THERE The run is located in Jasper National Park.

TAKE-OUT From Jasper, proceed 32 km east on Highway 16 to the bridge on the Rocky. If coming from Hinton, proceed west on Highway 16 toward Jasper. Note that there are two bridges on the Rocky; the first you reach going west from Hinton is not the correct one; continue to the second bridge, which is at the open gravel flats, 8.5 km west of the Miette Hot Springs Road.

PUT-IN Go 38 km west on Highway 16 to the junction with Highway 40 South. Turn south (right) on Highway 40 and follow the road for 48 km to a T intersection with Cadomin to the west (right) and Robb to the east (left). Turn right and follow the road for 17 km to the old townsite of Mountain Park. Continue south on the now smaller gravel road for 7.2 km to a trailhead on the west (right) side. Grab your boat and start hiking.

CAMPING There is undeveloped and developed camping along the road to the trailhead. You must get overnight permits for camping along the river.

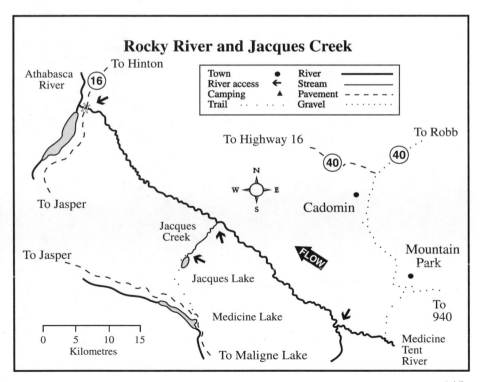

Rocky River and Jacques Creek

Town	●	River	———
River access	←	Stream	———
Camping	▲	Pavement	– – – – ·
Trail	· · · · ·	Gravel	· · · · · · ·

145

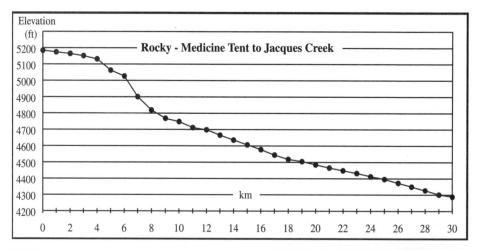

Rocky - Medicine Tent to Jacques Creek

Keith Klapstein at the outlet from Jacques Lake.

146

JACQUES CREEK   JACQUES LAKE TO ROCKY RIVER

GRADE	CLASS	FLOW	TIME	LENGTH
II⁺	II–V⁺	Low	2–4 hours	9 km (5.6 mi)
III	II⁺–V⁺	High		

Gradient   20 m/km (2%)
107 ft/mi

Max gradient   30 m in 1 km (3%)
100 ft in .6 mi

Put-in elevation   1490 m
4888 ft

Take-out elevation   1307 m
4288 ft

Shuttle   58 km (36 mi) one way

Season   June–August

Maps   83C13

Gauge   No

Craft   Canoes and kayaks

NOTES   There is a 13-km (8.1-mi) hike to reach the put-in. The run finishes with a 32-km (20-mi) paddle on the Rocky River (see page 140 for details).

CHARACTER   A small-volume creek run used to access the Rocky River. The creek flows in a meandering gravel-bottomed and often log-choked channel in the top section, then in a tight twisting bedrock channel in the lower bit.

FLOW INFORMATION   The only way to check the flow is to make the trek to the lake. The creek is fed by snowmelt and is uncontrolled.

TRAVEL   Access to the run and the shuttle are both on paved roads.

DESCRIPTION   The creek flows out of the east end of Jacques Lake, with incredible scenery as you leave the lake and travel through the open valley. In the first part, the creek runs in a single channel that is fairly open. A few kilometres from the lake, the creek begins to meander across flatter terrain and there are numerous log jams that must be portaged or crashed over. This is often trying, but carrying your boat is a much more painful task, so paddling a bit and portaging a bit is the lesser of two evils. The creek begins to cross bedrock outcrops in the last 3–5 km and enters a narrow channel that often goes around tight blind corners. Watch for a couple of small ledge drops over dark rock bands. Not far below, the creek makes a left turn with rock outcrops along the right bank. This leads immediately to a right turn and Sweet Spot, a 4–5-m fall into a shallow pool. You must land correctly in the right spot to avoid encounters with the bottom. Scout the fall from either side and portage through the trees on the left. Below the fall, the creek tears along in a constricted channel, then opens up just before you reach the Rocky.

GETTING THERE   The run is located in Jasper National Park, southeast of the town of Jasper, off Highway 16. See the map on page 145.

TAKE-OUT See the description for the Rocky River on page 140.

PUT-IN Refer to the description for the Rocky River on page 140. At the trailhead, follow the old fire road for about 5 km to where the road becomes a narrow trail. The remaining 8 km is a rutted, root choked horse trail.

CAMPING There is developed camping at the put-in, where you need a permit.

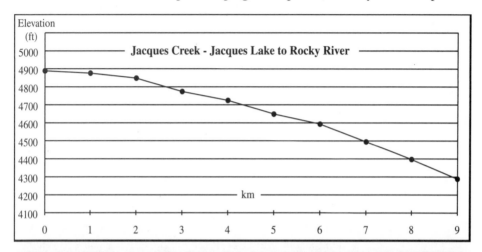

Stuart Smith in Sweet Spot. Photo: Keith Klapstein.

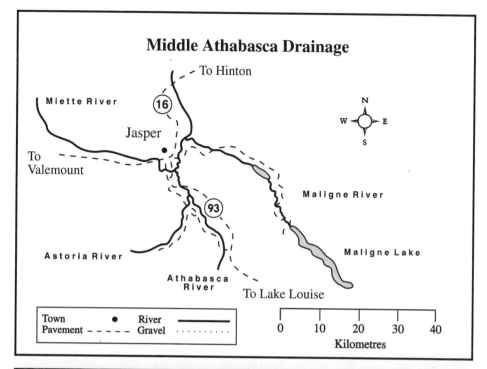

Middle Athabasca Drainage

To Hinton

Miette River

Jasper

16

To
Valemount

93

Maligne River

Maligne Lake

Astoria River

Athabasca
River

To Lake Louise

N
W E
S

| Town | ● | River | —— |
| Pavement | - - - - | Gravel | ·········· |

0   10   20   30   40
Kilometres

Donna Bradley and Stuart Smith on the Behind The Mountain run on the Maligne at low flow. Photo: Randy Clement.

GRADE	CLASS	FLOW	TIME	LENGTH
I⁺	I⁺–II	Most flows	3–5 hours	23 km (14 mi)

Gradient   1.1 m/km (.11%)   **Max gradient**   26 m in 23 km (.11%)
            6 ft/mi   85 ft in 14.3 mi

Put-in elevation   1030 m   **Take-out elevation**   1004 m
                         3379 ft   3294 ft

Shuttle   22 km (13.7 mi) one way   **Season**   May–October

Maps   83D16 and 83E1   **Gauge**   Yes

Craft   Canoes, kayaks and rafts

CHARACTER   A large-volume run on an open riverbed in spectacular scenery. There are no major rapids on this run; however, some manoeuvring is required.

FLOW INFORMATION   The river is uncontrolled and fed by snowmelt and glacial runoff. The river is on Alberta Environmental Protection's River Report recording. Use the flow at Hinton; low flow is 200 to 300 cms and high flow is 500 to 900 cms. At the take-out, you can expect 50–60 percent of that flow.

TRAVEL   Access to the run and the shuttle are on paved roads.

DESCRIPTION   At the put-in, the river flows in a open, braided channel with numerous large islands. This continues for most of the run, with a few sections where the river flows in a single channel. There are small riffles where the river drops off gravelbars. The scenery is spectacular and wildlife is abundant along the open shores. Near the take-out, the river flows in a single channel along a rock face on the right shore.

GETTING THERE   The run is located near Jasper, along Highway 16.

TAKE-OUT   From the lights at the junction of Highway 16 and Highway 93, go 22 km east on Highway 16 to the bridge over the Athabasca. If approaching the run from Hinton, you'll find the take-out bridge 30 km west of the park gate.

PUT-IN   Go west on Highway 16 to the first exit to the town of Jasper. Continue another 3 km to the junction with Highway 93A, which is on the south (left) side. Turn left and go 200 m to a junction, with a road on the left leading to Old Fort Point. Turn east (left) and follow the road down the hill and across three bridges to the parking area on the left, just past the third bridge.

CAMPING   There is developed camping just south of Jasper, off Highway 93, at Whistlers or Wapiti campgrounds.

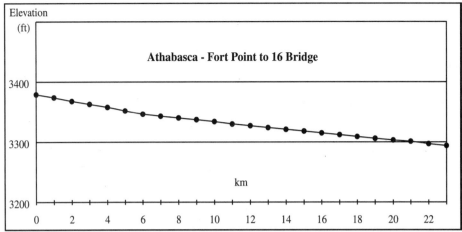

Athabasca - Fort Point to 16 Bridge

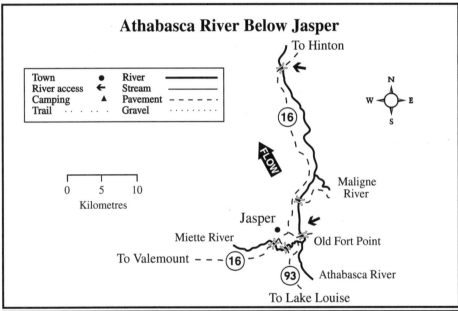

Athabasca River Below Jasper

To Hinton

Town	●	River	▬▬▬
River access	←	Stream	────
Camping	▲	Pavement	─ ─ ─
Trail	· · · · ·	Gravel	· · · · · ·

N
W ◆ E
S

FLOW

16

Maligne
River

Jasper

Miette River

Old Fort Point

To Valemount ─ ─ 16 ─

93

Athabasca River

To Lake Louise

0   5   10
Kilometres

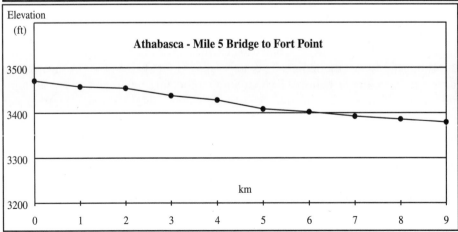

Athabasca - Mile 5 Bridge to Fort Point

GRADE	CLASS	FLOW	TIME	LENGTH
II	I–II	Low	1–2 hours	8.5 km (5.3 mi)
II	II–II⁺	High		

Gradient   3.3 m/km (.33%)   **Max gradient**   28 m in 8.5 km (.33%)
17 ft/mi   92 ft in 5.3 mi

Put-in elevation   1058 m   **Take-out elevation**   1030 m
3471 ft   3379 ft

Shuttle   8.5 km (5.3 mi) one way   **Season**   May–October

Maps   83D16   **Gauge**   Yes

Craft   Canoes, kayaks and rafts

CHARACTER A large-volume run with rapids at corners and constrictions. The scenery in the lower part of the run is outstanding. The numerous good play spots make this a popular run.

FLOW INFORMATION The river is uncontrolled and fed by glacial runoff and snowmelt. Assess the flow at the take-out, or see page 150 for an estimate of the flow level on the lower part of the river.

TRAVEL Access to the run and the shuttle are on paved roads.

DESCRIPTION At the put-in, the river flows in an open gravel flat with numerous channels around large islands. This continues for about 2 km, with short sections of small waves, to where the river assumes a single channel and makes a sharp right turn at an island. This is Beckers, a class II–II⁺ corner where the river is constricted and standing waves erupt, producing good surfing at most levels. A few large boulders also produce some good hole-riding. Below Beckers, the river has numerous class II rapids and play features that continue to the Rock Gardens. Here the river swings to the left side of the valley, then off a boulder shoal toward the right side, with lots of waves, small holes and strong eddies. The next rapid is just below a right turn with a large beach on the left shore. Expect some good surfing spots and a couple of midstream boulders that produce sharp eddies and holes. Below this, the river mellows until you reach Alpine Village (the log cabins on the left shore), where the whitewater crowd often exits. The river is easy to the take-out, with calm sections among islands and incredible scenery. The gradient profile is on page 151.

GETTING THERE The run is located south of Jasper, along Highway 93. See the map on page 156.

152

TAKE-OUT From the lights at the junction of Highway 16 and Highway 93, go 1.2 km east on Highway 16 to the junction with Highway 93A, which is on the south (right) side. Turn right and go 200 m to a junction, with a road on the left leading to Old Fort Point. Turn east (left) and follow the road down the hill and across three bridges, to the parking area on the left, just past the third bridge.

If you wish to skip the last 2 km of easy water and get the best whitewater, then, instead of turning off at Old Fort Point as described above, continue on Highway 93A for about 1.2 km to Alpine Village, a collection of cabins on the north (right) side. Across from the cabins is a small gravel pull-off near the river.

PUT-IN Return up the hill to the turn-off to Old Fort Point, at Highway 93A. Go south (left) and follow the road for 1.5 km to the junction with Highway 93, just past Alpine Village. Turn south (left) and follow Highway 93 for 5.7 km to a small road on the north (left) side, just before you reach the bridge over the Athabasca.

If you want only the best section of whitewater, you can put in at Beckers, which is 3.7 km south of the Highway 93/93A junction near Alpine Village.

CAMPING There is developed camping at Whistlers or Wapiti campgrounds on Highway 93 between the take-out and the put-in.

Stuart Smith, Rob Evans-Davies and Brock Wilson (left to right) employing unique hole-riding techniques at Beckers. Photo: Livia Stoyke.

Ron Steers (stern) and Bryn Thomas (bow) during an early season run on the Athabasca. Photo: Ifor Thomas.

GRADE	CLASS	FLOW	TIME	LENGTH
II	I–II	Most Flows	1–2 hours	11 km (6.8 mi)

Gradient 4.6 m/km (.46%) **Max gradient** 30 m in 6.5 km (.46%)
24 ft/mi 100 ft in 4 mi

Put-in elevation 1109 m **Take-out elevation** 1058 m
3638 ft 3471 ft

Shuttle 11 km (6.8 mi) one way **Season** May–September

Maps 83C12, 83C13 and 83D16 **Gauge** No

Craft Canoes, kayaks and rafts

CHARACTER A large-volume run on an open riverbed with excellent scenery. Rapids are created at channel constrictions and where the river drops off shoals.

FLOW INFORMATION The river is uncontrolled and fed by snowmelt and glacial runoff. Assess the flow at the take-out.

TRAVEL Access to the run and the shuttle are on paved roads.

DESCRIPTION At the put-in, the river is spread-out on a wide gravel channel. This continues for 3–4 km to just above Wabasso Campground, where a left turn with a series of standing waves on the right side provides some excitement. There is often good surfing on the right and an interesting whirlpool on river left. Below this the river eases for a few kilometres until a couple of sets of standing waves. This is followed by Dunk Corner, a sharp right turn with a wicked eddy on river right. Kayakers can do enders along the rock outcrop, but beware; swimmers can be in for a bit of a ride, doing laps in the recirculation! Not far below, the river drops in a long, class II–II+ rapid at Expressway. The rapid continues to just above the confluence with the Astoria River, which enters from the left. There is one set of standing waves below this, then the river is mellow to the take-out.

GETTING THERE The run is located south of Jasper, along Highway 93.

TAKE-OUT From the lights at the junction of Highway 16 and Highway 93, go south on Highway 93 for 7 km. Turn north (left) at a small road, just before you reach the bridge over the Athabasca. Follow the road to the parking area.

PUT-IN Continue 10.5 km south on Highway 93 to a left turn in the highway with a small gravel pull-out on the west (right) side.

CAMPING There is developed camping on Highway 93, about 4 km north of the take-out, at Wapiti Campground.

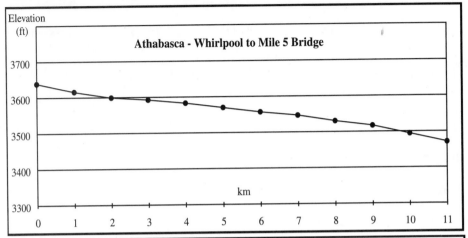

Athabasca - Whirlpool to Mile 5 Bridge

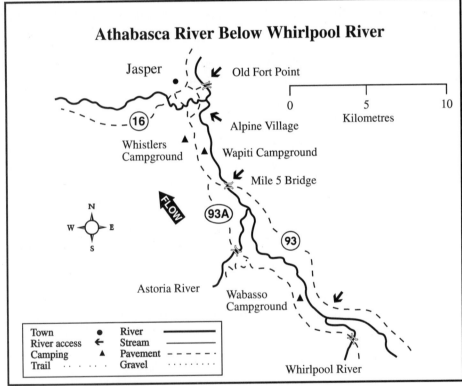

Athabasca River Below Whirlpool River

Jasper

Old Fort Point

Alpine Village

Whistlers Campground

Wapiti Campground

Mile 5 Bridge

0 5 10
Kilometres

FLOW

93A

93

N
W—◇—E
S

Astoria River

Wabasso Campground

Whirlpool River

Town	●	River	——
River access	←	Stream	—
Camping	▲	Pavement	– – –
Trail	· · · · ·	Gravel	· · · · · ·

GRADE	CLASS	FLOW	TIME	LENGTH
II	II–II⁺	Low	1–2 hours	2 km (1.3 mi)
III	II–III	High		

Gradient   9 m/km (.9%)
48 ft/mi

Max gradient   18 m in 2 km (.9%)
59 ft in 1.3 mi

Put-in elevation   1033 m
3389 ft

Take-out elevation   1015 m
3330 ft

Shuttle   2.5 km (1.6 mi) one way

Season   May–September

Maps   83D16

Gauge   Yes

Craft   Canoes, kayaks and rafts

CHARACTER   A high-speed, small to medium-volume run in an open riverbed, with rapids created by boulder gardens and tight corners. There can be sweepers on the narrow sections where the river undercuts the banks.

FLOW INFORMATION   Assess the flow at the take-out. The river is fed via underground sources from Medicine Lake and the flow increases as you descend. The river is fed by snowmelt and glacial runoff, and is uncontrolled. The run has higher flows in midseason when Medicine Lake is full.

TRAVEL   Access to the run and the shuttle are on paved roads.

DESCRIPTION   At the bridge, the river flows over a gravel-bed in a narrow fast-water channel. Just below the put-in watch for a large midstream rock. Below this the river splits at an island, where you stay left to avoid the sweepers in the right channel. The river then makes a sharp right turn and you encounter some class II standing waves. The river is open for about 350 m to a left turn. This leads to a boulder garden, then a set of standing waves that provide excellent surfing at lower flows. A calmer section leads to a small island, then the river turns left and heads toward a sharp right. Just below the right turn is the remains of an old weir, with a class II⁺–III rapid. Stay right to avoid the worst of it. Below this, the river has small class II features until the take-out.

GETTING THERE   The run is located near Jasper, off the Maligne Lake Road.

TAKE-OUT   From the eastern Highway 16 exit to Jasper, go east for 1.8 km to Maligne Lake Road on the south (right) side of the highway. Turn right and follow the road across the Athabasca River to a fork. Stay left and continue for 2 km to the Sixth Bridge turn-off, which is on the east (left) side of the road. Turn left and follow the road for about 1 km to an intersection on the north (left) side, which is marked for the Sixth Bridge. Turn left and follow the road for about another kilometre to the bridge and the parking lot.

PUT-IN   Return to the Maligne Lake Road, then turn south (left) and proceed for 800 m to the Fifth Bridge turn-off, on the (east) left side of the road. Turn left and follow the road to the parking lot by the bridge.

CAMPING   There are no campgrounds along the Maligne Road, but there is developed camping at Whistlers Campground, which is on Highway 93, 1.7 km south of the Highway 16/93 junction at Jasper.

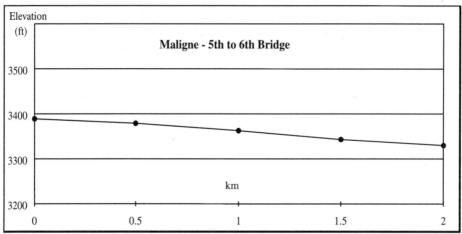

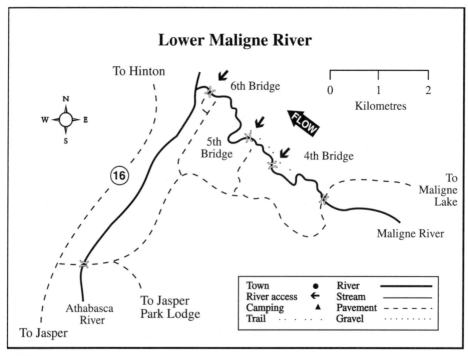

MALIGNE CANYON (4TH TO 5TH BRIDGES)

GRADE	CLASS	FLOW	TIME	LENGTH
III⁺	III–V	Low	1–2 hours	.8 km (.5 mi)
IV⁺	III–V	High		

Gradient 24 m/km (2.4%)
125 ft/mi

Max gradient 19 m in .8 km (2.4%)
62 ft in .5 mi

Put-in elevation 1052 m
3451 ft

Take-out elevation 1033 m
3389 ft

Shuttle A 900 m (.6 mi) carry

Season May–September

Maps 83D16

Gauge No

Craft Canoes and kayaks

NOTES There is a 900 m (.6 mi) carry to reach the put-in.

CHARACTER A small-volume run through a constricted bedrock canyon. The five major drops are steep and narrow, which makes the run a fast and exciting option for a short paddle. If you like throngs of cheering fans, try the weekends, when crowds of vicarious tourists will follow you to the put-in.

FLOW INFORMATION Check the flow at the take-out. The river is fed via underground sources from Medicine Lake and the flow increases as you descend. The river is fed by snowmelt and glacial runoff and is usually higher in midseason when Medicine Lake is full.

TRAVEL Access to the run and the shuttle are on paved roads.

DESCRIPTION The first big rapid, the Sickle, is about 150 m below the Fourth Bridge over the canyon. It begins at a low-angled rock outcrop on river left that constricts the flow into a narrow chute on the right. The river drops through three high-speed holes in a narrow flush, then screams into the rock headwall at the bottom. The river eases and makes a sharp right at the overhanging rock wall on the left. Many paddlers seal-launch off the rock ledge 2 m above water level on river right in order to avoid the stuff above.

Below the seal-launch, the river drops into a constricted class IV boulder garden, then makes a left turn into a very narrow canyon. Watch for logs here! The canyon then opens up and the river flows in an open channel to a right turn. Below the right turn, the river drops off a 1–2-m, class IV ledge. You will have walked by the ledge on the way up to the put-in. The river then swings left and heads into another constricted canyon. An eddy on the right,

Misunderstanding or Misinformation?

For me, it was just a run we did every Tuesday and Thursday night, and it was a bit familiar. Chuck and Stew were in town that weekend to paddle the good stuff around Jasper, so I said I would show them the run. Medicine Lake was not overflowing, and the water level in Maligne Canyon was the same moderated level that is common for most of the summer. Chuck was paddling his slalom C-1 and Stew was in his slalom kayak. Both were excited, though not nearly as excited as they soon would be.

We paddled the technical drops in the constricted canyon above the ledge with few problems. After we surfed a little above Two Timer, I checked that everyone was ready and peeled out into the low-walled canyon leading to the drop. I hadn't looked over my shoulder, and when I tucked into a micro eddy just above the drop to look up at the rest of the group, I got a big surprise!

There was Chuck, right on my tail. If I was surprised, there are no words for the look on his face. There was no room in my eddy, and he was too close for a hard run at the rapid. All I could hear was loud cursing as he disappeared over the edge into the fracas below. Stew was not far behind Chuck, but at least I had the opportunity to shout directions at him as he stroked past. Stew paddled hard, but hit the drop a bit right and slammed his bow into the bottom, then careened off the rocks and was swallowed up by the second hole. At that point I was sitting above the action, thinking I might have blown my role as leader that day. I ran the drop and eddied out to find an incredulous Chuck, who tore into me for ducking into the eddy to let him run the drop first. I tried to explain, but my appeal fell on deaf ears. Stew had seen enough and was in the trees, hiking for the take-out. At the take-out, the carnage was clearly visible. Chuck's boat was folded .5 m from the tail, with the hull completely parted, edge to edge. The fibres of the deck were all that was holding the flapping stern in place. Stew's front end was munched and both he and Chuck were less than enthusiastic about my directions on the river. So what really happened? I guess that depends on who you talk to. Whatever the story, our friendships endured and we still get along fine. Really!

below the cliff wall, lets you collect yourself for the class IV–V Two Timer. Here the river accelerates in the narrow canyon, through a set of exploding waves, then drops 1–1.5 m into a riverwide hole, followed 5 m below by a second diagonal riverwide hole. A short pool leads to the class IV–IV+ Turbo Booster, where the river charges into a narrow chute that slams the jutting cliff wall on the left at the bottom. Below Turbo Booster, the river opens up and there are some class II rapids until the take-out. There is no gradient profile for this run.

GETTING THERE   The run is located near Jasper, off the Maligne Lake Road. See the map on page 158.

TAKE-OUT From the eastern Highway 16 exit to Jasper, go east for 1.8 km to Maligne Lake Road on the south (right) side of the highway. Turn right and follow the road across the Athabasca River to a fork. Stay left and continue for 2.8 km to the Fifth Bridge turn-off, on the east (left) side of the road. Turn left and follow the road to the parking lot.

PUT-IN Grab your boat and carry across the bridge, then upstream along the river right shore. You reach a fork in about 200 m and stay right along the lower trail. Continue upstream to a constricted class V drop on a sweeping left bend in the river, where you look down from a low cliff into the canyon. There is a bridge across the river, about 150 m upstream.

CAMPING There are no campgrounds along the Maligne Road, but there is developed camping at Whistlers Campground, which is on Highway 93, 1.7 km south of the Highway 16/93 junction at Jasper.

Mike Price entering the Sickle at medium flows. Photo: Hugh Lecky.

GRADE	CLASS	FLOW	TIME	LENGTH
IV	III–VI	Medium	1–2 hours	2.7 km (1.7 mi)
V	III–VI	High		

Gradient   23 m/km (2.3%)   123 ft/mi

Max gradient   30 m in .6 km (5%)   100 ft in .37 mi

Put-in elevation   1443 m   4734 ft

Take-out elevation   1380 m   4528 ft

Shuttle   2.5 km (1.6 mi) one way

Season   June–August

Maps   83C13

Gauge   No

Craft   Kayaks and canoes

CHARACTER   A medium-volume run over a riverbed of huge boulders. The rapids at the start are extremely difficult, with a high trash factor should you make any mistakes. The whole run is hazardous, since water rarely flows in the channel, so sweepers, logs and unnatural features are common. The river is fed by snowmelt and glacial runoff and is uncontrolled.

FLOW INFORMATION   Assess the flow at the put-in. This run only has water in it about every four years, when the lake overflows. Do not be too surprised if all you see are huge boulders in the riverbed!

TRAVEL   Access to the run and the shuttle are on paved roads.

DESCRIPTION   Carry upstream from the parking area, along the river, to where you can launch at the lake. From the lake outlet, the river flows in a smooth water surge, with incredible power, through a narrow channel with a few trees across it. You encounter some class II–III rapids before you reach the pool near the road, just above Excalibur. Here the river funnels into a steep exploding chute through bedrock and hammers off the rock wall on the left, then plunges 2–3 m into a terminal hole. The whole thing is class V⁺–VI. Directly below the hole in Excalibur, the river blasts off another drop into a smaller hole, then tears into a long, constricted class IV boulder garden that eases at the left turn where the river leaves the road. When the river turns right just below, it plunges off the class V⁺–VI Carom Shot, a steep 3–5-m chute that lands in a shallow hole backed up by a downstream ledge. There is one clean slot on the left that avoids smacking onto the second rock outcrop, but contacting the bottom with your bow is a real possibility. The rest of the run is a tight class III⁺–IV⁺ channel that howls over the boulders. Watch for a couple of constricted drops and possible sweepers, though there is nothing as difficult as the first big drops.

Excalibur

Each day we drove up the road, past the jumbled, chaotic boulderfield at the north end of Medicine Lake. Each day my mind wandered back to another time, when I stood beside the exploding chaos thundering over those same rocks. Although the lake was filling up quickly, I doubted the rapid would form. But I prepared myself all the same. Those days, I worked with Tom Thompson, and we always laughed about the day I would paddle that rapid. The Maligne River normally drains out of Medicine Lake through underground channels, and emerges many kilometres away in the lower canyon. Each year the lake goes through the same cycle, filling as the river rises, then draining as the river drops. About every four years the unbelievable happens. The lake rises 90 metres, fills to the brim, then pours out onto the boulders on the north end. The resulting whitewater is something to behold.

That summer the lake rose quickly, then levelled off for a while. It was teasing me. When I returned from my days off, water was flowing through the rocks; paddleable, but hardly terrific. That week the river rose again and each day the flow increased. After years of coulda's, shoulda's and woulda's, it was time to put up or shut up. Events like this happen only so often in one's life. It reminded me of the Olympics; occurring every four years, and when the time comes you have to be there, at that place, at that time, completely ready.

I called friends and coerced them into helping out. People for throw bags, a paddler for on-water safety, and of course Tom would be there for the photos. We drove up after work and got there around 8 p.m.. The water was flowing, but it wasn't really kicking, so after some debate I called it off. The next day the lake rose and again we drove up after work. Kim Prevost, Chris Burgstaller, Mike Price, Tom Thompson, Tom Mountain and I found the water was pumping, creating a roadside spectacle of massive proportions. It was time.

We discussed the strategy of my line, the possible screw-ups, then arranged the group. On the water, the river had little gradient coming out of the lake, but flowed with incredible power. In the first few rapids I was late on the moves and got pasted in a small hole. After jumping a couple of logs, I arrived above the drop. The crowd had mushroomed, and the distractions were many as I walked along the bank trying to get the moves straight in my mind. Then back in my boat, I stroked toward the lip and was suddenly screaming along the rock wall, on the boiling water. Smashing through the entrance waves, I slammed into the exploding pillow that hit me like a freight train, tossing me diagonally across the river. I took one stroke and reached for a jet of water that was blasting through that frothing, seething hole. Hauling on the jet I erupted out of the foam and into the lower part of the rapid, my heart racing. At the bottom were friends' faces, and the wild exuberance that comes from too much adrenaline. It was over so quickly and so cleanly that all the preparation seemed superfluous, as it always does when you get things just right.

Stuart Smith pounding into the hole in Excalibur. Photo: Ben Gadd.

GETTING THERE The run is located south of Jasper, along the Maligne Lake Road off Highway 93.

TAKE-OUT At the eastern Highway 16 exit to Jasper, go east for 1.8 km to Maligne Lake Road on the south (right) side. Turn right and follow the road across the Athabasca River to a fork. Stay left, and go 6 km to Maligne Canyon. Continue for about 12 km, to the Watchtower trailhead, which is on the west (right) side of the road. The trailhead is on a long, flat straight as you head up toward Maligne Lake. Turn right and follow the road to the parking lot.

PUT-IN Go upstream on the Maligne Lake Road for about 2.2 km to a parking lot on the west (right) side of the road, just past the huge rapid beside the road. At appropriate flows, the parking lot will be inundated with water.

CAMPING There are no campgrounds along the Maligne Road, but there is developed camping at Whistlers Campground, which is on Highway 93, 1.7 km south of the Highway 16/93 junction at Jasper.

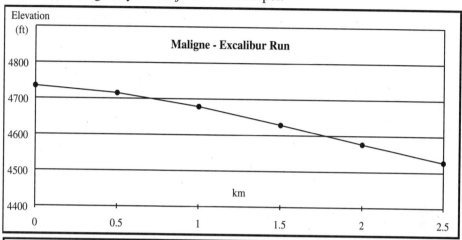

Maligne - Excalibur Run

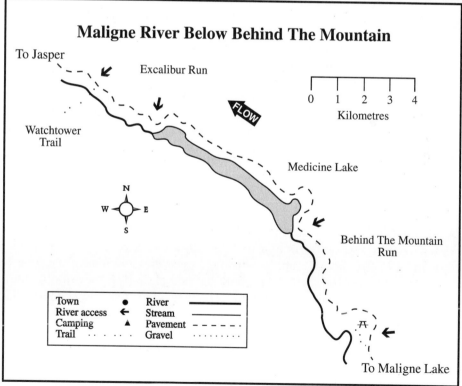

Maligne River Below Behind The Mountain

GRADE	CLASS	FLOW	TIME	LENGTH
III	II–V	< 5	2–3 hours	6 km (3.7 mi)
III⁺	II⁺–V	5–8		
IV	III–V⁺	> 8		

Gradient   18 m/km (1.8%)   **Max gradient**   30 m in .7 km (4.3%)
           95 ft/mi   100 ft in .43 mi

Put-in elevation   1542 m   **Take-out elevation**   1434 m
                        5058 ft   4705 ft

Shuttle   6 km (3.7 mi) one way   **Season**   May–August (see notes)

Maps   83C13   **Gauge**   Yes

Craft   Canoes, kayaks and rafts

NOTES   The river is closed to all paddling activities in May and June. See the story on page 172 for details.

CHARACTER   A small to medium-volume run that flows in a constricted channel, with massive broken boulders that create steep, well-defined drops. The toughest section runs in a continuous 2-km barrage of whitewater. Canoeists and rafters must be very hot, or they will have to wrestle their boats along a steep, narrow and highly unpleasant portage.

FLOW INFORMATION   Check the flow at the put-in. If you have to seal-launch more than 30 cm off the grass bank, the river is low. If the grass bank is level with the water, the river is high. See the flow information on page 173 for references to the specific stage readings above. The river is uncontrolled and fed by snowmelt and glacial runoff.

TRAVEL   Access to the run and the shuttle are on paved roads.

DESCRIPTION   At the start, the river flows on a gravel-bed. Below the first corner to the right, boulders constrict the flow into a class II–II⁺ drop that leads to 150 m of class II⁺ rapids with standing waves and holes. The river is then open and easy for about 1 km, with the odd class II–II⁺ section. A sharp jog to the left with a set of large boulders on the right is the start of the harder drops. This is followed not far below by a class II⁺–III drop, with a big boulder on the left and high-speed waves and holes in the narrow chute. A second jog to the left, with huge boulders on the right, is followed by a constricted section with some good surfing. The river eases, then things pick up at a turn to the left, where mammoth boulders on the left constrict the flow. From the eddy at the top, on river right, you can look down at Hypertension, a class III–IV drop where

Maligne River Madness

They scouted briefly, then headed back up to run the drop. It was Curly's second try; a bitter swim was the result of his previous attempt. Now he wanted to follow Mo down, while Larry came behind. Larry and Mo just looked at each other and laughed. "No way, Curly! We'll wait halfway down in case you mess up, but that's it." Curly wasn't pleased; he was, however, persistent. So Larry and Mo paddled down and eddied out. Then down came Curly, off line and getting hammered, just above the nasty pourover. He dropped in, then miraculously shot out. He was now heading backwards toward the big, flat recirculation in the middle of the drop. Curly was clearly mixed up, but he started sprinting anyway. Unfortunately, he was sprinting upstream. He slipped slowly into that nasty hole and was promptly sucked sideways in the foam.

Curly is a one-armed bandit; he can roll and brace on one side, but only one side. Fortunately, he landed in the hole on his good side. After a couple of moments watching Curly's ride, Larry and Mo were yelling at him to paddle, so he could get out. Curly took their advice and valiantly started stroking. But all that happened was that he reached the edge of the hole, spun around, and was now on his bad side. After a weak attempt at survival, he was windowshaded and disappeared into the froth. When he surfaced, out of his boat, he was sucked back in for round two, boat and all. Then his helmet surfaced in the foam, followed by . . . no, not his shoulders, but his arm! Curly had taken his helmet off! As his head cleared the froth, he heaved his helmet and went back in for a bareheaded round three. After several amazing tricks, he washed free and was flopping about in the huge waves, tumbling in holes and generally getting throbbed. Then abruptly he halted, pinned spread-eagle on the upstream side of a boulder. With grim determination, he struggled onto the top, stranded but safe. But Curly, it seems, had other plans. In a wild, arm-flailing flop, he leapt out at the back of Larry's boat. He was woefully off the mark and swimming once again. Larry, unaware of the events just behind him, eddied out. Curly was then swept toward a downstream log that was swinging back and forth, like a primitive egg beater. It was pulled downstream by the current, where it would spring free, then rebound upstream to be caught again, repeating the cycle.

In an impossible combination of timing, Curly swept under the log. Just when it looked like he would make it, he was whacked in the back of the head, as the log rebounded. He rolled over face down, then revived somewhat and fluttered onto his back, alive but not much more. Larry caught up with Curly and promptly hauled his butt to shore. On the opposite shore, Mo had Curly's boat and was about to ferry it across when Curly spotted him. Curly staggered toward the river, yelling "I'll swim across". Mo was dumbfounded. In a last-ditch effort to halt Curly's progress, he heaved Curly's paddle, spear-like, across into the trees. Curly halted, transfixed by his paddle high in the air above, and turned to follow it. When Mo reached the other side, Larry had a firm grip on Curly. Larry and Mo were simply shocked. What could they say? Curly was completely out of his mind! It was simply another instance of Staircase Mania.

exploding waves and holes produce the white froth. The rapid runs straight, with diagonal holes off both sides, then disappears to the right, with more holes and big waves. Below Hypertension the river opens up and tears over a shallow boulder-bed. A turn to the right at a huge midstream boulder leads to 100–150 m of fast water, where the trees on the banks close in and the riverbed narrows. At the end of the straight, the river curves right to a huge boulder on the right bank, just above the class IV+–V+ Staircase. Stop on the right to scout or portage along the well-worn trail. At all flows except high water, the lower trail is the easier option. At high flows you may want to carry up the steep slope, then along the valley rim to the cutline that leads down to below the Staircase.

The Staircase begins with a class III–IV lead-in of waves and holes, followed by a turn to the left and a hole. Next is the crux move, a sharp, 1.5-m class V drop into a tight recirculation. The river then erupts into a narrow chute that ends in a flat hole. Immediately below is a steep drop off a shallow boulder ledge, and exploding waves that lead to a diagonal hole at a right bend. About 25 m below the diagonal hole a midstream boulder splits the flow, with a drop into a hole on the right and a shallow, constricted chute on the left. The gradient eases for about 100 m to where a cutline descends to the river. The whole rapid drops a long way in a very short distance.

Below the cutline, the river flows into a narrow, class IV boulder barrage that ends in a short pool with a massive boulder on the left. After this, the river opens up and the water flows with speed over the shallow rock-bed in a long section of class III–III+ whitewater. The river comes close to the road, then leaves it again. Watch for a long, open section ending in a sweeping turn to the left, followed by a turn to the right. At the right turn is a log jam, which often blocks most of the channels. Stay to the right, down a narrow channel, to avoid the logs. Below the log jam, the river is open class II–III until you reach a huge gravel plain. When the lake is low, you paddle down a gravel-lined channel to the take-out, but when the lake is high, you paddle 400–500 m across the lake. At the end of the run, where the valley opens up at the lake, is one of the most spectacular on-river vistas you will find.

GETTING THERE   The run is located south of the town of Jasper, along the Maligne Lake Road, off Highway 93. See the map on page 165.

TAKE-OUT   From the eastern Highway 16 exit to Jasper, go east for 1.8 km to Maligne Lake Road on the south (right) side of the highway. Turn right and follow the road across the Athabasca River to a fork. Stay left and go 21 km to a parking lot on a sharp right turn, at the north end of Medicine Lake. From there, continue for about 7.5 km to the south end of the lake, where a large looping turn to the right (around a side valley on the left) is followed by a sharp left turn. Just before a straight leading up a hill is a small gravel road on the west (right) side of the road, with a gate about 40 m beyond the turn-off.

Park by the gate and follow the road to the gravel pit, then bear right to the riverbank so you will recognize the take-out from the river.

PUT-IN Continue upstream on the Maligne Lake Road, for about 5.5 km, to a small gravel road on the right that doubles back at 45 degrees to the road. You will recognize the approach to the road by a steep ascent, followed by a left, then a right and finally a steep descent. At the bottom of the hill, watch for the gravel road on the right side, where the river is close to the road.

CAMPING There are no campgrounds along the Maligne Road, but there is developed camping at Whistlers Campground, which is on Highway 93, 1.7 km south of the Highway 16/93 junction at Jasper.

Stuart Smith in the Staircase at medium–high flows. Photo: Keith Klapstein.

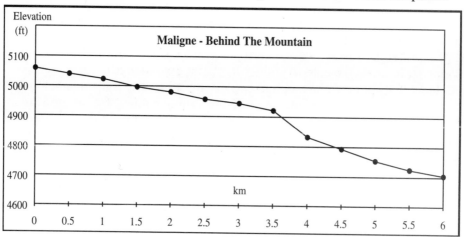

GRADE	CLASS	FLOW	TIME	LENGTH
II	II–II+	< 6	1–2 hours	4.5 km (2.8 mi)
II+	II–III	> 7		

Gradient   9.2 m/km (.92%)   **Max gradient** 30 m in 3 km (.1%)
           49 ft/mi   100 ft in 1.9 mi

Put-in elevation   1583 m   **Take-out elevation**   1542 m
                5194 ft   5058 ft

Shuttle   4 km (2.5 mi) one way   **Season**   May–August (see notes)

Maps   83C13   **Gauge**   Yes

Craft   Canoes, kayaks and rafts

NOTES The river is closed to all paddling activities in May and June. See the story on page 172 for details.

CHARACTER A small to medium-volume run on a beautiful river that flows over an open riverbed of broken boulders. The toughest rapids are created at constrictions in the channel and by huge boulders. The run has a great ender spot, and some play sites which are suitable for novice to intermediate paddlers.

FLOW INFORMATION There is a gauge on the bridge at the outlet of Maligne Lake, where you can get a specific reading. View the gauge from the river left shore, just upstream of the bridge. Low flow is 4 and high flow is 10. Flows above 7 are fun. The river is uncontrolled and fed by snowmelt and glacial runoff. The upstream lake helps buffer flow variations.

TRAVEL Access to the run and the shuttle are on paved roads.

DESCRIPTION The river at the put-in is on an open gravel-bed, with a few boulders producing features. Below the bridge, the river flows in a wide channel with a few small surfing waves, until you reach a sharp right turn at the end of a long straight. At the class II+ Ender Rock, the river dodges between massive boulders that split the channel into two narrow slots. The right channel makes a sharp turn to the right, plunges off the pillow formed by the midstream monolith, then opens up. A convenient eddy on the right allows recycling at the play hole. The left channel disappears around the midstream monolith, down a narrow channel, with an easier drop over bedrock.

Below Ender Rock are a few class II–II+ rapids as the river flows beside the road. Look for a midstream hole named the Whopper, at a narrow constriction with a bedrock outcrop on the left just above it. The river leaves the road, with easier rapids until a long straight ending at a sharp left turn. A large, flat midstream rock just above the left turn signals the entrance to Jacknife Bend. Here the river turns 90 degrees, and a couple of large boulders on the right produce pressure waves off the shore and squirrelly boiling water. Below the first corner, the river turns right, with midstream boulders creating defined features and fun eddy-hopping. After the right turn the river has a long section of class II rapids until you reach the road again. The river twists to the left, then a sharp right turn leads back to the road. Below this is another turn to the left with an island just downstream. The head of the island often has logs piled against it or sweepers extending off the sides, so be aware! The river then flows quietly through gravelbars to the take-out.

GETTING THERE The run is located south of Jasper, along the Maligne Lake Road, off Highway 93. See the map on page 175.

TAKE-OUT From the eastern Highway 16 exit to Jasper, go east for 1.8 km to Maligne Lake Road on the south (right) side of the highway. Turn right and follow the road across the Athabasca River to a fork. Stay left, and go 20 km to the north end of Medicine Lake. From there, continue south for 13 km to a small gravel road on the right that doubles back at 45 degrees to the road. You will recognize the approach to the gravel road by a steep ascent, followed by a left, then a right and finally a steep descent. At the bottom of the hill watch for the gravel road on the right side, where the river is close to the road.

PUT-IN Continue upstream on the Maligne Lake Road to the first bridge across the river. Just before the bridge is a small picnic area on the east (left) side of the road.

CAMPING There are no campgrounds along the Maligne Road, but there is developed camping at Whistlers Campground, which is on Highway 93, 1.7 km south of the Highway 16/93 junction at Jasper.

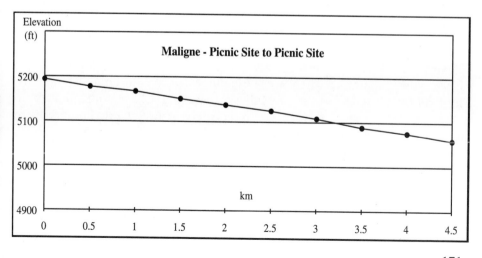

171

Duck Soup

From the outside, it looks like a reasonable recipe for doing the right thing; close a section of the river to paddling in order to save Harlequin Ducks. If you look beyond the popular propaganda, things are not quite so clear.

The Harlequin Duck, it must be noted, is not an endangered species, only the eastern population is endangered. The bird was still hunted in the eastern U.S. until 1989, and is a legal game bird in most of the western states. You can hunt Harlequins in both B.C. and Alberta. In 1993 the Maligne River from Maligne Lake to Medicine Lake was closed to all paddling activities in May and June by Parks Canada. The closure decision was based on data that was collected by one individual over a period of 6 years. Despite identifying this data as subjective, this information was used to show that there was a decline in ducks at the outlet of Maligne Lake. Later this data was again used in a statistical analysis of duck observations and rafting use of the river. Far ranging and speculative interpretations of data have been used to state that rafting has caused a decline in ducks. The outlet at Maligne Lake is said to be special habitat, supporting huge numbers of ducks. Yet data collected by Parks Canada between 1992 and 1994 shows that the Medicine Lake Delta consistently has nearly double the amount of ducks, yet those findings are not reported as significant. Nor has anyone gone to great lengths to study ducks in that area.

Other research indicates that water levels and the availability of fish roe (as a food source) are important ecological factors that impact Harlequin Ducks. Despite identifying these key elements in the earliest study, these factors have not been correlated with duck observations. Even if you accept one individuals observations, the data shows a sudden decline of observations in 1989—the year the Exon Valdez oil spill decimated bird populations along the west coast. Yet that point is completely overlooked as a possible contributing factor. The data also shows that the number of duck observations has steadily increased since then. What about the effects of the petroleum pollution produced by the tour boats on Maligne Lake? Or the increased tourist use of the Maligne Valley? Or population cycles? Or the cessation of fish stocking in Maligne Lake? There are numerous factors overlooked by the current investigations.

I have paddled nearly every river and creek in the Rockies, from north of Jasper to the U.S. border. There are Harlequin Ducks on most of those streams. The road bridge at the outlet of Maligne Lake might have something to do with the numerous sightings there, and the study focused there. Perhaps there are too many rafts on the Maligne River. That is, however, very far from stating that rafting or other river use has caused a decline in Harlequin Ducks. But don't just believe this brief discussion, get the reports yourself. Look beyond the wide generalizations, based on data interpretations, to the actual facts. I support protecting our environment, but rational, open minded scientific research is what decisions should be based on. It is clear to me that paddlers, and rafters in particular, are getting an undeserved dunking in this soup.

GRADE	CLASS	FLOW	TIME	LENGTH
II⁺	II–III	< 6	1–2 hours	6.5 km (4 mi)
III	II–III⁺	> 7		

Gradient 13.5 m/km (1.4%)
71 ft/mi

Max gradient 30 m in 1.5 km (2%)
100 ft in .9 mi

Put-in elevation 1671 m
5482 ft

Take-out elevation 1583 m
5194 ft

Shuttle 6 km (3.7 mi) one way

Season May–August (see notes)

Maps 83C12 and 83C13

Gauge Yes

Craft Canoes, kayaks and rafts

NOTES The river is closed to all paddling activities in May and June. See the story on page 172 for details.

CHARACTER A small to medium-volume river that rips along the jagged boulder-bed, with crystal-clear high-speed water, excellent technical paddling and lots of defined features. The scenery at the put-in is amazing.

FLOW INFORMATION Check the gauge painted on the river right bridge piling at the put-in. View the gauge from the river left shore, just upstream of the bridge. Low flow is 4 and high flow is 10. Flows above 7 are great fun. The river is uncontrolled and fed by snowmelt and glacial runoff.

TRAVEL Access to the run and the shuttle are on paved roads.

DESCRIPTION Below the lake, the river enters a long stretch of class II–II⁺ rapids. After a couple of turns you reach a narrow section that leads to The Fence, a class II⁺ rapid with a hole in the centre of the river. Below this, the river pools, then rushes down another narrow chute to The Wall, a class II⁺–III⁺ hole that extends off the shore. Below The Wall the river has some steep wave surfing and well-defined class II–II⁺ features. A left turn, at an old log jam on the right, leads to a short straight. This is followed by a right turn and a longer straight, with an island on the left. At the end of the straight the river turns left and rips into Z-Drop, a long, high-intensity, class III rapid with lots of holes, rocks and exploding waves. The drop has two main sections. The first is a left/right/left zigzag through sharp boulders, with numerous waves and holes. Below is a short calmer section, then a long arcing turn to the right. The second section starts with holes and waves where the river turns right, and finishes where the river splits around a boulder island, with narrow channels on either side. The action continues for 200 m below the bridge then the gradient decreases, and class II rapids are separated by longer calm sections until the take-out.

173

Humble and Well-Battered Pie

It began as just another trip down the river with a raft-load of folks who entrusted their safety to me, their guide. The weather was hot and sunny, so I wore my nylon shorts, a ridiculously small racing PFD and a tiny excuse for a helmet. If I hadn't oozed confidence, you might have thought me a bit underprepared. My crew was wildly excited. At least that's how they started the run.

The most difficult rapid is Z-Drop, named for the wicked picket fence of sharp boulders that lies diagonally across the start of the rapid. At the top of the drop I leaned way out to get a good sweep, feet hooked in the webbing on the thwart. My body was extended parallel to the water, held up by my legs, which were levered against the outside tube. I had performed the manoeuvre a hundred times before, and until that moment it had been pretty routine. As I put my weight on it, the blade caught between two rocks and I was pitched forward. The last thing I saw, before I hit the water face-first, was the crew stroking in unison, powering the boat away from me. I came up gasping, and in total disbelief. Yes, I was swimming! Then I hit the first rock in the picket fence. I smacked it so hard that I spun into the air, executing a back-abrading shoulder roll off the point. I landed on another jagged boulder and was swept to the right, where my bare legs hammered the next rock in the line. To say I was swimming is a blatant misinterpretation. I bounced off rocks, tumbling and cartwheeling along the jagged boulders. The "swim" lasted only about 200 m, but I hit every rock even remotely near me, with the misguided accuracy of a tossed rag doll. Then I saw the raft, a blue beacon of hope, just ahead. I smacked the upstream side and was immediately sucked downward. Despite my wild clawing, I slid beneath it, trapped in the sieve of sharp rocks that had stranded the raft, with the boat directly above me. I started hammering on the thick foam floor of the raft, but that was futile. Nearly out of breath, I suddenly found the whole episode less than amusing. The boat had a sewn-in floor, with a line of rope woven around the inside perimeter of the ring, to secure the floor. Reaching upstream, I was barely able to get my fingers on the rope. With a massive heave, I reached my other hand out on the upstream side and grasped the safety line. Then in a final trout-like lunge against the current, I threw my arm around the upstream tube and surfaced in a sputtering, gasping surge. The crew was all gawking downstream when in unison, they spun around to see me, dripping blood, flopping over the edge of the boat. They were somehow a lot less excited than they had been before.

At the take-out the other guides were busy, and it looked like I might just slip it by. Then someone leaked the news. Perhaps it was my shocky shade of pale white, the numerous contusions or the way I hobbled around, but suddenly everyone noticed. To make things worse my paddle had stuck in place, perfectly vertical in the current, to be plucked by one of the rival raft companies. But hey, my ego would heal and eventually my body as well. Unfortunately, the incident is still much too popular with certain people around here.

GETTING THERE The run is located south of Jasper, along the Maligne Lake Road, off Highway 93.

TAKE-OUT At the eastern Highway 16 exit to Jasper, go east for 1.8 km to Maligne Lake Road on the south (right) side. Turn right and follow the road across the Athabasca River to a fork. Stay left and continue for 20 km to Medicine Lake. From there, go 17 km south to the first bridge across the river. Just before the bridge is a small picnic area on the west (left) side.

PUT-IN Continue upstream for 6 km to the bridge at the outlet from Maligne Lake. Go to the parking lot at the end of the road and use the boat launch.

CAMPING There is developed camping at Whistlers Campground, which is on Highway 93, 1.7 km south of the Highway 16/93 junction at Jasper.

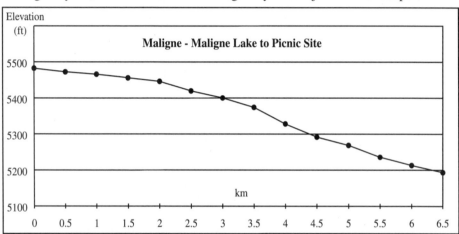

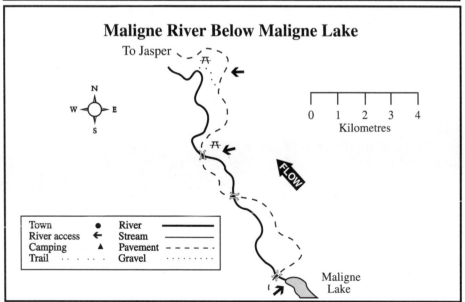

GRADE	CLASS	FLOW	TIME	LENGTH
I	I⁺	Most Flows	1–2 hours	3 km (1.9 mi)

Gradient   .7 m/km (.07%)   **Max gradient** 2 m in 3 km (.07%)
              3.7 ft/mi   7 ft in 1.9 mi

Put-in elevation   1035 m   **Take-out elevation**   1033 m
                      3396 ft   3389 ft

Shuttle   3 km (1.9 mi) one way   **Season**   May–September

Maps   83D16   **Gauge**   Yes

Craft   Canoes, kayaks and rafts

CHARACTER   A small-volume float trip on a meandering, mud-bottomed channel with no major rapids. There is one class II drop just upstream of the bridge at the take-out, but you can exit above it. The run is a good way to get up close to the many elk, deer, beaver, moose and coyotes in the area.

FLOW INFORMATION   Flow level variations make little difference on this mellow float. The river is uncontrolled and fed by snowmelt and glacial runoff.

TRAVEL   Access to the run and the shuttle are on paved roads.

DESCRIPTION   There are few outstanding features on the run. The river flows in an exaggerated set of meanders with flat water for the duration of the run. There are many logs and sweepers on the river; however, they are easy to avoid. The river is removed from the highways, except at the bridge midway through the run, and is quiet and peaceful.

GETTING THERE   The run is located near Jasper, off Highway 16.

TAKE-OUT   From the lights at the junction of Highway 16 and Highway 93, go 1.2 km east on Highway 16 to the junction with Highway 93A. Turn south (right) and go 700 m to the bridge over the river.

PUT-IN   Return to the Highway 16 junction with Highway 93A, then go west (left) on Highway 16 until you reach the lights. Continue west for 800 m to a small pull-off on the south (left) side of the highway just before the bridge.

CAMPING   There is developed camping at Whistlers Campground, which is on Highway 93, 1.7 km south of the 16/93 junction at Jasper.

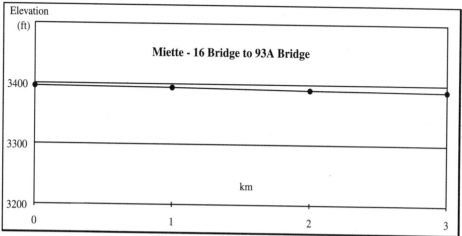

Elevation (ft)

Miette - 16 Bridge to 93A Bridge

km

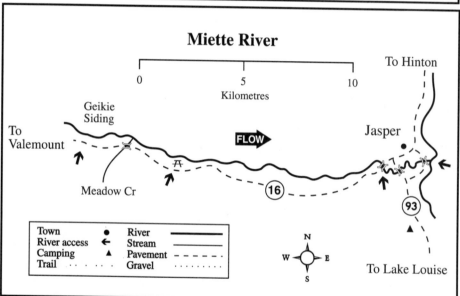

Miette River

To Hinton

Geikie
Siding

To
Valemount

0   5   10
Kilometres

FLOW

Jasper

Meadow Cr

16

Town	●	River	———
River access	←	Stream	——
Camping	▲	Pavement	– – –
Trail	· · · · ·	Gravel	· · · · · ·

93

N
W · E
S

To Lake Louise

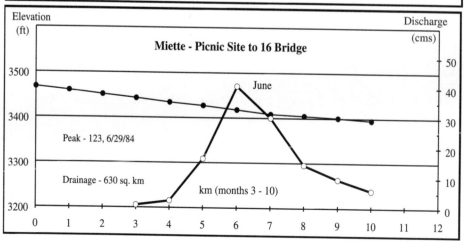

Elevation (ft)

Discharge (cms)

Miette - Picnic Site to 16 Bridge

June

Peak - 123, 6/29/84

Drainage - 630 sq. km

km (months 3 - 10)

GRADE	CLASS	FLOW	TIME	LENGTH
II	I⁺–II⁺	Low	2–3 hours	10 km (6.2 mi)
II	I⁺–III	High		

Gradient 2.2 m/km (.22%)
12 ft/mi

Max gradient 22 m in 10 km (.22%)
72 ft in 6.2 mi

Put-in elevation 1057 m
3468 ft

Take-out elevation 1035 m
3396 ft

Shuttle 8 km (5 mi) one way

Season May–August

Maps 83D16

Gauge Yes

Craft Canoes, kayaks and small rafts

CHARACTER A small-volume trip in a meandering channel. There are a couple of major rapids where the river encounters boulder gardens.

FLOW INFORMATION Assess the flow at the take-out. The river is fed by snowmelt and glacial runoff and is uncontrolled. The hydrograph is on page 177. High flows make the major rapids harder but the rest of the run changes little.

TRAVEL Access to the run and the shuttle are on paved roads.

DESCRIPTION The run begins in a gravel channel but the river is soon flowing between mud banks. The river meanders in the open valley and wildlife can often be seen. About two-thirds of the way into the run the river is close to the highway, then 300–400 m below drops into a constricted class II–III boulder garden that is 200 m long. Below this the rapids ease until 1.5 km downstream, where you encounter another class II–II⁺ boulder garden. The river runs in easy class I to the take-out, where you encounter some small waves at a broken ledge under the take-out bridge. The gradient profile is on page 177.

GETTING THERE The run is located west of Jasper, off Highway 16. See the map on page 177.

TAKE-OUT From the lights at the junction of Highway 16 and Highway 93, go 800 m west on Highway 16 to the bridge. There is a pull-off on the south (left) side of the highway just before you reach the bridge.

PUT-IN Continue 8 km west on Highway 16 to a large, paved pull-out on the north (right) side, with a picnic area by the river.

CAMPING There is developed camping at Whistlers Campground, which is on Highway 93, 1.7 km south of the 16/93 junction at Jasper.

GRADE	CLASS	FLOW	TIME	LENGTH
II	II–II⁺	Low–Medium	1–2 hours	3.5 km (2.2 mi)
III	II–III	Medium–High		

Gradient 9.4 m/km (.94%)   **Max gradient** 30 m in 3 km (1%)
50 ft/mi   100 ft in 1.9 mi

Put-in elevation 1090 m   **Take-out elevation** 1057 m
3576 ft   3468 ft

Shuttle 2.8 km (1.7 mi) one way   **Season** May–August

Maps 83D16   **Gauge** Yes

Craft Canoes, kayaks and small rafts

CHARACTER A small-volume run that starts in a constricted narrow channel, then flows over an open gravel-bed in the lower part. The rapids are created by the tight, twisting channel that flows over boulders and bedrock ledges.

FLOW INFORMATION Assess the flow at the take-out. Higher flows make for much larger features and faster water in the constricted channel. The river is uncontrolled and fed by snowmelt and glacial runoff.

TRAVEL Access to the run and the shuttle are on paved roads.

DESCRIPTION At the put-in the river drops over a small broken ledge in a narrow canyon, then opens up to a calm and wandering channel. Flat water continues for about 1 km to where the river speeds up as it flows along a bedrock wall on river left. This leads to a left turn and a long class II rapid composed of standing waves. At the bottom of the rapid, a small ledge that extends off the right side has good surfing at higher flow levels. The river passes under a footbridge and makes a left, where it drops off a constricted class II–III chute on the right. Below this the river runs over a broken bedrock and boulder channel then makes a right. A class II–II⁺ broken ledge is just above the railroad bridge. The river then turns left and flows onto a more open, but steep boulder-bed. The remaining rapids are formed where the river splits into narrow channels around boulder islands. There are a couple of class II–II⁺ drops, then the rapids ease to the take-out. In the lower section, watch for logs and log jams in the shifting channels.

GETTING THERE The run is located west of Jasper, off Highway 16. See the map on page 177.

TAKE-OUT From the lights at the junction of Highway 16 and Highway 93, go 9 km west on Highway 16 to a large, paved pull-out on the north (right) side. There are picnic tables and washrooms near the river.

PUT-IN Go 2.8 km west on Highway 16, to a pull-off on the north (right) side where the highway goes up a hill to a left corner. The old pull-off has boulders blocking the entrance. Park there and carry down the embankment, across the tracks and through the meadow to the river.

CAMPING There is developed camping at Whistlers Campground, which is on Highway 93, 1.7 km south of the 16/93 junction at Jasper.

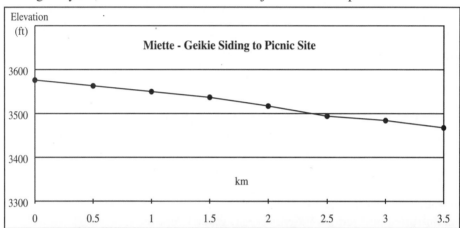

The usual gear chaos at the put-in. Photo: Gilbert Wall.

GRADE	CLASS	FLOW	TIME	LENGTH
III$^+$	II$^+$–IV$^+$	Medium	1–2 hours	3.5 km (2.2 mi)
IV$^+$	III–V	High		

Gradient   37 m/km (3.7%)
193 ft/mi

Max gradient   30 m in .7 km (4.3%)
100 ft in .4 mi

Put-in elevation   1200 m
3937 ft

Take-out elevation   1072 m
3517 ft

Shuttle   5 km (3.1 mi) one way

Season   May–August

Maps   83D16

Gauge   No

Craft   Kayaks and rubber canoes

NOTES   The trip ends with a 2-km (1.2-mi) run on the Athabasca.

CHARACTER   A small-volume run down a steep boulder-strewn hillside. The lower section flows through trees, over log jams and across shifting boulders.

FLOW INFORMATION   The river is dam-controlled and fed by snowmelt and glacial runoff. Check the flow at the put-in. At low flows the run is a boulder bash, and at high flows a high-pressure flush. The upstream dam diverts about 1 cms for power production, which is a problem only at low flows.

TRAVEL   Access to the run and the shuttle are on paved roads.

DESCRIPTION   There is 300 m of steep, class IV above the bridge. The river then turns left and drops into a convoluted class IV–IV$^+$ boulder garden and rips toward the 2–3-m chute under the bridge. The river pools, then tumbles off a boulder fence and drops steadily over a steep boulder-bed. The gradient decreases slightly just above a sharp left turn. Here the river accelerates around a huge boulder near the right shore and into a class IV rapid. The river then enters a narrow bedrock canyon and makes a sharp, blind right turn at the bottom. There is a class IV–IV$^+$ drop in the middle that is difficult to scout. Below the canyon, the river opens up and flows quickly over a shallow boulder-bed. The rapids below the canyon are class II$^+$–III$^+$, but the log jams, trees and narrow boulder chutes create constant hazards as you navigate the steep slope.

GETTING THERE   The run is located south of Jasper, off Highway 93A. See the map on page 187.

TAKE-OUT   From the lights at the junction of Highways 16/93, go 7 km south on Highway 93 to a small road on the north (left) side, just before you reach the bridge over the Athabasca. Turn left and park out of the way.

PUT-IN Go back north for 600 m on Highway 93, to the junction with Highway 93A, which is on the west (left) side. Turn left and follow the road for 5 km to the bridge. Park on the east (left) side of the road just before the bridge and descend the steep slopes upstream of the bridge, on river left. You can also carry upstream along the river left bank for 200–300 m, to just below the wild gorge beneath the dam. The carry gets you a couple of extra class IV drops.

CAMPING There is developed camping at Wabasso Campground, 4 km south of the put-in bridge on Highway 93A, or at Wapiti Campground, 4 km north of the take-out, on Highway 93.

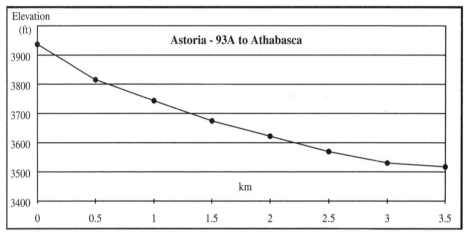

Jim Orava under the bridge on the Astoria. Photo: Robert Beaudry.

GRADE	CLASS	FLOW	TIME	LENGTH
IV–IV⁺	II–V	Low	4–6 hours	8.5 km (5.3 mi)
IV⁺–V	III–V⁺	Medium		
V–V⁺	III–V⁺	High		

Gradient 36 m/km (3.6%)   **Max gradient** 30 m in .5 km (6%)
191 ft/mi   100 ft in .3 mi

Put-in elevation 1558 m   **Take-out elevation** 1250 m
5110 ft   4101 ft

Shuttle 13 km (8 mi) one way   **Season** June–August
plus a 1.2-km (.7-mi) carry

Maps 83D9 and 83D16   **Gauge** No

Craft Kayaks and canoes

NOTES The road to the put-in does not open until June 10–June 15.

CHARACTER A small-volume run that tears over a steep boulder-bed in the top section, then enters continuous whitewater in a canyon. The canyon section requires either paddling long class V–V⁺ rapids, or a strenuous portage.

FLOW INFORMATION Assess the flow at the take-out bridge. If the drop just above the bridge looks as though it has a clean line, the river is medium high. If the rocks on the river left of the drop look like a bouncy waterslide, the river is low. The river is uncontrolled and fed by snowmelt and glacial runoff. The upstream dam diverts about 1 cms of the flow above the take-out.

TRAVEL Access to the run and the shuttle are on paved roads.

DESCRIPTION At the put-in, the river flows placidly in a meandering gravel channel. About 300 m below, the river turns right and takes off. The rapids increase in difficulty, from open class II to steeper class III, as the river descends through a convoluted bed of boulders. The gradient increases and the river becomes entrenched in a narrow, class III⁺–IV channel, with larger boulders. The river runs as class IV for about 3 km, then the gradient increases again. At a long island with a narrow channel on the right, the river drops off Escapade, a class IV⁺–V boulder-choked series of steps in the left channel. You can look downstream along the white ribbon that snakes its way toward the dark rock walls of the canyon. Below Escapade, the river runs in class IV–IV⁺ boulder drops until a rock wall on the right side constricts the flow into Gas Pedal, a tight chute that drops 1–2 m. This is followed 80 m downstream by Foreplay, a class IV⁺–V rapid split by a massive boulder into a steep-angled chute on the right and a convoluted boulder-choke on the left.

Boondoggled on the Astoria

Sometime in the distant past, Ifor and I hauled our boats down the steep, jumbled boulders to reach the put-in. We then prepared ourselves for the descent down the mountainside. Ifor is a good friend and a solid paddler, whose sound judgement balances my more reckless and cocky style. He also has a great sense of humour, accompanied by a wicked gleam in his eye. Most of the time you have to watch him out of the corner of your eye, in case he is up to something. We paddle well together and have enjoyed many great trips.

That day, the river was reasonably high and the added water made the run soft and, for the most part, bouncy. But in places the river would turn abruptly and fan-out over steep, boulder-choked passages where the water, oblivious to the obstacles, kept up its thundering pace. At one wild corner, my bow was deflected by a rock and I found myself momentarily sideways. In a valiant attempt to straighten my boat, I threw in a huge sweep on the upstream side. Halfway through the sweep, the paddle wedged between two rocks, and I was yanked over. There was hardly sufficient water to get upside down, but what water there was continued howling downhill, hammering me and my boat off the numerous obstacles. During a roll attempt, my paddle again hit the bottom and stuck, this time dragging me from my boat.

I was pounding along a steep waterslide, tumbling off numerous boulders. Just when I really wanted out of there, I landed in a deeper channel and took off in a surging rush of exploding waves. Now I was really flying down the mountainside! After a couple of resounding ricochets off boulders, I dragged my trembling body onto shore. Somehow, Ifor had managed to trap my boat against some rocks. After a miraculously short swim I was back in my boat, somewhat bruised and more than a bit embarrassed. At the canyon, we portaged the top drop and scouted downstream as far as possible. The stuff below the first drop was difficult, but what bothered me was the waterfall Ifor said lay below, around the blind corner. Since I had not paddled the run before, I assumed he would lead. When he got in his boat first, on a narrow ledge, he affirmed this. Then he looked up at me holding my boat, waiting for him to get in, and said nonchalantly "Oh, there is room for you here." So I passed him my boat. He set it down just to the outside of his, and I climbed in. It wasn't until I had my spraydeck on and paddle in hand, that I realized the situation. I looked at him, wondering how he was going to launch first. He looked back with that gleam in his eye, shrugging his shoulders. I started to protest, then realized the futility, as he sat there grinning innocently at me. What could I say? He had just saved my boat for me! I owed him one.

So I launched and we paddled the rest of the run without incident. From that day on, I was always much more aware of his sense of humour on the river. It is something I have come to appreciate greatly. However, since then I have also tried to avoid being duped too often!

Brock Wilson in the boulder garden below Freeze Frame at low flow.

The canyon mouth is 30 m downstream of Foreplay. As you descend, it is best to start looking for a place to stop before you enter Gas Pedal. Below this the current speed is such that stopping is very difficult. Scout the canyon on river left by scrambling along the cliff face, about 8–10 m above the water, where you can descend below the canyon mouth to check what lies downstream. About 30 m below Foreplay the river drops into the canyon at Howler, a steep, 2–4 m, class V–V$^+$ drop in a narrow chute. The action intensifies as you exit the 20-m-long, boiling slot at a riverwide 1–2-m drop into a vacuum-cleaner hole. Below this the river rushes headlong at a class V boulder sieve, with a narrow, twisting chute on the left. The river then drops off bedrock into a long, low-angled ramp that screams down to a left turn, hits a boiling hole at the bottom and rips through a narrow, overhung slot in the bedrock. About 20 m below, the river drops off Freeze Frame, a 2–4-m, class IV$^+$–V waterfall. The above 200–300-m section of whitewater is an incredible, high-intensity, grade V$^+$ masterpiece. At all but the lowest flows, the whole thing runs together into one wet whitewater dream.

If you wish to portage the Howler, you have two options. The first is a steep and arduous climb up the rock face on the left, followed by an equally harrowing descent back to the river. At low to medium flows you can seal-launch just to the left of the Howler, off a small boulder-worn pothole. Once at river level below the Howler, you can portage; or you can selectively run the drops until just above the narrow slot through the bedrock that is upstream of Freeze Frame. At this point, you must either portage up and around another rock outcrop, or run the slot and eddy out on the right, in the short pool just above Freeze Frame.

Ifor Thomas in Freeze Frame at low–medium flow. Photo: Derek Thomas.

Ian Mackay taking a breather on the open upper section, with Mount Edith Cavell in the background. Photo: Robert Beaudry.

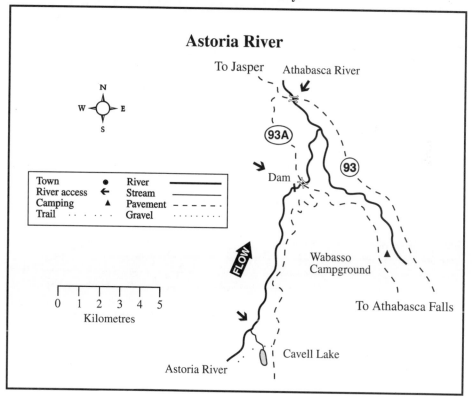

Astoria River

To Jasper   Athabasca River

93A

93

Dam

Town	●	River
River access	←	Stream
Camping	▲	Pavement
Trail	· · · · ·	Gravel

FLOW

Wabasso Campground

To Athabasca Falls

0 1 2 3 4 5
Kilometres

Astoria River

Cavell Lake

You can scout Freeze Frame from the rock outcrop on river right, just above the drop. Below Freeze Frame the river makes a wild, class IV–IV⁺ left/right/ left carom shot off rock outcrops, then enters a 200-m-long boulder garden. The excitement ends in a flatwater pool that is backed up by the dam. Exit on the left, just above the concrete wall, and carry your boat down the road to your vehicle. Do not miss the take-out on this one!

GETTING THERE The run is located south of Jasper, off Highway 93A.

TAKE-OUT From the lights at the junction of Highway 16 and Highway 93, go 6.6 km south on Highway 93 to the junction with Highway 93A, which is on the west (right) side. Turn right and follow the road for 5 km to a bridge. Park on the east (left) side of the road just before the bridge.

PUT-IN Go south across the bridge, then in 200 m turn west (right) on the Edith Cavell Road. Follow the road for 12 km, to the hostel on the left side of the road. About 100 m past the hostel is a parking area on the right side, at the Tonquin Valley trailhead. Park there, then follow the trail down to a bridge on Cavell Creek. At the bridge, follow the moraine downhill across the steep boulders. Walking on the boulders is the easiest way down. After 600–700 m, take to the east (right) shore and cross through the open forest to the river. If you follow the moraine along the creek, you will make a slightly longer, but assured path to the river.

CAMPING There is developed camping at Wabasso Campground, on Highway 93A, 4 km south of the take-out bridge.

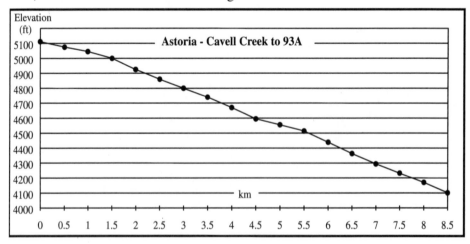

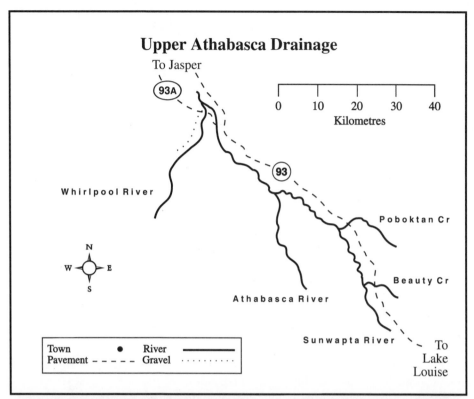

Upper Athabasca Drainage

To Jasper

93A

| 0 | 10 | 20 | 30 | 40 |

Kilometres

93

Whirlpool River

Poboktan Cr

N
W — E
S

Beauty Cr

Athabasca River

Sunwapta River

To
Lake
Louise

| Town | ● | River | ——— |
| Pavement | – – – – – | Gravel | ·········· |

Will the unknown rafter please reveal himself! Photo: Tom Thompson.

GRADE	CLASS	FLOW	TIME	LENGTH
II	II–II⁺	Low	2–3 hours	9.5 km (5.9 mi)
II⁺	II–III	High		

Gradient   2.8 m/km (.28%)   **Max gradient**   27 m in 9.5 km (.28%)
15 ft/mi   88 ft in 5.9 mi

Put-in elevation   1155 m   **Take-out elevation**   1128 m
3789 ft   3701 ft

Shuttle   13.5 km (8.4 mi) one way   **Season**   May–September

Maps   83C12   **Gauge**   No

Craft   Canoes, kayaks and rafts

CHARACTER   A scenic medium to large-volume run with most of the rapids in the first half. The rapids are created by bedrock ledges, boulders and sharp turns in a constricted canyon. At high flows, expect some great surfing.

FLOW INFORMATION   The river is uncontrolled and fed by snowmelt and glacial runoff. Assess the flow at the take-out.

TRAVEL   Access to the run and the shuttle are on paved roads.

DESCRIPTION   The run starts in an open channel just downstream of the canyon below the fall. The river flows around a huge midstream boulder, then drops through a class II–II⁺ set of rapids into a canyon. Though in a canyon, the river channel is open at water level, with lots of exploding standing waves in the first few kilometres of the run. There are a couple of great surf spots, lots of well-defined features and great views looking upstream. The rapids ease and the river opens up, then closes in to a calm-water canyon. The roar at the end is Kerkeslin Ledge, a class II–III double drop off a bedrock outcrop. The first part of the drop has a few standing waves on the right, followed by a short pool. The second drop has a sharp chute on river left, up against an undercut rock face, and the left side has a pourover drop into a tight hole. Below this, the river takes on the character of the rest of the run, with long calm sections broken by short rapids created by midstream boulders and channel constrictions. Take out on the right where you first see the highway, or continue to just below the confluence with the Whirlpool River, which enters from the left. Between the upper take-out and the Whirlpool, there is one 200-m-long section of class II–II⁺ rapids known as the Rock Gardens.

GETTING THERE   The run is located south of Jasper, along Highway 93. See the map on page 193.

TAKE-OUT From the lights at the junction of Highway 16 and Highway 93, go south on Highway 93 for 7 km, to the bridge over the Athabasca. Continue south for 10.3 km, to a left bend in the highway. Look for the small gravel pull-out on the west (right) side. If coming from the south, look for the gravel pull-out on the west (left) side 12.5 km north of the Highway 93A junction at the turn-off to Athabasca Falls. If you want to use the upper take-out, then go 3 km south of the gravel pull-out to where the river is close to the road, just before a steep hill. Park well off the highway.

PUT-IN Go south on Highway 93 to the junction with Highway 93A, which is on the west (right) side. Turn right and cross the Athabasca in 400 m, then continue for 500 m to the parking area on the west (left) side of the road. This is the Geraldine Lakes trailhead. Park there and carry across the road, then down a small road that leads to the river after a series of switchbacks.

CAMPING There is developed camping about 4 km south of Athabasca Falls, on Highway 93, at Kerkeslin Campground. There is also camping at Wabasso Campground, which is 13.5 km north of the put-in, on Highway 93A.

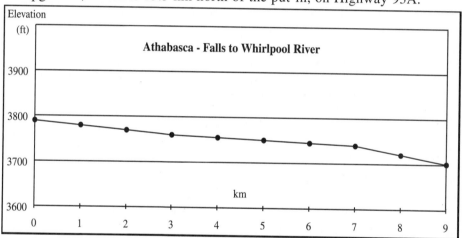

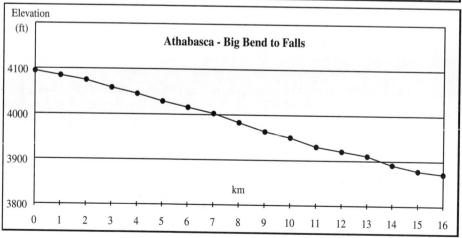

191

GRADE	CLASS	FLOW	TIME	LENGTH
II	II–II+	Low	2–3 hours	15.5 km (9.6 mi)
II	II+	High		

Gradient 4.4 m/km (.44%)
23 ft/mi

Max gradient 30 m in 6.8 km (.44%)
100 ft in 4.2 mi

Put-in elevation 1248 m
4094 ft

Take-out elevation 1180 m
3871 ft

Shuttle 15 km (9.3 mi) one way

Season May–September

Maps 83C12

Gauge No

Craft Canoes, kayaks and rafts

CHARACTER A scenic medium to large-volume run on an open riverbed with spectacular vistas. The rapids are created at channel constrictions and where the river drops off rock bars and gravel shoals.

FLOW INFORMATION The river is uncontrolled and fed by glacial runoff and snowmelt. Assess the flow at the take-out. At medium to high flows the river has much better playing on the fast surfing waves.

TRAVEL Access to the run and the shuttle are on paved roads.

DESCRIPTION At the put-in, the river is in an open single channel, and flows swiftly around tight corners. Not far below, the river opens up with large islands and multiple channels. Watch for a class II–II+ rapid at a narrowing of the channel. There are great views of the surrounding mountains. The major rapids consist of standing waves produced by constriction of the flow. The rapids are more powerful and distinct at lower flows when the water is funnelled into narrow chutes. About 1 km above the take-out, the river constricts and accelerates through a class II–II+ set of large standing waves, then the highway comes into sight. Head for the right shore, because as the river turns left, it drops off the class VI+ Athabasca Falls. If you are pushing your limits on the river, or unsure of your ability to rescue swimmers in a short time period, you may wish to take out well above the fall. Though one fortunate individual survived the drop after an inadvertent plunge, the fall has been fatal in every other case. The gradient profile is on page 191.

GETTING THERE The run is located south of Jasper, along Highway 93.

TAKE-OUT From the lights at the junction of Highway 16 and Highway 93, go 30 km south on Highway 93. Look for the junction with Highway 93A at the turn-off to Athabasca Falls. If coming from the south, proceed to the junction with Highway 93A at the turn-off to Athabasca Falls. At the Highways 93 and 93A junction, go south on Highway 93 for about 700 m to where the road is close to the river. Park well of the highway and ensure you know where the take-out is from the river.

PUT-IN Go 15 km south on Highway 93 to a small picnic area on the west (right) side of the highway. The pull-off is at an exaggerated bend in the river, just before a long ascent.

CAMPING There is developed camping about 4 km south of the take-out, at Kerkeslin Campground. There is also camping at Wabasso Campground, which is 14 km north of Athabasca Falls on Highway 93A.

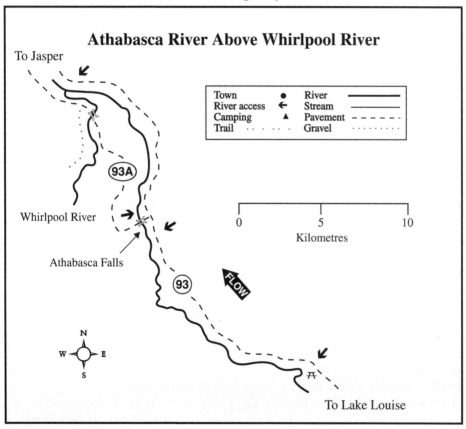

Athabasca River Above Whirlpool River

Town	●	River ————
River access	←	Stream ————
Camping	▲	Pavement – – – –
Trail · · · · ·		Gravel · · · · · · ·

GRADE	CLASS	FLOW	TIME	LENGTH
I⁺	I⁺–II	Low	1–2 hours	2.5 km (1.6 mi)
II	II	High		

Gradient   6.7 m/km (.67%)   **Max gradient**   17 m in 2.5 km (.67%)
              35 ft/mi   55 ft in 1.6 mi

Put-in elevation   1127 m   **Take-out elevation**   1110 m
                        3697 ft   3642 ft

Shuttle   2.4 km (1.5 mi) one way   **Season**   May–August

Maps   83C12   **Gauge**   No

Craft   Canoes, kayaks and rafts

CHARACTER   A small to medium-volume float trip on an open riverbed, with excellent views of the surrounding area.

FLOW INFORMATION   Assess the flow at the take-out. Low flows are a problem, as the river is very spread-out in the lower section. The river is uncontrolled and fed by snowmelt and glacial runoff.

TRAVEL   Access to the run and the shuttle are on paved roads.

DESCRIPTION   At the bridge, the river flows in a swift single channel. This continues for about 1 km. The river then spreads out on a gravel plain, with wide, shallow channels. There are a few riffles where the river drops off gravelbars. Take out just prior to the confluence with the Athabasca.

GETTING THERE   The run is located south of Jasper, off Highway 93A.

TAKE-OUT   From the lights at the junction of Highway 16 and Highway 93, go 6.6 km south on Highway 93 to the junction with Highway 93A, which is on the west (right) side. Turn right and follow the road for 13 km to the Meeting of the Waters pull-out on the east (left) side of the road. If coming from the south, look for the junction with Highway 93A at the turn-off to Athabasca Falls. Turn west (left) onto Highway 93A and go north for 10.5 km to the Meeting of the Waters pull-out on the east (right) side of the road.

PUT-IN   Go 2.3 km south on Highway 93A to the put-in bridge.

CAMPING   There is developed camping at Wabasso Campground, 6 km north of the put-in, on Highway 93A.

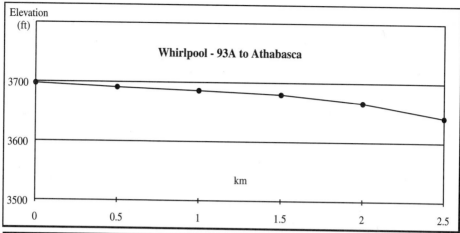

Whirlpool - 93A to Athabasca

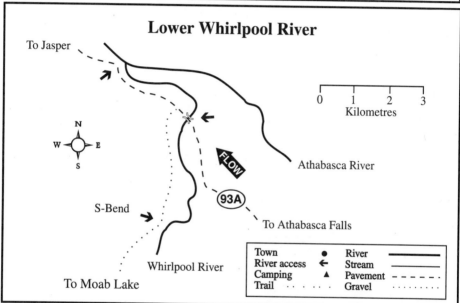

Lower Whirlpool River

To Jasper

N
W — E
S

Kilometres
0 1 2 3

Athabasca River

FLOW

93A

To Athabasca Falls

S-Bend

Whirlpool River

To Moab Lake

Town	●	River	▬▬▬
River access	←	Stream	▬▬
Camping	▲	Pavement	– – – –
Trail	· · · · ·	Gravel	· · · · · ·

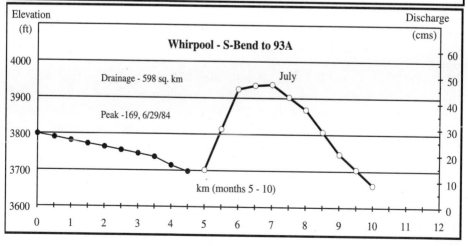

Whirlpool - S-Bend to 93A

Drainage - 598 sq. km

July

Peak -169, 6/29/84

km (months 5 - 10)

GRADE	CLASS	FLOW	TIME	LENGTH
II	I–II	Low	1–2 hours	4.5 km (2.8 mi)
II	II–II⁺	High		

Gradient 7 m/km (.7%)
37 ft/mi

Max gradient 30 m in 4.2 km (.7%)
100 ft in 2.6 mi

Put-in elevation 1158 m
3800 ft

Take-out elevation 1127 m
3697 ft

Shuttle 4 km (2.5 mi) one way

Season May–August

Maps 83C12

Gauge Yes

Craft Canoes, kayaks and rafts

CHARACTER A small to medium-volume run on an open gravel-bed. The one major rapid is formed where the river flows through a long boulderfield.

FLOW INFORMATION Assess the flow at the take-out. Low flows provide much more technical paddling. The river is uncontrolled and fed by snowmelt and glacial runoff. The hydrograph is on page 195.

TRAVEL The shuttle is on gravel roads.

DESCRIPTION The river at the start is narrow and constricted, but quickly spreads out over the rocky riverbed. The first 1–2 km are easy, then the river drops through a boulderfield in a long class II–II⁺ rapid. At low flows the river is channelled between boulders, while at high flows, the rapid is a set of standing waves. Below this the river has a couple of corners, but is open until the take-out. There are good views in the lower half of the run. The gradient profile is on page 195.

GETTING THERE The run is located south of Jasper, off Highway 93A. See the map on page 195.

TAKE-OUT From the lights at the junction of Highway 16 and Highway 93, go south on Highway 93 for 6.6 km. At the junction with Highway 93A, which is on the west (right) side, turn right and follow the road for 15 km to the bridge. If coming from the south, look for the junction with Highway 93A at the turn-off to Athabasca Falls. Turn west (left) onto Highway 93A and go north for 8.3 km to the bridge.

PUT-IN Go 100 m north, then turn west (left) onto the gravel Moab Lake Road, and follow it for 3.9 km to a small pull-off on the left, near the river's edge. A rock berm leads out along the river, just below the S-Bend.

196

CAMPING There is developed camping on Highway 93A at Wabasso Campground, 6 km north of the turn-off to Moab Lake.

Donna Bradley in the upper part of the S-Bend rapid. Photo: Keith Bobey.

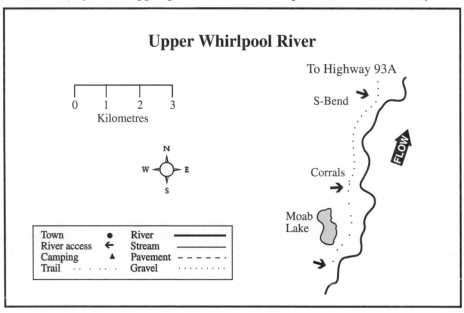

GRADE	CLASS	FLOW	TIME	LENGTH
II	II–II+	Low	1–2 hours	2.5 km (1.6 mi)
II+	II–III	High		

Gradient 8 m/km (.8%) **Max gradient** 20 m in 2.5 km (.8%)
42 ft/mi   64 ft in 1.6 mi

Put-in elevation 1178 m   **Take-out elevation** 1158 m
3864 ft   3800 ft

Shuttle 2.5 km (1.6 mi) one way   **Season** May–August

Maps 83C12   **Gauge** Yes

Craft Canoes, kayaks and rafts

CHARACTER A small to medium-volume run on an open riverbed, with rapids created by constrictions, bedrock outcrops and boulderfields. The views are outstanding. There are numerous spots where you can spend hours surfing.

FLOW INFORMATION Assess the flow at the take-out. The river is fed by snowmelt and glacial runoff and is uncontrolled.

TRAVEL The shuttle is on gravel roads.

DESCRIPTION At the put-in the river is open, with fast current flowing over the boulder-bed. About 100 m downstream, the river drops off a rock bar at a constricted class II–II+ rapid that often has some good surfing. The next 900 m has short class II–II+ rapids interspersed with easier sections. Watch for a sharp right turn with a rock outcrop on the left, where the river flows through a constricted class II+ rapid. Just below that, the river pools for a short distance, then drops off a bedrock outcrop that has fine surfing below it. After a calm stretch there is a long set of standing waves and small holes that leads to a calmer open section. Below this, the river flows toward the right side of the channel, then splits into a series of narrower channels that twist through boulder fences in constricted class II+–III drops. At the end of a long island the channels rejoin and the river flows over the shallow boulder-bed into the S-Bend, which has a rock fence along the far left and a sharp hole at the bottom on the right. The take-out is on the left shore.

GETTING THERE The run is located south of Jasper, off Highway 93A. See the map on page 197.

TAKE-OUT From the lights at the junction of Highway 16 and Highway 93, go 6.6 km south on Highway 93 to the junction with Highway 93A, on the west (right) side. Turn right and follow the road for 15 km to the Moab Lake

"Safety" and Rescue

It was a Friday evening, after a particularly long day of work. I was to attend a river rescue course the next day, which would involve a lot of standing around. So I wanted some solitude, some relaxation and a little fun. I grabbed my canoe and carried it for a couple of kilometres, to the Upper Whirlpool. I had been diligent in learning what to do on the river when things went wrong, and having rock-climbed before, I knew the mechanics of rope and pulley systems well. By the end of the evening, I would tax my skills to the limit and require every scrap of my ingenuity to get home with all my gear.

Just above the take-out is a rapid known as the S-Bend. By the time I got to the S-Bend, I had carried, surfed, hole-ridden and played myself to exhaustion. I got a bit casual about zipping between boulders in a narrow drop and flipped after catching my paddle on the bottom. Into the ice-cold water I went! I was bouncing along the bottom, upside down, with my canoe strapped firmly to my butt. After a couple of exasperated roll attempts, I bailed. As I ejected from my thigh straps, the boat caught a sharp midstream rock in a fast chute. The boat halted abruptly, and I was swept downstream. After bouncing over the boulders, I leapt out of the river and raced back up to my boat, which was still pinned on the rock. Twice I waded out to the boat, but was swept away. In desperation, I attempted to swim down on the boat and grab it, but the current was too swift and I could not hold on. I could wade out to about 2 m from my the boat, but that was it. Since this was an "easy" run, I had left my throwbag at home, in a misguided effort to keep my boat light.

During a sudden brainstorm, I ran to the car to retrieve a few items that might assist me. I taped open the carabiner from my PFD tow system, then taped it to the kayak paddle I had in the car. After 20 minutes of fishing for the grab loop on the canoe, I had the open carabiner snagged on the boat, and the thin cord from my roof rack served as a line to shore. Despite several minutes of tugging, hauling and grunting, the boat hadn't moved. I looked around for a tree to anchor a haul system, but the only things close were a few skimpy willows. With the second rope from my roof rack, I created an equalized anchor on the multiple stems of the willow bush, but I was one carabiner short of the system I was rigging! I raced back to the car once again and rooted in the glove compartment for an old D-ring, left over from my boat outfitting. Back at the willow, I used the line from my tow system as a prussik to attach the D-ring to the haul line. After a brief moment of silence, in deference to all willows, I began to pull on the system. The willow shifted and bent a bit, but held firm as the stretch in the ropes was taken up, then after more cautious hauling on the line, the boat came free and swung to shore. It was 11:30 p.m. when I returned to the car and headed for home. The next morning the river rescue course instructors introduced themselves, then asked if anyone had any experiences to share with the group. I could only grin as I raised my hand to reply!

Road, which is on the west (right) side. If coming from the south, look for the junction with Highway 93A at the turn-off to Athabasca Falls. Turn west (left) onto Highway 93A and go 8.5 km north to the Moab Lake Road on the west (left) side. At the Moab Lake Road junction with Highway 93A, turn west onto the gravel road and go for 3.9 km to a small gravel pull-off on the left.

PUT-IN Go 2.5 km upstream to a set of corrals on the south (left) side of the road. Immediately past the corrals, a small trail on the left leads across the meadow, through the trees and to the river in about 600 m.

CAMPING There is developed camping on Highway 93A at Wabasso Campground, 6 km north of the turn-off to Moab Lake.

Sean Pander surfing one of the many play waves below the corrals.

GRADE	CLASS	FLOW	TIME	LENGTH
II	II–III⁺	Low	1–2 hours	3 km (1.9 mi)
II⁺	II–IV	High		

Gradient 7.3 m/km (.73%)   **Max gradient** 22 m in 3 km (.73%)
　　　　　　39 ft/mi   72 ft in 1.9 mi

Put-in elevation 1200 m   **Take-out elevation** 1178 m
　　　　　　　　　3937 ft   3864 ft

Shuttle 2.5 km (1.6 mi) one way   **Season** May–August

Maps 83C12   **Gauge** Yes

Craft Canoes, kayaks and rafts

NOTES You must carry 2 km (1.2 mi) along a trail to reach the put-in.

CHARACTER A small to medium-volume run that flows on an open gravel-bed for most of the run, with spectacular views. The one major rapid is formed where the river is constricted between huge boulders.

FLOW INFORMATION The river is uncontrolled and fed by snowmelt and glacial runoff. Assess the flow at the take-out.

TRAVEL Access to the run is via 7 km of gravel roads.

DESCRIPTION At the put-in, the river flows in an open gravel plain with incredible views looking upstream. About 1 km below the put-in, the river drops into a boulder-garden rapid that leads to the constricted slots in the class III⁺–IV Boulder Drop. Here the river splits into two chutes around the midstream boulders. The river then drops off convoluted boulder fences into a single channel. Below this, the river runs in a more open channel with class II rapids and a couple of easy play spots until you reach the take-out. Rather than carry the 600 m to the corral, most folks combine this run with the section down to the S-Bend. The rest of the run is described on page 198.

GETTING THERE The run is located south of Jasper, along Highway 93. See the map on page 197.

TAKE-OUT From the lights at the junction of Highway 16 and Highway 93, go 6.6 km south on Highway 93 to the junction with Highway 93A, which is on the west (right) side. Turn right and follow the road for 15 km to the Moab Lake Road, which is on the west (right) side. If coming from the south, look for the junction with Highway 93A at the turn-off to Athabasca Falls. Turn west (left) onto Highway 93A and go 8.5 km north to the Moab Lake Road on the west (left) side. At the Moab Lake Road junction with Highway 93A, turn west and go 3.9 km to a small gravel pull-off on the left that leads out onto a rock berm. This is the same take-out as used for the run on page 198, since the easiest way to finish the run is by doing the run down to the S-Bend.

PUT-IN Go upstream for 2.5 km to a set of corrals on the south (left) side. Continue past the corrals for 500 m to where the road ends. Grab your boat and carry/drag along the trail. Just past the trailhead the trail forks, the right fork leading to Moab Lake. Stay left and you will reach the river in about 2 km.

CAMPING There is developed camping on Highway 93A at Wabasso Campground, 6 km north of the turn-off to Moab Lake.

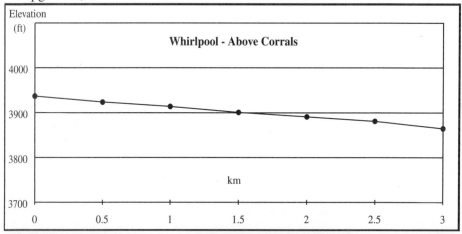

Aaron Darkes in Boulder Drop. Photo: Corina Ramsey.

SUNWAPTA BELOW FALLS TO ATHABASCA

GRADE	CLASS	FLOW	TIME	LENGTH
II–II+	II–III	Most Flows	2–3 hours	11 km (6.8 mi)

Gradient 5.7 m/km (.57%) 30 ft/mi   **Max gradient** 30 m in 3.5 km (.86%) 100 ft in 2.2 mi

Put-in elevation 1310 m 4298 ft   **Take-out elevation** 1248 m 4094 ft

Shuttle 9 km (5.6 mi) one way plus a 2-km carry   **Season** May–August

Maps 83C12   **Gauge** No

Craft Canoes, kayaks and rafts

NOTES You must carry 2 km (1.2 mi) along a trail to reach the put-in.

CHARACTER A medium-volume river flowing over a boulder-bed. The whitewater section below the falls is short, and the scenery is excellent.

FLOW INFORMATION The river is uncontrolled and fed by snowmelt and glacial runoff. Assess the flow at the put-in.

TRAVEL Access to the run and the shuttle are on paved roads.

DESCRIPTION At the put-in, the river is class II–III in a narrow channel. This continues for 500–600 m, the gradient decreasing all the time. The river then mellows, with some class II rapids at bends and channel constrictions. Once you enter the Athabasca there are a few small rapids, and the scenery is outstanding. The Athabasca flows in an open channel, with some islands about 2 km below the confluence, then assumes a single channel until the take-out.

GETTING THERE The run is located south of Jasper, along Highway 93.

TAKE-OUT From the lights at the junction of Highway 16 and Highway 93, go 30 km south on Highway 93 to the junction with Highway 93A, at the turn-off to Athabasca Falls. Continue south on Highway 93 for 15 km to a small picnic site on the west (right) side of the road. If coming from the south, the take-out is on the west (left) side 8.6 km north of the Sunwapta Falls turn-off.

PUT-IN Go 8.6 km south on Highway 93 to the Sunwapta Falls Road, which is on the west (right) side of the highway. Turn right and go for 700 m to the parking lot. Carry your boat down the well-worn footpath along the river right side. There is a series of falls in the canyons, with an easier section in the middle. Be certain to put-in below the lower fall! Scout downstream to be sure.

CAMPING There is developed camping on Highway 93, 5 km south of the take-out, at Honeymoon Lake.

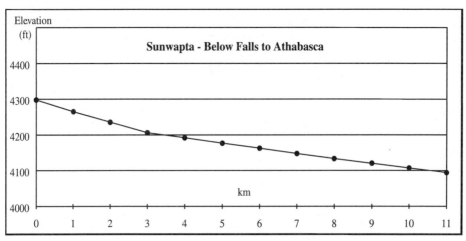

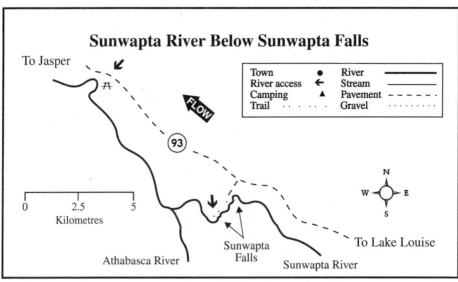

GRADE	CLASS	FLOW	TIME	LENGTH
II	II–II⁺	Low	1–2 hours	8 km (5 mi)
III	II⁺–III⁺	High		

Gradient 9.5 m/km (1%)
50 ft/mi

Max gradient 30 m in 2 km (1.5%)
100 ft in 1.2 mi

Put-in elevation 1468 m
4816 ft

Take-out elevation 1392 m
4567 ft

Shuttle 6.5 km (4 mi) one way

Season May–August

Maps 83C12

Gauge No

Craft Canoes, kayaks and rafts

CHARACTER A short low to medium-volume run that flows over a shallow and continuous riverbed of boulders. There are several constricted drops, with a few calm sections that provide opportunities to relax. The views are outstanding.

FLOW INFORMATION Assess the flow at the take-out. The river is fed by snowmelt and glacial runoff and is uncontrolled.

TRAVEL Access to the run and the shuttle are on paved roads.

DESCRIPTION The river is open and easy for about 1–2 km. After a left turn at a long boulder garden, the rapids are continuous class II. The action alternates with short, easier sections and the rapids build to class II⁺–III in a couple of spots. About halfway down the run, the river flows off a boulder bar on a left turn/right turn combination, in a constricted class II–III drop. Not far below this is a constricted chute where the river drops through a narrow class III channel with huge boulders in it. Near the take-out, the river makes a sharp left turn at a narrow gap, with a rock wall on the right, then flows through a boulder garden. Below this are some islands, where you take the right channel along islands piled with logs, to a sharp left turn at a grassy bank. The take-out has a small eddy on the right that can be difficult to catch, particularly for rafts. Sunwapta Falls is about 1 km below, and though the river is not difficult past the take-out, you have little time to recover from any mishaps, so be sharp!

GETTING THERE The run is located south of Jasper, along Highway 93.

TAKE-OUT From the lights at the junction of Highway 16 and Highway 93, go 54 km south on Highway 93 to the Sunwapta Falls turn-off, on the west (right) side. If coming from the south, the Sunwapta Falls turn-off is on the west (left) side about 48 km north of the Columbia Icefields Centre. From the Sunwapta Falls turn-off, go 400 m south on Highway 93 to a small gravel pull-off on the west (right) side. Walk along the old road for 500 m, across the meadow and through the trees, to the river. Mark the take-out.

PUT-IN Go 5.5 km south on Highway 93 to Bubbling Springs, where there is a small parking area on the east (left) side of the highway. Continue 1 km south to where the road makes a right turn and there is a guardrail on the right side. At the south end of the guardrail a small trail on the right leads into the trees. Park well off the road and follow the trail for 300–400 m to the river.

CAMPING There is developed camping 15 km south of the put-in, at Jonas Creek, or 4 km north of the take-out, at Honeymoon Lake.

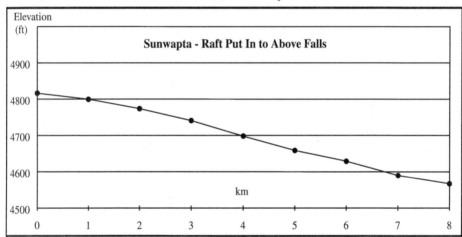

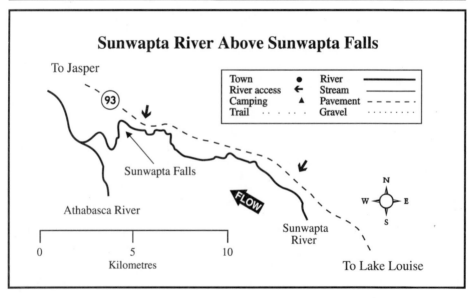

GRADE	CLASS	FLOW	TIME	LENGTH
II	II–IV	Most Flows	2–4 hours	23 km (14 mi)

Gradient 3.8 m/km (.38%) 20 ft/mi

Max gradient 30 m in 4.2 km (.71%) 100 ft in 2.6 mi

Put-in elevation 1555 m 5102 ft

Take-out elevation 1468 m 4816 ft

Shuttle 22 km (13.7 mi) one way

Season May–September

Maps 83C6, 83C5 and 83C12

Gauge Yes

Craft Canoes, kayaks and rafts

CHARACTER A scenic low to medium-volume run on an open riverbed, in spectacular scenery. There are a couple of distinct rapids, but otherwise the river flows in an open channel with a few easy class II rapids at sharp corners and where the river drops off gravel shoals.

FLOW INFORMATION Assess the flow at the put-in. The river is fed by snowmelt and glacial runoff and is uncontrolled.

TRAVEL Access to the run and the shuttle are on paved roads.

DESCRIPTION At the put-in, the river flows in a braided gravel flat, then about 3 km into the run becomes a single channel. There are no major rapids until about 9 km into the run, when you reach a huge rockslide that comes down to the river on the right. Scout the class III⁺–IV drop on the left shore. Below this, the river is mellow again until 800 m downstream of the confluence with Poboktan Creek, which enters on the right. At a turn to the right, watch for a class II–II⁺ rapid consisting of boulders and broken bedrock. Below this point the river has a couple of easy class II rapids at sharp turns and small boulder gardens until the take-out.

GETTING THERE The run is located south of Jasper, along Highway 93.

TAKE-OUT From the lights at the junction of Highway 16 and Highway 93, go 54 km south on Highway 93 to the Sunwapta Falls turn-off. Continue 6 km south to Bubbling Springs, where there is a small parking area on the east (left) side of the highway. If coming from the south, Bubbling Springs is 17 km north of the Jonas Creek Campground. At Bubbling Springs, go 1 km south to where the road makes a right turn and there is a guardrail on the west (right) side. At the south end of the guardrail a small trail on the right leads into the trees. Park well off the highway and follow the trail for 300–400 m to the river. Mark the take-out at the river.

PUT-IN Go 22 km south on Highway 93 to a viewpoint pull-off on the west (right) side of the highway. This is 6 km south of the Jonas Creek Campground.

CAMPING There is developed camping at the Jonas Creek Campground, 6 km north of the put-in.

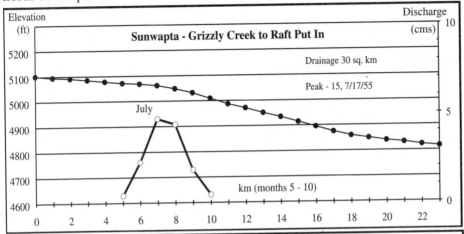

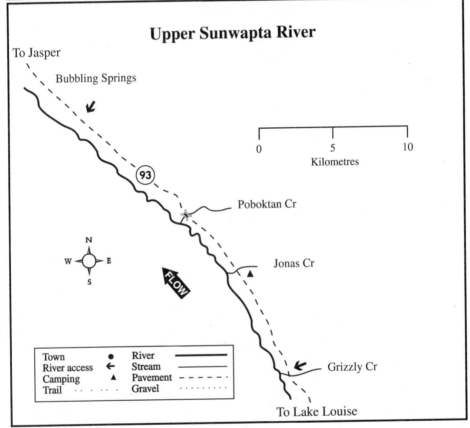

GRADE	CLASS	FLOW	TIME	LENGTH
IV⁺	IV–VI⁺	Medium	3–5 hours	5 km (3 mi)
V	IV⁺–VI⁺	High		

Gradient   37 m/km (3.7%)
          198 ft/mi

Max gradient   30 m in .6 km (5%)
              100 ft in .37 mi

Put-in elevation   1720 m
               5643 ft

Take-out elevation   1533 m
                 5029 ft

Shuttle   A 5-km (3.1-mi) carry

Season   May–August

Maps   83C6

Gauge   No

Craft   Kayaks

NOTES   You must carry 5 km (3.1 mi) up the trail to the put-in, and you will probably portage more than once on the way back down!

CHARACTER   A small-volume creek run in a steep canyon, with several falls and numerous tight drops in a narrow channel filled with broken boulders.

FLOW INFORMATION   Assess the flow at the take-out. The creek is fed by snowmelt and glacial runoff and is uncontrolled.

TRAVEL   Access to the run is on paved roads.

DESCRIPTION   Above the canyon, the creek tears along on a steep and open gravel-bed. This changes abruptly at Hell Fire, a class V⁺–VI⁺ fall, where the creek drops 1–2 m into a narrow chute, then smashes off the rock wall on the left and drops 4–6 m into a pool. About 50 m below Hell Fire, the creek drops out of the pool, over a 1-m ledge, then narrows and accelerates. Immediately below is the class V–V⁺ Pitfall, where the creek plunges 3–5 m into a nasty hole. About 20 m below this, the creek drops 1–2 m through a narrow slot in the bedrock, then opens up. The creek continues over broken bedrock and huge boulders in a class IV–V barrage of steep drops. This continues for about 1 km, then the creek makes a right turn and enters a constricted canyon. The canyon ends in a steep class V⁺–VI chute that drops 4–6 m onto a shallow landing. This can be portaged on the right from above the right turn. Downstream, the creek has more steep drops in the tight, low-walled canyon, then eases onto a gravel-bed and flows the last 1–2 km in gravel-lined channels.

GETTING THERE   The run is located south of Jasper, off Highway 93.

TAKE-OUT   From the lights at the junction of Highway 16 and Highway 93, go 30 km south on Highway 93 to the junction with Highway 93A, at the turn-off

Primitive Man Goes Kayaking

By the mid-1980's, we had paddled all the regular runs and most of the remote rivers in the area. That left us searching for those last, hard-to-get-to runs, the ones most people would never bother with. But we were driven, and pushing the limits at every opportunity. After a lengthy map search, I came up with a run on Poboktan Creek, above Highway 93. At the time, we paddled big-volume composite kayaks on stuff we were not familiar with, in order to give ourselves a safety margin (psychological or otherwise). But those boats were incredibly heavy and didn't stand up to dragging all that well. Ifor and I figured we needed some sort of boat buggy for the haul to the put-in. Several mental gymnastics sessions led to a design; a visit to the local bike shop, then the welder, consolidated our schemes into reality.

The rig was pretty simple: two small bike wheels, with a single steel bar bolted to the axles, connecting the two wheels. At the trailhead we were really excited! This wouldn't be another of those incredible boat-wrestling escapades that left us exhausted at the put-in! We strapped our boats together and secured them to the buggy, then gave it a test run around the parking lot to be sure the unit actually worked. It was almost like a regression to a time when wheels were unknown, and we had just assembled a brand new contraption. We couldn't help standing around, congratulating ourselves.

About 20 minutes up the trail, we began to have doubts. The trail was rutted and had boulders alongside that bounced the boats back and forth, applying forces we had not planned for. Not only that, it seemed to require a lot of effort to manipulate the rig over the boulders and roots. Too often we found ourselves lifting the whole rig up and over rocks. The trail was so narrow that one wheel rode in the rut with the other bouncing along outside it, which canted the whole rig on its side. It was apparent that there were some serious flaws in our proudly designed creation!

With copious amounts of care and attention we babied that rig up hills, through ruts and over boulders. We took turns stepping into the traces, to haul the heavy rig up the trail. We thought one guy should be able to tow the rig while the other rested. However, the "resting" guy would usually end up pushing and lifting on the rear of the rig. Despite our plans, we were both sweating profusely and getting rather tired. At the end of one of the shifts, the accumulated flexing reached the critical point, and with a sudden snap the rig self-destructed. One wheel shot off into the trees, while the other remained strapped to the boats and twisted up in the air as the whole thing rolled over. We held a brief ceremony, then heaved the debris into the bush and carried our boats toward the sound of the first fall, which was nearby. We had just managed to reach the put-in. The result of our hours of scheming, engineering and welding lay in a heap in the trees. A day or so later I returned, conscience-driven, to recover the pieces and deposit them in the dump!

to Athabasca Falls. From the junction with 93A, continue south on Highway 93 for 41 km to the bridge on Poboktan Creek. Just south of the bridge is a trailhead parking lot on the east (left) side. If coming from the south, look for the Jonas Creek campground 26 km north of the Columbia Icefields Centre. The bridge is 5.4 km north of the campground, and the trailhead is on the east (right) side just before you reach the bridge.

PUT-IN Follow the trail from the east end of the parking lot through the trees, then across the creek and upstream along the river right bank. The trail is very rutted from the horse traffic. The trail leaves the creek and you will travel through the heavy forest up some switchbacks. Continue upstream to the open gravel flats. If you wish to avoid hiking any higher than required, listen for the sound of the fall at the start of the canyon and head right, away from the trail at that point. Above the canyon the creek is open and easier.

CAMPING There is developed camping 5 km south of the take-out, at Jonas Creek Campground.

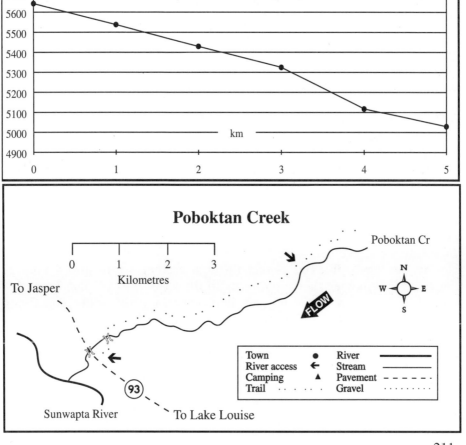

GRADE	CLASS	FLOW	TIME	LENGTH
V	V–VI⁺	Most Flows	2–3 hours	1.5 km (.9 mi)

Gradient   53 m/km (5.3%)   **Max gradient** 30 m in .5 km (6%)
281 ft/mi   100 ft in .3 mi

Put-in elevation   1640 m   **Take-out elevation**   1560 m
5380 ft   5118 ft

Shuttle   A 1.5-km (.9-mi) carry   **Season**   May–August

Maps   83C6   **Gauge**   No

Craft   Kayaks

NOTES You must carry 1.5 km (.9 mi) up the steep trail to the put-in, and portage at least once during the descent.

CHARACTER A small-volume plummet off a series of waterfalls in a very tight canyon. There is little attraction other than photographs, adrenaline and airtime. Climbing skills come in handy for getting around on the steep walls.

FLOW INFORMATION Assess the flow at the take-out. The creek is fed by snowmelt and glacial runoff and is uncontrolled.

TRAVEL Access to the run is on paved roads.

DESCRIPTION The canyon starts with The Big One, a class VI–VI⁺ fall that tears out of a narrow gorge and shoots into space, landing 15–19 m below in a short pool. Below The Big One, the creek flows through boulder debris rapids and drops off a class VI two-tiered cascade. Then it runs in the open canyon to the brink of the class V–V⁺ Lumbarsis, a 10–12-m vertical fall into a boiling pool. With any error here, the hapless victim flushes rapidly toward the severely undercut left wall. At the end of a short pool, the creek drops into a tight slot, then plunges 2–4 m through a steep chute into a vicious recirculation. Another short pool leads to the class V–V⁺ Canon Fodder, a steep drop off a submerged log jam into a narrow gorge with water flying about in the tight slot. Below this, the creek flows in a tight canyon with easier water. You then reach Stutter Speed, a sharp turn to the left that drops 1–2 m into a narrow slot then ricochets off the left wall and drops another 2–4 m into the pool. The canyon below this point is deep, with vertical or overhung walls, but little current. The canyon then opens up and runs for about 150 m to just above Hat Trick, a series of three wild drops. The rapid starts with a 2–3-m drop off a rock ledge into a crazy recirculation, tears into a narrow slot and

Stuart Smith in Lumbarsis, in the Beauty Creek canyon. Photo: Brock Wilson.

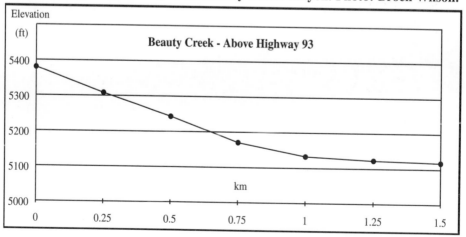

finally careens off the rock wall on the left into an undercut crack. Higher flows and hot moves are the only way through this class V+ drop. Below Hat Trick, the river drops off a 9–11-m fall into a narrow slot, then squeezes into a log-jammed crack, which means portage time. Carry down to below the gorge, then bounce and grind your way back to the parking lot. All the drops between Lumbarsis and Hat Trick have been run, but it takes a good day and good flows to pull it off.

GETTING THERE The run is located south of Jasper, along Highway 93.

TAKE-OUT From the lights at the junction of Highway 16 and Highway 93, go 30 km south on Highway 93 to the junction with Highway 93A, at the turn-off to Athabasca Falls. From the junction with 93A, continue south on Highway 93 for 56 km to the Beauty Creek Hostel. Go another 2 km south to a small gravel pull-off on the east (left) side of the road. If coming from the south, watch for the trailhead pull-off on the east (right) side 15 km north of the Columbia Icefields Centre.

PUT-IN Follow the trail east along the gravel berm, then to the right through the trees and onto the old highway where you go right. When you reach the creek, turn left and follow the rooted trail upstream along the river right shore. Continue upstream until fear or good judgement prompts you to stop. Most paddlers will put in near Lumbarsis (see photo) and paddle only a couple of drops.

CAMPING There is developed camping 11 km north of the trailhead at Jonas Creek Campground.

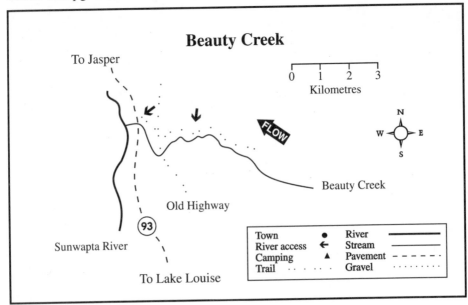

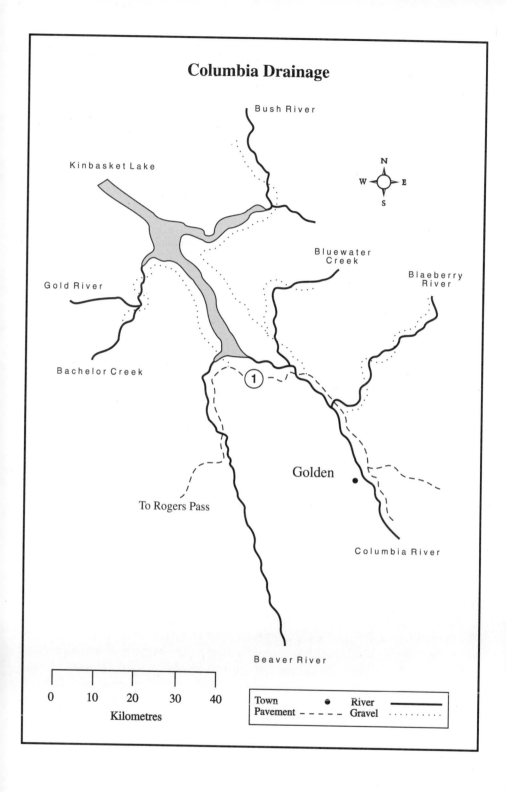

Columbia Drainage

Bush River

Kinbasket Lake

Bluewater
Creek

Blaeberry
River

Gold River

Bachelor Creek

1

Golden

To Rogers Pass

Columbia River

Beaver River

| 0 | 10 | 20 | 30 | 40 |

Kilometres

Town ● River ──────
Pavement ─ ─ ─ ─ Gravel ··········

GRADE	CLASS	FLOW	TIME	LENGTH
III–IV	III-VI	Medium	1–2 hours	4.5 km (2.8 mi)
IV–V	IV-VI⁺	High		

Gradient   26 m/km (2.6%)   **Max gradient**   30 m in .9 km (3.3%)
134 ft/mi   100 ft in .56 mi

Put-in elevation   872 m   **Take-out elevation**   757 m
2860 ft   2485 ft

Shuttle   6 km (3.7 mi) one way   **Season**   May–August

Maps   82N12   **Gauge**   Yes

Craft   Kayaks and canoes

CHARACTER A small-volume run that cuts through bedrock canyons with waterfalls and constricted drops in tight quarters.

FLOW INFORMATION The river is uncontrolled and fed by snowmelt and glacial runoff. Assess the flow at the take-out.

TRAVEL Access to the run and the shuttle are on gravel roads.

DESCRIPTION The run begins in an open gravel-bed with few rapids in the first 1–2 km. You then encounter class II rapids and small ledges before reaching Shooting Star, a constricted class V chute through bedrock, with a sneak route on the right. Below this is 100 m of class IV–IV⁺ as the river cuts into the bedrock. Not far below is calmer water at a tight, overhung canyon that ends in a blind right turn. Around the corner you will find The Jam. This is a class IV–IV⁺ boulder garden of immense stones, with a sharp right turn, then a sharp left turn. Below The Jam, the canyon opens up to a set of short pools above a picket fence of boulders. A 150-m stretch of class IV⁺–V leads to the brink of a class VI–VI⁺ waterfall in the narrow gorge. Get out on the right shore below The Jam and scramble up the steep downsloping rock ledges to an old logging road that runs along the top of the canyon. Carry along the old road for about 200 m, then bear left through an old clear-cut. Descend 60 m, in a steep bush thrash, to reach the river. The river is easy until just below a gauging station, where a rock outcrop from the left forces the river into The Slot, a narrow 3–4-m, class VI–VI⁺ waterfall on the right. Below The Slot, the river is easy until you reach the take-out.

GETTING THERE The run is located north of Golden, off Highway 1, along the West Columbia Forest Service Road.

TAKE-OUT If coming from Golden, go to the junction of Highway 1 and Highway 95. Proceed 47 km north on Highway 1 to the Kinbasket Lake Lodge turn-off (the West Columbia Forest Service Road), which is on the north (right) side of the highway.

If coming from Rogers Pass, go 13 km east on Highway 1 to the bridge over the Beaver River. Continue east for 18 km to the Kinbasket Lake Lodge turn-off (the West Columbia Forest Service Road), which is on the north (left) side of the highway.

At the junction of Highway 1 and the West Columbia Forest Service Road, turn north. Follow the West Columbia Forest Service Road for 5 km, down the steep switchbacks to the bridge over an arm of the lake. From there, proceed north for 35 km to the bridge at the take-out. The bridge is 1 km past the junction of Black Road, which is on the west (left) side of the road.

PUT-IN Return 1 km south along the West Columbia Forest Service Road to Black Road. Turn west (right) and follow the road for 5 km to the bridge.

CAMPING There is undeveloped camping at the take-out.

Ian Taylor above the lower canyon.

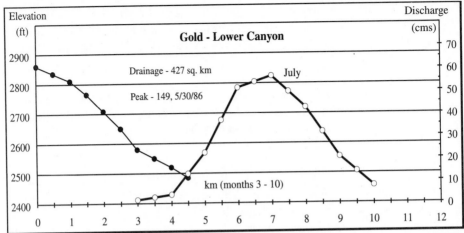

Gold - Lower Canyon

Drainage - 427 sq. km

Peak - 149, 5/30/86

July

km (months 3 - 10)

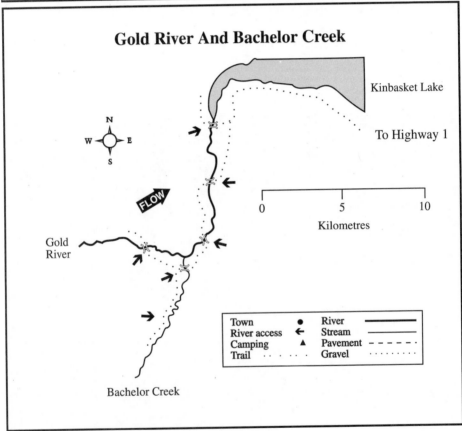

Gold River And Bachelor Creek

Kinbasket Lake

To Highway 1

FLOW

Gold
River

Bachelor Creek

Town	●	River	———
River access	←	Stream	——
Camping	▲	Pavement	– – –
Trail	· · · ·	Gravel	· · · · · ·

GRADE	CLASS	FLOW	TIME	LENGTH
II⁺	II⁺–IV	Low	1 hour	3 km (1.9 mi)
III⁺	III–IV⁺	High		

Gradient   22 m/km (2.2%)   **Max gradient** 30 m in 1.2 km (2.5%)
              115 ft/mi   100 ft in .75 mi

Put-in elevation   937 m   **Take-out elevation**   872 m
                      3075 ft   2860 ft

Shuttle   3 km (1.9 mi) one way   **Season**   May–August

Maps   82N12   **Gauge**   Yes

Craft   Canoes, kayaks and small rafts

CHARACTER A short, small-volume run in a remote valley with rapids created by boulders and bedrock outcrops.

FLOW INFORMATION The river is uncontrolled and fed by snowmelt and glacial runoff. Assess the flow at the take-out.

TRAVEL Access to the run and the shuttle are on gravel roads.

DESCRIPTION The run begins as a 1-km section of easy whitewater, with a couple of small class II–II⁺ rapids. You then reach a creek, which enters from the right. Below this, a rock outcrop produces a constricted class IV⁺ rapid, then the river eases to class III with a couple of class III⁺ rapids. Finally, a long class II–III rapid ends near the take-out. This run can be combined with the lower portion of the upper run to get the best section of easier whitewater on the river (see the run on page 221 for details).

GETTING THERE The run is located north of Golden, off Highway 1, along the West Columbia Forest Service Road. See the map on page 218.

TAKE-OUT If coming from Golden, go to the junction of Highway 1 and Highway 95. Proceed 47 km north on Highway 1 to the Kinbasket Lake Lodge turn-off (the West Columbia Forest Service Road), which is on the north (right) side of the highway.

If coming from Rogers Pass, go 13 km east on Highway 1 to the bridge over the Beaver River. Continue east for 18 km to the Kinbasket Lake Lodge turn-off (the West Columbia Forest Service Road), which is on the north (left) side of the highway.

At the junction of Highway 1 and the West Columbia Forest Service Road, turn north. Follow the West Columbia Forest Service Road for 5 km, down the steep switchbacks, to a bridge over an arm of the lake. From there, proceed north for 34 km to the Black Road, which is on the west (left) side of the road. Turn left and follow the road for 5 km to a bridge.

PUT-IN   Go upstream for another 3 km to the put-in bridge.

CAMPING   There is undeveloped camping along the road to the put-in.

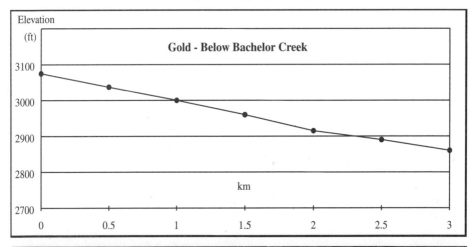

Paddling in British Columbia means logs—anytime and anywhere.

GRADE	CLASS	FLOW	TIME	LENGTH
IV+	III–V+	Low	2 hours	5 km (3 mi)
V	III–VI	Medium		

Gradient 26 m/km (2.6%)
137 ft/mi

Max gradient 30 m in .6 km (5%)
100 ft in .37 mi

Put-in elevation 1067 m
3500 ft

Take-out elevation 937 m
3075 ft

Shuttle 5 km (3 mi) one way

Season May–August

Maps 82N12

Gauge Yes

Craft Kayaks and canoes

CHARACTER A short run on a small-volume river that tears over a steep and convoluted boulder-bed. There is difficult whitewater right from the start.

FLOW INFORMATION The river is uncontrolled and fed by snowmelt and glacial runoff. Assess the flow at the put-in, where the river is constricted.

TRAVEL Access to the run and the shuttle are on gravel roads.

DESCRIPTION The run begins directly below the bridge, with class IV–IV+ rapids in a maze of boulders and small ledges. The river turns to the right and enters 1–1.5 km of class V–V+ rapids in a boulder-choked channel, where the river flows through a bedrock canyon. A short section of class III leads to a small creek entering from river right. This is just above a class IV+–V rapid that is filled with logs. Below this the gradient eases and the river flows through a class II–II+ section to a gauge station. Downstream of the confluence with Bachelor Creek, which enters from the right, the river spreads out in much easier rapids. A kilometre-long section of easy water leads to a sharp left turn, followed closely by a sharp right turn. This starts a constricted class III–III+ set of rapids which ends just above the take-out bridge.

GETTING THERE The run is located north of Golden, off Highway 1, along the West Columbia Forest Service Road. See the map on page 218.

TAKE-OUT If coming from Golden, go to the junction of Highway 1 and Highway 95. Proceed 47 km north on Highway 1 to the Kinbasket Lake Lodge turn-off (the West Columbia Forest Service Road), which is on the north (right) side of the highway. If coming from Rogers Pass, go 13 km east on Highway 1 to the bridge over the Beaver River. Continue east for 18 km to the Kinbasket Lake Lodge turn-off (the West Columbia Forest Service Road), which is on the north (left) side of the highway.

At the Highway 1/West Columbia Forest Service Road junction, turn north. Follow the West Columbia Forest Service Road for 5 km to the bridge over an arm of the lake. From there, go north for 34 km to the Black Road, which is on the west (left) side. Turn left and follow the road for 5 km to a bridge, then continue upstream for another 3 km to the take-out bridge.

PUT-IN Go upstream for 2.5 km to a bridge on Bachelor Creek, then continue just past the bridge to a fork. Stay right and follow the road for 2.5 km to a bridge. If you wish to avoid the difficult whitewater in the upper canyon, you can get in on the right, 300 m past the Bachelor Creek bridge.

CAMPING There is undeveloped camping along the road to the put-in.

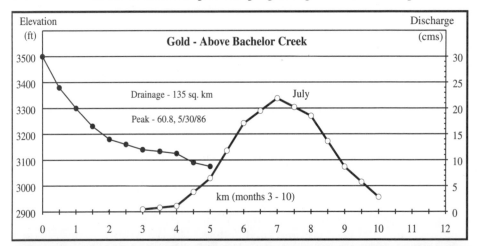

Looking downstream from just below the put-in at low flows.

GRADE	CLASS	FLOW	TIME	LENGTH
V	IV–V+	Low	1–2 hours	4.5 km (2.8 mi)
V+	IV–V+	Medium		

Gradient   49 m/km (4.9%)
              257 ft/mi

Max gradient   30 m in .5 km (6%)
                   100 ft in .31 mi

Put-in elevation   1189 m
                       3900 ft

Take-out elevation   969 m
                         3180 ft

Shuttle   5 km (3 mi) one way

Season   May–August

Maps   82N12

Gauge   No

Craft   Kayaks and canoes

CHARACTER   An intense small-volume run that pounds through a low-walled bedrock canyon, with numerous class V and V+ drops. Any portaging requires desperate bush thrashing in the dense undergrowth.

FLOW INFORMATION   The creek is uncontrolled and fed by snowmelt and glacial runoff. Check the flow at the put-in as follows: on the downstream side of the river right bridge support are four timbers lying perpendicular to the shoreline. If the lower edge of the fourth timber from the top is just in the water, the creek is medium to low. If the top of that timber is covered, the creek is medium. At medium to high flows the creek is a very serious outing.

TRAVEL   Access to the run and the shuttle are on gravel roads.

DESCRIPTION   The run begins quietly with a short, easy section that quickly becomes class II+–III. You then reach a sharp right turn followed by a sharp left turn, where the creek drops into Bachelor Party, a tight canyon that is a grade V torrent. The canyon begins with three back-to-back, class V drops that lead to yet another class V drop. This is immediately followed by Hoover, a narrow class V+ chute that plunges into a vicious recirculation. The bedrock closes in just above Hoover and scouting is a desperate affair. You can portage on the river left bank by scrambling up just above Hoover, then thrashing through the undergrowth to a gully that leads down to a small ledge and seal-launch below Hoover. The canyon is then more open class IV, but still contains plenty of class V–V+ boulder-choked mazes. Near the end of the run, the creek spreads out and cascades down a steep boulderfield, which is visible from the road. The best stuff cannot be seen from the road and you should be prepared to paddle the tough stuff or face insane portages!

GETTING THERE The run is located north of Golden, off Highway 1, along the West Columbia Forest Service Road. See the map on page 218.

TAKE-OUT If coming from Golden, go to the junction of Highway 1 and Highway 95. Proceed 47 km north on Highway 1 to the Kinbasket Lake Lodge turn-off (the West Columbia Forest Service Road), which is on the north (right) side of the highway.

If coming from Rogers Pass, go 13 km east on Highway 1 to the bridge over the Beaver River. Continue east for 18 km to the Kinbasket Lake Lodge turn-off (the West Columbia Forest Service Road), which is on the north (left) side of the highway.

At the junction of Highway 1 and the West Columbia Forest Service Road, turn north. Follow the West Columbia Forest Service Road for 5 km, down the steep switchbacks to the bridge over an arm of the lake. From there, proceed north for 34 km to the Black Road, which is on the west (left) side of the road. Turn left and follow the road for 5 km to a bridge, then in another 3 km, a second bridge. Continue for 2.5 km to the bridge over Bachelor Creek.

PUT-IN Go across the bridge to a fork. Stay left and go 4.5 km upstream to a narrow bush-lined track that leads 400 m down to an old bridge. The track is solid, but you need high clearance and sharp eyes to avoid the numerous rocks.

CAMPING There is undeveloped camping at the take-out or at the put-in.

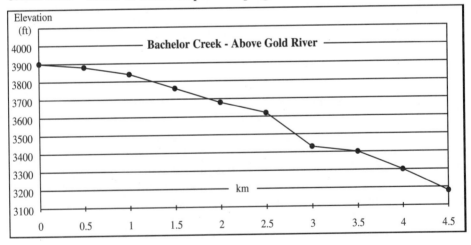

BUSH — BRIDGE TO VALENCIENNES RIVER

GRADE	CLASS	FLOW	TIME	LENGTH
I⁺	I⁺–II	Low	1–2 hours	6 km (3.7 mi)
II	I⁺–II⁺	High		

Gradient 8.1 m/km (.81%)
43 ft/mi

Max gradient 30 m in 2 km (1.5%)
100 ft in 1.2 mi

Put-in elevation 811 m
2660 ft

Take-out elevation 762 m
2500 ft

Shuttle 5.3 km (3.5 mi) one way

Season May–August

Maps 82N14

Gauge No

Craft Canoes, kayaks and rafts

CHARACTER A short run on a medium-volume river with great scenery, and a short, narrow canyon. There are few rapids except at high flows.

FLOW INFORMATION The river is uncontrolled and fed by snowmelt and glacial runoff. Check the flow at the take-out. When Kinbasket Lake is full, it backs up above the take-out and you have to check the water level at the put-in.

TRAVEL Access to the run and the shuttle are on gravel roads.

DESCRIPTION The river runs in an open gravel-bed at the put-in, with some braiding below. Enjoy the scenery and the great views. The river is open, with a few small sets of waves in the often braided channel. Watch for Surprise Canyon, about three-quarters of the way down the run; it is the only real action on the run. Here the river makes a sharp right turn into a narrow canyon at a bedrock outcrop. At most flows you can paddle part of the way into the canyon to see the exit, before committing to the whole thing. If this is not feasible, it is a steep climb on the right shore to look down into the canyon. Below this the river opens up again with a few sets of small waves before you reach the take-out.

GETTING THERE The run is located north of Golden, off Highway 1, along the Bush River Forest Service Road.

TAKE-OUT At the junction of Highway 1 and Highway 95 in Golden, proceed 25 km north on Highway 1 to Donald Road, which is on the north (right) side of the highway. If coming from Rogers Pass, watch for Donald Road on the north (left) side, 800 m east of the Highway 1 bridge over the Columbia.

At the junction of Highway 1 and Donald Road, turn north and follow the road for 800 m to a junction with a paved road on the right. Stay left, then go for 700 m to a bridge on Waitabit Creek. Follow the Bush River Forest Service Road along Kinbasket Lake for 61 km to a junction with the Bush Road North on the left. Continue straight, 6.3 km past the junction, to a bridge over the Valenciennes River at the confluence with the Bush River.

PUT-IN Continue 4.9 km upstream along the Bush River to a fork. Stay left and in 700 m you reach the put-in bridge.

CAMPING There is developed camping at a site on the Valenciennes River near the take-out, or undeveloped camping on the road to the put-in.

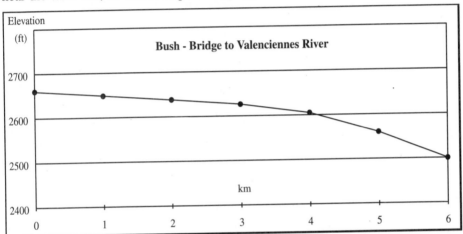

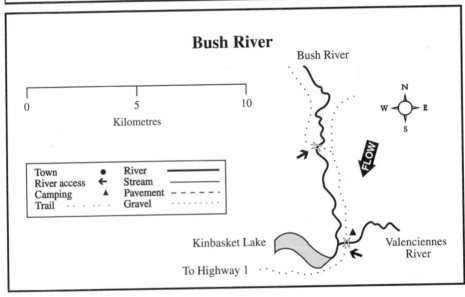

GRADE	CLASS	FLOW	TIME	LENGTH
II–III	III–VI	Most Flows	1 hour	6 km (3.7 mi)

Gradient   12 m/km (1.2%)   **Max gradient** 30 m in 2.5 km (1.2%)
65 ft/mi   100 ft in 1.6 mi

Put-in elevation   805 m   **Take-out elevation**   731 m
2640 ft   2399 ft

Shuttle   16 km (10 mi) one way   **Season**   May–August

Maps   82N6 and 82N11   **Gauge**   Yes

Craft   Canoes, kayaks and rafts

NOTES   When Kinbasket Lake is low, you may encounter other rapids below the Gnarler, since the lake covers an underwater canyon. Scout ahead to be sure!

CHARACTER   A short run on a medium-volume river that flows through an open valley in the top part, then a short canyon at the bottom.

FLOW INFORMATION   The river is uncontrolled and fed by snowmelt and glacial runoff. Call Environment Canada's Water Survey Branch for current flow. Use the flow at the mouth, where low flow is 30 to 50 cms and high flow is 160 to 200 cms.

TRAVEL   Access to the run and the shuttle are on gravel roads.

DESCRIPTION   The river runs in an open channel for the first 2–3 km until you encounter small rapids above the railroad bridge. Below the bridge are a couple of class II–II⁺ rapids leading to a diagonal ledge extending off the river left side. The river is forced through a narrow class III–IV slot into a short pool. Then 150 m of class III leads to the Gnarler, a class V–VI constricted chute that drops 2–5 m. Scout the drop from the right. Below this the river enters Kinbasket Lake, then passes through the Gateway, a narrow slot in a rock fin. Paddle the remaining 1.5 km across the lake.

GETTING THERE   The run is located west of Golden, off Highway 1.

TAKE-OUT   If coming from Golden, go to the junction of Highway 1 and Highway 95. Proceed 47 km north on Highway 1 to the Kinbasket Lake Lodge turn-off (the West Columbia Forest Service Road), which is on the north (right) side of the highway. If coming from Rogers Pass, go 13 km east on Highway 1 to the bridge over the Beaver River. Continue east for 18 km to the Kinbasket Lake Lodge turn-off (the West Columbia Forest Service Road), which is on the north (left) side of the highway.

Railroad Blues

It was labelled "Beaver Canyon" and there was also a named rapid on the map, so I figured that they must be some sort of significant features. Perhaps I was getting older, a little wiser, or maybe I just recalled the last time I got burned by jumping blindly onto an unknown river with a distinct canyon on the map. Whatever the reason, I decided to scout the canyon before committing to the run. I'm not the lazy type, but when I looked at the map and saw the railroad running along the canyon, I figured the smart thing to do was to grab my motorcycle, rip up the tracks real quick-like, survey the whitewater and zip back out. No one would be the wiser!

I had just finished unloading my bike, when a train went tearing by. That was perfect, since I figured as soon as the train was gone, I could head out assured there wouldn't be any trains for some time. When the last car was out of sight, I fired up my cycle and started down the gravel along the tracks. When the tracks reached a rock face on the left, everything got a bit narrower, and eventually I had to ride alongside the track. It was pretty rough, bouncing over all those railroad ties. Every once in a while I would nearly pile it, as the front wheel rubbed the rail, while I was busy gawking around trying to see the river.

When I reached a long trestle across a gully, the very obvious, and very first, thing to cross my mind was, what would happen if I encountered a train while on the trestle. I hesitated a moment, then looked over my shoulder. All clear behind, and all clear ahead. So I jumped the bike over one track, into the space between the two rails and hit the throttle. It was one of those wildly exhilarating moments when you do something not only devious, but a little foolish.

That's how I felt that day. That is, until I saw that locomotive come smoking around the corner just ahead. Then everything was fear, a massive wave of the stuff. I had the throttle twisted wide open, but it was clear I wasn't going to make it. Going back was out, since my tiny motor would never outrace that throbbing diesel, with a full head of steam. I was about to panic, when I spotted it. The tiny little balcony, with the flimsy little railing, hanging out over the void just ahead. The engineer was hard on the horn, as if I might not realize I was about to be flattened by a screaming locomotive! I jumped off the bike and headed straight for that tiny little balcony. In a grunting heave, I threw my bike over the rail and onto that platform, then scrambled madly to the edge. I was cowering there with mostly air under my butt, praying that tiny little platform would hold. The train howled past, shaking the trestle with the violent thunder of the throbbing engines. The wind that accompanied the train swept over me, and the noise was deafening as the cars screamed by less than a metre away. I was trembling uncontrollably, helpless on that micro ledge. By the time the last car cleared the trestle, I could barely function. Next time I'll be sure to walk. The exercise will be much easier on my heart!

Turn north and follow the West Columbia Forest Service Road for 5 km, down a steep set of switchbacks to a bridge over the arm of the lake.

PUT-IN Return to Highway 1, turn right and go west for 6.3 km to the top of a hill, where the highway makes a left turn. Watch for the unlabelled gravel road on the west (right) side of the highway. Follow the winding road downhill for 4.3 km to the bridge over the river.

CAMPING There is developed camping near the take-out.

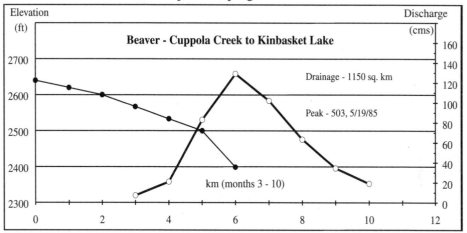

Beaver - Cuppola Creek to Kinbasket Lake

Drainage - 1150 sq. km

Peak - 503, 5/19/85

km (months 3 - 10)

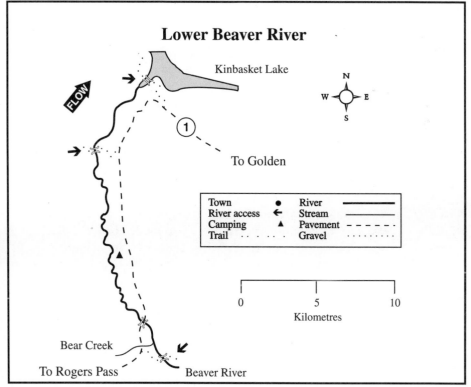

Lower Beaver River

BEAVER   BEAR CREEK TO CUPPOLA CREEK

GRADE	CLASS	FLOW	TIME	LENGTH
I⁺	II	Most Flows	3–5 hours	20 km (12 mi)

Gradient   2.4 m/km (.24%)   **Max gradient** 30 m in 12 km (.25%)
13 ft/mi   100 ft in 7.5 mi

Put-in elevation   853 m   **Take-out elevation**   805 m
2800 ft   2640 ft

Shuttle   19 km (11.7 mi) one way   **Season**   May–September

Maps   82N6   **Gauge**   Yes

Craft   Canoes, kayaks and rafts

CHARACTER A scenic medium-volume run that flows through an open valley, with few whitewater features. Watch for sweepers and log jams.

FLOW INFORMATION The river is uncontrolled and fed by snowmelt and glacial runoff. Call Environment Canada's Water Survey Branch for current flow. Use the flow at the mouth, where low flow is 30 to 50 cms and high flow is 160 to 200 cms.

TRAVEL Access to the run and the shuttle are on paved roads.

DESCRIPTION At the put-in the river flows in a single channel, over an open gravel-bed. This continues for a few kilometres until you encounter islands in the meandering channel. The river then passes through a marshy section, with dense growth along the shores. Enjoy the scenery and quiet, though the highway is never more than 1–2 km from the river. Near the take-out the river flows swiftly in a single channel again.

GETTING THERE The run is located near Rogers Pass, off Highway 1. See the map on page 229.

TAKE-OUT If coming from Golden, go to the junction of Highway 1 and Highway 95. Proceed 47 km north on Highway 1 to the Kinbasket Lake Lodge turn-off (the West Columbia Forest Service Road), which is on the north (right) side of the highway. Continue west for 6.3 km to the top of a hill, where the highway makes a left turn. Watch for the unlabelled gravel road on the west (right) side of the highway. If coming from Rogers Pass, go 13 km east on Highway 1 to the bridge over the Beaver River. Continue east for 11.5 km to the top of a hill, where the highway turns right. Watch for the unlabelled gravel road on the west (left) side of the highway. At the gravel road, turn west and follow the winding road 4.3 km to the bridge over the river.

PUT-IN Return to Highway 1, turn right and go 11.5 km to the highway bridge. Continue 2 km past the bridge and watch for the Beaver Valley Road on the south (left) side. Turn left and follow the road for 1 km to the put-in.

CAMPING There is camping at the Beaver Valley Campground, which is 1.2 km east of the Glacier National Park Gate.

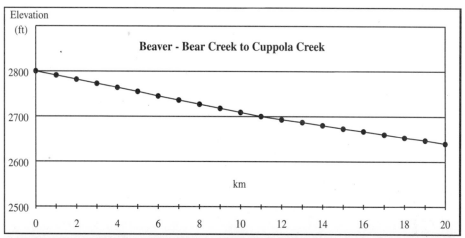

Ty Trand experiencing the "British Columbia Jungle" up close and in person.

GRADE	CLASS	FLOW	TIME	LENGTH
III–III+	II+–V+	Low	2–3 days	36 km (22 mi)
III+–IV	III–VI	Medium		

Gradient 12.1 m/km (1.2%)
64 ft/mi

Max gradient 30 m in 1 km (3%)
100 ft in .62 mi

Put-in elevation 1311 m
4300 ft

Take-out elevation 876 m
2875 ft

Shuttle 270 km (168 mi) one way

Season June–September

Maps 82N3 and 82N6

Gauge Yes

Craft Canoes and kayaks

NOTES There is a 2-km (1.2-mi) carry over the pass to the Beaver valley, and a 2-km (1.2-mi) carry to the river. The trail to the pass is well-defined.

CHARACTER A remote run on a small to medium-volume river flowing through excellent scenery. The run has good sections of boulder-garden rapids and a very difficult canyon near the end of the run. There are an incredible number of portages around the trees and log jams in the river.

FLOW INFORMATION The river is uncontrolled and fed by snowmelt and glacial runoff. Call Environment Canada's Water Survey Branch and use the reading at the mouth. Low flow is 30 to 50 cms and high flow is 160 to 200 cms. You begin with almost none of the flow and end the run with nearly all of it.

TRAVEL Much of the shuttle is on paved roads.

DESCRIPTION When you reach the river, the water flows in a small trickle. Drag or carry downstream along the river for about 1–2 km, until the volume is such that paddling is feasible. In this section the river is full of logs and log jams and the portages are numerous. As you descend, the volume is increased by the many small side creeks tumbling off the steep valley walls. About 5 to 6 km below the pass, the river begins to drop into a continuous boulder-bed of class III rapids. This continues for much of the run, with a couple of harder drops, and a few calmer sections where the river flows through meadows. Logs are a problem for most of the run. About 8 km from the end of the run, the gradient increases and the river flows into a steep-sided valley, then a canyon. The rapids increase in difficulty, to class IV with several class V–VI drops. Many of the rapids in the canyon are clogged with logs, and some of the portages border on desperate. You could portage the entire canyon on river right, where a trail parallels the river. Not far below Grizzly Creek, the river flows in a more open valley, with easier rapids until you reach the take-out.

232

GETTING THERE The run is located between Golden and Rogers Pass.

TAKE-OUT If coming from Golden, go to the junction of Highway 1 and Highway 95. Proceed west on Highway 1 until you reach the Glacier National Park gate. Continue past the park gate until you reach a bridge on the Beaver River. Go 2 km further, to a small gravel road on the south (left) side of the highway (labelled Beaver Valley Road). If coming from Rogers Pass, go east on Highway 1 until you exit the final snowshed across the road. Watch for the Beaver Valley Road on the south (right) side of the highway in 4.9 km. If you miss the road on the way down the hill and end up at the bridge, turn around and go 2 km west to the gravel road. At the junction of Highway 1 and the Beaver Road, turn south and follow the road for 1 km to a bridge. Park well off the road.

PUT-IN Go west on Highway 1 to Revelstoke, then south on Highway 23 until you reach the ferry at Shelter Bay. Once across the ferry, go south on Highway 23 until you reach the junction with Highway 31. Turn north (left) and follow the gravel road, via Trout Lake, to the small town of Cooper Creek, just north of Lardeau Provincial Park. Just south of Cooper Creek, turn east (left) and cross the Duncan River. Continue to the junction with the Duncan Forest Service Road, which is on the north (left) side. Turn left and follow the gravel road to its end.

CAMPING There is undeveloped camping along the river, though you must get an overnight permit from Glacier National Park for back-country camping.

One of the boulder-garden rapids below Beaver Glacier.

233

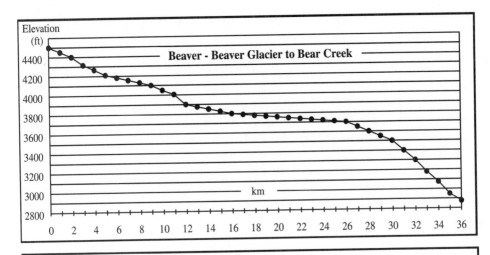

Beaver - Beaver Glacier to Bear Creek

Upper Beaver River

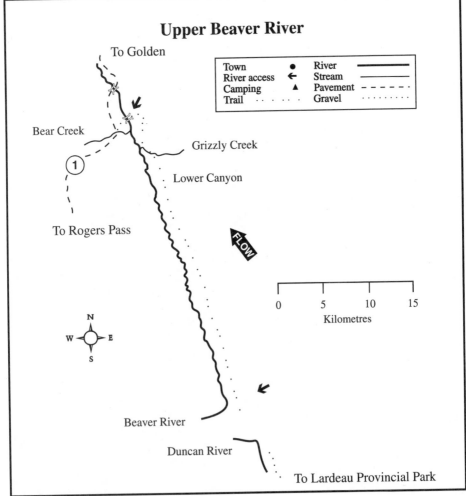

To Golden

Legend			
Town	●	River	—
River access	←	Stream	—
Camping	▲	Pavement	– – –
Trail	· · · · ·	Gravel	· · · · · · ·

Bear Creek

Grizzly Creek

①

Lower Canyon

To Rogers Pass

FLOW

N
W ◆ E
S

0   5   10   15
Kilometres

Beaver River

Duncan River

To Lardeau Provincial Park

BLUEWATER CREEK   BLACKWATER CR TO KINBASKET

GRADE	CLASS	FLOW	TIME	LENGTH
II	I–II	Most Flows	1 hour	3.5 km (2.2 mi)

Gradient 8.7 m/km (.86%)
46 ft/mi

Max gradient 30 m in 3.5 km (.86%)
100 ft in 2.2 mi

Put-in elevation 794 m
2605 ft

Take-out elevation 764 m
2505 ft

Shuttle 6.5 km (4 mi) one way

Season May–August

Maps 82N11

Gauge No

Craft Canoes, kayaks and rafts

CHARACTER A short run on a small to medium-volume creek that flows in an open gravel channel. There are a couple of short class II rapids, and a scenic, open canyon.

FLOW INFORMATION The creek is uncontrolled and fed by snowmelt and glacial runoff. You can estimate the flow at the put-in as described on page 237.

TRAVEL Access to the run and the shuttle are on gravel roads.

DESCRIPTION At the put-in, the creek is in a single channel on a gravel-bed, with waves at the corners as you descend. There are a couple of spots where small bedrock outcrops produce rapids, but the creek is open for the most part. The canyon under the road bridge is scenic, but without major drops. Near the end of the run, the creek flows in an open gravel channel in the scenic valley.

GETTING THERE The run is located north of Golden, off Highway 1, along the Bush River Forest Service Road.

TAKE-OUT At the junction of Highway 1 and Highway 95 in Golden, proceed 25 km north on Highway 1 to Donald Road, which is on the north (right) side of the highway. If coming from Rogers Pass, watch for Donald Road on the north (left) side, 800 m east of the Highway 1 bridge over the Columbia.

At the Donald Road junction, turn north and follow the road for 800 m, to a junction with a paved road on the right. Stay left on the Bush River Forest Service Road for 700 m to a bridge on Waitabit Creek. Continue for 2.5 km to a junction with a road on the west (left) side. Turn left and follow the road for 2 km to the site of an old bridge, just above Kinbasket Lake.

PUT-IN   Return to the Bush River Forest Service Road and turn north (left). Go 2.5 km to a fork with an unlabelled road on the east (right) side. Stay right and follow the road for 800 m to another fork, where you go left and continue for 1.3 km. This brings you to a recreation site at the confluence of Bluewater Creek and Blackwater Creek.

CAMPING   There is developed camping at the put-in.

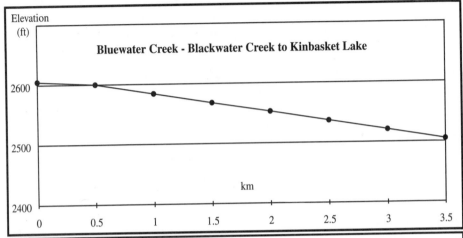

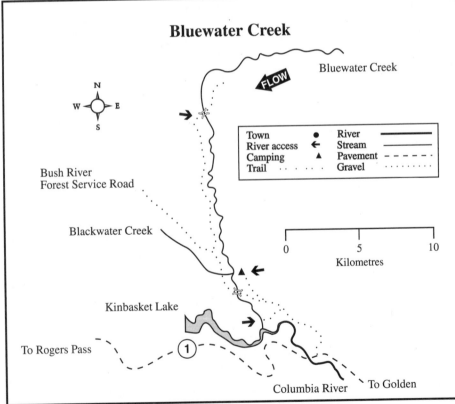

BLUEWATER CREEK　　BRIDGE TO BLACKWATER CR

GRADE	CLASS	FLOW	TIME	LENGTH
II⁺	II–III⁺	Low	2–4 hours	13.5 km (8.9 mi)
III	II⁺–IV	High		

Gradient　16 m/km (1.6%)　　　　**Max gradient**　30 m in 1.8 km (1.7%)
　　　　　　　83 ft/mi　　　　　　　　　　　　　　　100 ft in 1.1 mi

Put-in elevation　1006 m　　　　**Take-out elevation**　794 m
　　　　　　　　　　3300 ft　　　　　　　　　　　　　　2605 ft

Shuttle　18 km (11 mi) one way　　**Season**　May–August

Maps　82N11　　　　　　　　　　**Gauge**　No

Craft　Canoes, kayaks and rafts

NOTES There is a 5.3 km carry to the put-in. See the put-in section for details.

CHARACTER A great small to medium-volume run through a series of scenic canyons, with lots of easy playing and well-defined features. The rapids are caused by rock outcrops in the narrow creekbed, and occasional boulder gardens.

FLOW INFORMATION The creek is uncontrolled and fed by snowmelt and glacial runoff. Check the flow at the take-out as follows: find the downstream side of the old bridge support on the river left bank. There are seven timbers lying parallel to the bank. If the bottom of the seventh timber from the top is just in the water, the creek is low. If the lower edge of the sixth timber from the top is just in the water, the creek is medium. If the top of the sixth timber from the top is covered, the creek is high.

TRAVEL Access to the run and the shuttle are on gravel roads.

DESCRIPTION At the put-in you are amidst spectacular peaks that line the valley. From the bridge, the creek flows in a single fast channel over a gravel-bed. This continues, with some class II⁺–III rapids, until you reach a sharp left turn with huge boulders on the right bank. The creek is compressed into a 100-m-long class III–III⁺ set of rapids, which end in a class III⁺–IV drop at a constricted chute through a bedrock outcrop. Below this, the rapids ease to class II⁺–III, then to class II, with short class II⁺–III rapids at ledges across the river. This continues until you reach a set of hoodoos on the right shore. The valley then constricts into a beautiful open-bottomed canyon, with occasional class II⁺–III rapids. This continues to the take-out, with many well-defined features.

GETTING THERE   The run is located north of Golden, off Highway 1, along the Bush River Forest Service Road. See the map on page 236.

TAKE-OUT   At the junction of Highway 1 and Highway 95 in Golden, proceed 25 km north on Highway 1 to Donald Road, which is on the north (right) side of the highway. If coming from Rogers Pass, watch for Donald Road on the north (left) side, 800 m east of the Highway 1 bridge over the Columbia.

At the junction of Highway 1 and Donald Road, turn north and follow the road for 800 m to a junction with a paved road on the right. Stay left and follow the Bush River Forest Service Road for 700 m to a bridge on Waitabit Creek. Continue for 5 km to a fork with an unlabelled road on the east (right) side. Go right and follow the road for 800 m to another fork, where you stay left. Proceed 1.3 km to a recreation site at the confluence of Bluewater Creek and Blackwater Creek.

PUT-IN   Return to the Bush River Forest Service Road and turn north (right). Go 4.8 km to a junction with the Bush-Bluewater Forest Service Road on the east (right) side. Turn right and follow the road for 5.5 km to an old junction with a road on the left. The put-in is at the bridge 5.3 km further on the road to the right, but at this point there is a sign stating that the road is closed ahead. You can find out more information on the road closure by calling (604) 344-7585. If you choose not to drive further, you can carry your boat down the road to the put-in. It is your call!

CAMPING   There is developed camping at the take-out, or undeveloped camping along the road to the put-in.

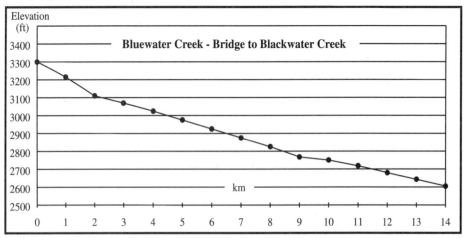

BLAEBERRY REDBURN CR TO BRIDGE

GRADE	CLASS	FLOW	TIME	LENGTH
I⁺	II	Low	1–2 hours	9.5 km (5.9 mi)
II	II	High		

Gradient 4.7 m/km (.47%)
25 ft/mi

Max gradient 30 m in 6.4 km (.47%)
100 ft in 4 mi

Put-in elevation 838 m
2750 ft

Take-out elevation 794 m
2605 ft

Shuttle 10.5 km (6.5 mi) one way

Season May–September

Maps 82N7 and 82N6

Gauge Yes

Craft Canoes, kayaks and rafts

CHARACTER A scenic medium-volume run through an open valley with great views. There are a few small rapids, but sweepers and log jams are the main hazard.

FLOW INFORMATION The river is uncontrolled and fed by snowmelt and glacial runoff. Estimate the flow at the take-out.

TRAVEL The shuttle is on gravel roads.

DESCRIPTION At the put-in, the river flows in a single channel, but it soon enters an open braided section. Enjoy the views and the open, easy river. Take out at the bridge.

GETTING THERE The run is located north of Golden, off Highway 1.

TAKE-OUT At the junction of Highway 1 and Highway 95 in Golden, proceed 16 km north on Highway 1 to the Blaeberry School Road. This road is on the east (right) side of the highway, 1 km past the highway bridge on the Blaeberry. If coming from Rogers Pass, the road is on the east (left) side 9.7 km south of the bridge on the Columbia. Turn east and go 1.7 km to a junction with the Golden-Donald Upper Road. Turn south (right) and go 2 km to the bridge.

PUT-IN Go south for 1.4 km to the junction with the Oberg-Johnston Road. Turn east (left) and proceed for 1.8 km to the junction with the Moberley School Road. Turn east (left) and go 600 m to a fork, where you stay right on the Blaeberry Road. You continue along the Blaeberry Road for 6.5 km to a junction with a bridge on the north (left) side.

CAMPING There is developed near the put-in.

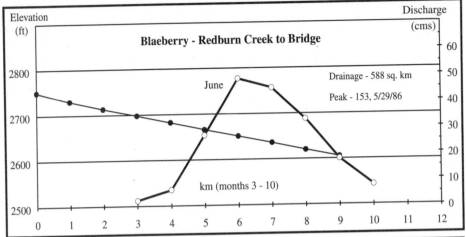

Blaeberry - Redburn Creek to Bridge

June

Drainage - 588 sq. km

Peak - 153, 5/29/86

km (months 3 - 10)

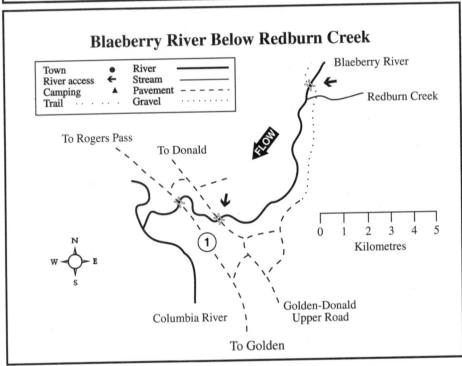

Blaeberry River Below Redburn Creek

Town ● River ——
River access ← Stream ——
Camping ▲ Pavement – – –
Trail · · · · · · Gravel · · · · · · ·

Blaeberry River

Redburn Creek

FLOW

To Rogers Pass

To Donald

N
W ◆ E
S

①

0 1 2 3 4 5
Kilometres

Columbia River

Golden-Donald
Upper Road

To Golden

GRADE	CLASS	FLOW	TIME	LENGTH
II⁺–III	III–IV	Low	1–2 hours	5 km (3 mi)
III–III⁺	III–V	High		

Gradient 10.5 m/km (1.1%)
55 ft/mi

Max gradient 30 m in 2.8 km (1.1%)
100 ft in 1.9 mi

Put-in elevation 974 m
3195 ft

Take-out elevation 922 m
3025 ft

Shuttle 5.6 km (3.5 mi) one way

Season May–September

Maps 82N10

Gauge Yes

Craft Canoes, kayaks and rafts

CHARACTER A small to medium-volume run with a short whitewater section that offers some great playing and several constricted rapids. The whitewater is formed by bedrock outcrops that funnel the river into narrow slots.

FLOW INFORMATION The river is uncontrolled and fed by snowmelt and glacial runoff. Estimate the flow level at the bridge just downstream of Split Creek (2 km west of the Split Creek Forest Recreation Site) as follows: on the river left bridge support is a concrete wall. If the water is lapping below the concrete, the river is low. If the water is covering the bottom of the concrete then count the number of horizontal lines on the concrete wall, until you reach the small ledge running horizontally across the abutment. If just one line is showing, the river is very high. If two lines are showing, the river is medium to high.

TRAVEL Access to the run and the shuttle are on gravel roads.

DESCRIPTION The river flows away from the put-in as a single channel in an open riverbed. This continues, with easy class II rapids, until you reach a narrow low-walled canyon with a short class III rapid. Below this, the river opens up to Split Creek, which enters from the left. Directly below the creek confluence is Split Falls, where the right side drops into a narrow, 100-m-long class IV chute. The left side flows along the rock outcrop producing the chute on the right, then cascades off in a class IV–V, 2–3-m drop. The river then flows into 400 metres of narrow class III⁺–IV boiling and exploding whitewater in a low-walled canyon. A couple of short canyons with class III rapids lead to the calmer section at the bridge. Below the bridge are a couple of class III–III⁺ rapids in beautiful low-walled canyons. The last 1–1.5 km of the run are open and easy. At a straight, watch for a set of old bridge pilings high above the water on river left. The take-out is just below. Thrill seekers can run the 2–4-m class IV⁺–V drop at the take-out, but this is no place for mistakes. About 100 m below this drop is the class VI–VI⁺ Blaeberry Falls, which drops 9–12 m into a horrendous recirculation.

GETTING THERE   The run is located north of Golden, off Highway 1.

TAKE-OUT   The area is crisscrossed with numerous roads, so pay attention to the directions and trust your odometer. From the junction of Highway 1 and Highway 95 in Golden, proceed 9.6 km north on Highway 1 to Hartley Road, which is on the east (right) side of the road. Continue north for another 1.1 km, to the Moberley Bridge Road, which is also on the east (right) side of the road. If coming from Rogers Pass, the Moberley Bridge Road is on the east (left) side 15.1 km south of the bridge on the Columbia. Turn east on the Moberley Bridge Road, then go up the hill and continue to a junction with the Golden-Donald Upper Road. This is 2.1 km from the highway. Turn south (right) and go 1.3 km to the junction with the Moberley School Road, which is on the east (left) side. Turn left and go 2.1 km to the junction with the Oberg-Johnston Road, which is on the north (left) side. Continue past that junction for 600 m to a fork, where you stay right on the Blaeberry Road.

Continue 6.5 km along the Blaeberry Road to a junction with a bridge on the north (left) side. Stay left, cross the bridge, then continue along the road for 6.7 km to a small gravel road on the south (right) side of the road. Turn right and follow the road for 200 m to the parking area. Take a look at the river at the take-out so you will recognize the drop above the fall.

PUT-IN   Continue upstream for 3.4 km to a bridge on the river (where you can estimate the flow as described in the flow information section). Go 2 km further to the Split Creek Forest Service Recreation Area, which is on the north (left) side of the road.

CAMPING   There is developed camping at the put-in.

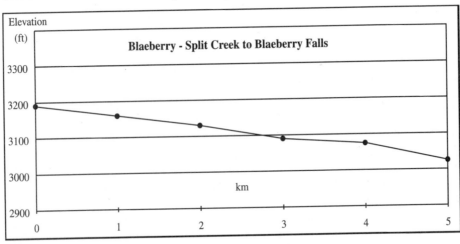

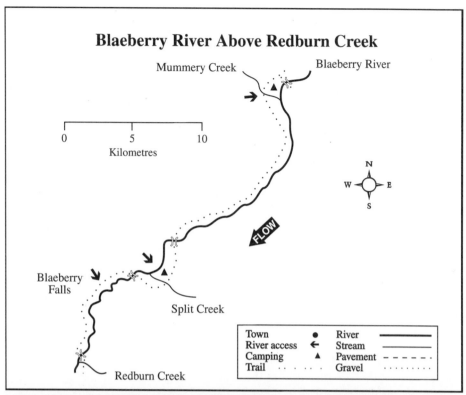

Blaeberry River Above Redburn Creek

Mummery Creek

Blaeberry River

0   5   10
Kilometres

N
W — E
S

FLOW

Blaeberry
Falls

Split Creek

Town	●	River	———
River access	←	Stream	———
Camping	▲	Pavement	– – – –
Trail	· · · · ·	Gravel	· · · · · · ·

Redburn Creek

Looking upstream at Split Falls.

GRADE	CLASS	FLOW	TIME	LENGTH
II	I–II	Most Flows	3–5 hours	20 km (12.4 mi)

Gradient 5.9 m/km (.59%)   **Max gradient** 30 m in 5 km (.6%)
31 ft/mi   100 ft in 3 mi

Put-in elevation 1091 m   **Take-out elevation** 974 m
3580 ft   3195 ft

Shuttle 20 km (12.4 mi) one way   **Season** May–September

Maps 82N10   **Gauge** Yes

Craft Canoes, kayaks and rafts

CHARACTER A scenic small to medium-volume run, with spectacular peaks surrounding the valley. The river flows in an open gravel plain, with many small braided channels. The challenges are finding the deep-water channels, and avoiding log jams and sweepers.

FLOW INFORMATION The river is uncontrolled and fed by snowmelt and glacial runoff. Assess the flow at the take-out.

TRAVEL Access to the run and the shuttle are on gravel roads.

DESCRIPTION The river just below the put-in is typical of the entire run. Finding deep water in the braided channels is the biggest challenge. The trip is a scenic float with little real whitewater. There are a couple of tight corners and the odd sweeper and log jam. The road is close to the river for most of the run.

GETTING THERE The run is located north of Golden, off Highway 1. See the map on page 243.

TAKE-OUT The area is crisscrossed with numerous roads, so pay attention to the directions and trust your odometer. From the junction of Highway 1 and Highway 95, in Golden, proceed 9.6 km north on Highway 1 to Hartley Road, which is on the east (right) side of the road. Continue north for another 1.1 km to the Moberley Bridge Road, which is also on the east (right) side of the road. If coming from Rogers Pass, the Moberley Bridge Road is on the east (left) side of the highway 15.1 km south of the bridge on the Columbia. Turn east on the Moberley Bridge Road, then go up the hill and continue to a junction with the Golden-Donald Upper Road. This is 2.1 km from the highway. Turn south (right) and go 1.3 km to the junction with the Moberley School Road, which is on the east (left) side. Turn left and go 2.1 km to the junction with the Oberg-Johnston Road, which is on the north (left) side. Continue past that junction for 600 m to a fork, where you stay right on the Blaeberry Road.

Continue 6.5 km along the Blaeberry Road to a junction with a bridge on the north (left) side. Stay left, cross the bridge, then follow the road for 9.2 km to the junction with the Blaeberry-Mather Forest Service Road, which is on the north (left) side. Stay right and follow the road upstream. You will cross the river in about 1 km; then 2 km past the bridge, you reach the Split Creek Forest Service Recreation Site, which is on the north (left) side of the road.

PUT-IN Go 3 km upstream to another bridge over the river, then continue for 16.5 km to the Mummery Creek Forest Recreation Site, which is on the south (right) side. About 400 m past the recreation site, you will reach a junction on the south (right) side that leads to the bridge at the put-in.

CAMPING There is developed camping at the take-out or at the Mummery Creek Forest Recreation Site. There are many undeveloped sites in the area.

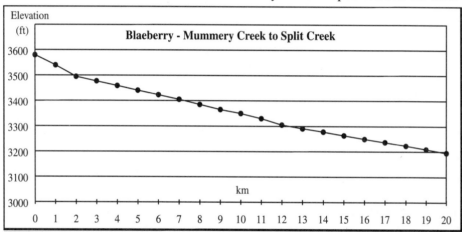

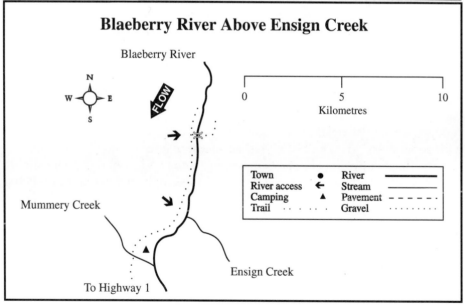

Blaeberry River Above Ensign Creek

BLAEBERRY   BRIDGE TO ENSIGN CREEK

GRADE	CLASS	FLOW	TIME	LENGTH
V	IV–VI	Low	2–3 hours	5 km (3 mi)
V⁺	V–VI	Medium		

Gradient 26 m/km (2.6%)   **Max gradient** 30 m in .8 km (3.8%)
135 ft/mi   100 ft in .5 mi

Put-in elevation   1262 m   **Take-out elevation**   1134 m
4140 ft   3720 ft

Shuttle 6 km (3.7 mi) one way   **Season** May–September

Maps 82N10   **Gauge** Yes

Craft Kayaks

CHARACTER A small-volume run that flows in an open gravel plain for the first part of the run, then drops through a narrow and boulder-choked channel for the last half. The lower part of the run is a continuous series of high-pressure moves through a maze of boulders with unending horizon lines.

FLOW INFORMATION The river is uncontrolled and fed by snowmelt and glacial runoff. Assess the flow at Terminus rapid, on the way to the put-in.

TRAVEL Access to the run and the shuttle are on gravel roads.

DESCRIPTION The river runs over a gravel-bed, with some braiding in the first 2 km. It then changes character with a class II⁺–III rapid at a collection of huge boulders. The river is close to the road before it swings left, away from the road, to a right turn. Below the right turn is Cornerstone, a class IV–IV⁺ rapid that starts the wild stuff. The river flows through jagged bedrock and boulders, with logs in and around the channels. The rapids increase in difficulty to class V, and the water flows with incredible speed through the convoluted channel. There are a couple of class V–V⁺ rapids, before you reach a riverwide class V⁺ broken ledge. There is a chute into a vicious recirculation on the right, and a narrow obstructed channel on the left. Below this is more class V with some class V⁺. The river then accelerates into a chute with a distinct horizon line below. This is The Quickening, a class VI drop that pours slickly off a 2–4-m ledge into a sickening reversal on the right and onto a rock outcrop on the left. You can portage along the right shore. Just below The Quickening is Bazooka, a class V explosion through a narrow bedrock pinch. Below this, the gradient eases and the river opens up. An easier section leads to Terminus, the class IV–IV⁺ rapid that can be seen from the road on the way up.

GETTING THERE The run is located north of Golden, off Highway 1. See the map on page 245.

The Fright Night Run

As I drove up that evening it was raining, and the clouds were thick and dark. In the heavy cloud the valley seemed sombre and subdued. I paddled the open upper part, then reached a rapid with dark, looming rocks sticking out of the ice-cold glacial meltwater, and the character of the run changed. The river disappeared into a narrow channel, with logs thrusting out at odd angles amidst jagged boulders. The scene had an unnatural feel to it. As I paddled on, dusk was closing in, and the wet rocks were dark and gloomy. The run began to feel desperate. Each move was just above something a little scary: an unknown horizon line, a log jam, or an undercut boulder. A couple of times I stopped to check over my shoulder, expecting to see something creepy following me down the river. I was definitely getting a bit spooked. The whitewater got harder and after a wicked ledge, I reached a horizon line. It was dry in my boat, and the lurking quality of the surroundings did not encourage me to get out and scout. I tried in vain to get a look below that horizon line. Finally in exasperation, I swung the boat around and sprinted at the drop. Luckily I was going fast, for the river slid off a 3-m ledge into a horrendous recirculation. At the brink I swept my bow out over the void, and came down in a wild ricochet off the rock outcrop on the left. I was stroking frantically, the boat hanging on the edge of the recirculation. As I windmilled over the boil line, I erupted blindly into the next drop. If I was a little nervous before, now my heart was pounding, and I was gasping for breath. I could hear myself grunting with each frantic stroke, as I shot between the dark boulders. At the take-out, all I could recall were nasty features; the kind of things that are usually called a hazard. Cold water, dark rocks, unending horizon lines, log jams, gloomy lighting, jagged undercut boulders, and a drop in the middle that is so ugly, it alone will frighten you. The whole thing reminded me of all the worst nasties gathered together into one of those nightmares that, as a kid, scared you silly. Maybe it was just the light, the approaching darkness, the rain, or who knows what, but I left that run with the distinct feeling I had brushed up against something evil. It was years later, when I needed the information for this book, before I finally returned. For security, I paddled in the brilliant sunshine, with a couple of friends. Oh, and I carried my lucky crystal with me!

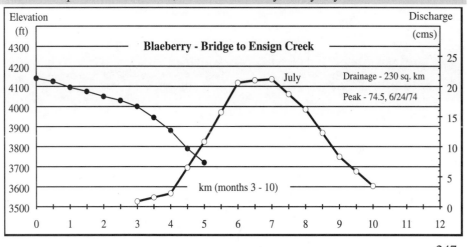

247

TAKE-OUT At the junction of Highway 1 and Highway 95 in Golden, proceed 10.6 km north to the Moberley Bridge Road, which is on the east (right) side of the highway. If coming from Rogers Pass, the Moberley Bridge Road is on the east (left) side of the highway 15.1 km south of the bridge on the Columbia. Turn east on the Moberley Bridge Road, then go up the hill to a junction with the Golden-Donald Upper Road. This is 2.1 km from the highway. Turn south (right) and go 1.3 km to the junction with the Moberley School Road, which is on the east (left) side. Turn left and go 2.1 km to the junction with the Oberg-Johnston Road, which is on the north (left) side.

Continue straight past that junction for 600 m to a fork, where you stay right on the Blaeberry Road. In 6.5 km you reach a junction with a bridge on the north (left) side. Stay left, cross the bridge, then continue along the road for 9.2 km to the junction with the Blaeberry-Mather Forest Service Road, which is on the north (left) side. Stay right and follow the road upstream to where you cross the river in about 1 km, then again in about another 5 km. Continue for another 16.5 km to the Mummery Creek Forest Recreation Site, which is on the south (right) side. About 2.6 km past the recreation site, is a road on the south (right) side, labelled Amiskwi Pass, with a bridge over the river. You continue past that road for 1.2 km to where the river is close on the south (right) side of the road. Park well off the road.

PUT-IN Continue upstream for 6 km to the bridge over the river at the Cairnes Creek Forest Service Road.

CAMPING There is undeveloped camping at the put-in.

Looking upstream at Terminus in low flows.

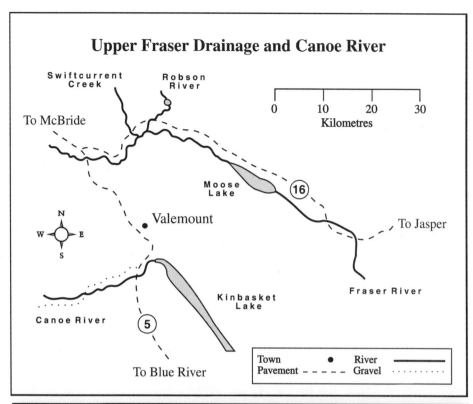

Upper Fraser Drainage and Canoe River

Swiftcurrent Creek

Robson River

To McBride

0   10   20   30
Kilometres

Moose Lake

16

Valemount

To Jasper

Fraser River

N
W   E
S

Kinbasket Lake

Canoe River

5

To Blue River

Town ●   River ———
Pavement – – – –   Gravel · · · · · · · ·

James Van Camp after a brisk encounter with a hole on the Canoe River.

GRADE	CLASS	FLOW	TIME	LENGTH
II	II–IV$^+$	Low	1–3 hours	11 km (6.8 mi)
II$^+$	II–V	Medium		
III	II–V$^+$	High		

Gradient 3.6 m/km (.36%)
19 ft/mi

Max gradient 30 m in 7.5 km (.4%)
100 ft in 4.7 mi

Put-in elevation 792 m
2600 ft

Take-out elevation 753 m
2470 ft

Shuttle 9 km (5.7 mi) one way

Season May–October

Maps 83D14

Gauge Yes

Craft Canoes, kayaks and rafts

CHARACTER A medium to large-volume run that flows in an open valley, with a couple of short constricted sections and one waterfall. The portage at the fall requires quite a bit of work, particularly for rafters.

FLOW INFORMATION The river is uncontrolled and fed by snowmelt and glacial runoff. Assess the flow at the take-out.

TRAVEL Access to the run and the shuttle are on paved roads.

DESCRIPTION At the put-in, the river flows in an open gravel flat, then assumes a single channel not far from the start. A 2–3-km section of open river follows, with a couple of small rapids. The river then enters a closed-in valley and narrows at a low-walled canyon where at low flows, broken bedrock ledges create narrow class II–III chutes. At higher flows the river blasts through the narrow section, producing large standing waves. The river opens up for a bit, then makes a sharp right turn at a distinct horizon line. This is Rearguard Falls, a class IV$^+$–V$^+$ set of broken bedrock ledges. There are a couple of routes down the drop. The easiest is on river left, along the shelf off the left shore. The route on the right double-drops through a couple of big holes. You can scout from the right shore, where a trail takes you to the viewpoint. Portage by scrambling over the fence, then down the steep bedrock to the river. Folks with large inflatables can carry up the path for about 100 m, to a set of poles that allow you to lower your boat down the inclined ramp to below the fall. Below Rearguard Falls, the river flows through a constricted set of class II$^+$–III rapids, with standing waves and holes. The river then mellows and there are few rapids until you reach the take-out.

GETTING THERE The run is located west of Jasper along Highway 16. See the map on page 253.

TAKE-OUT From the lights at the junction of Highway 16 and Highway 93 in Jasper, proceed west on Highway 16. Go approximately 100 km to a picnic site on the south side of the highway. You will pass a weigh scale just before you reach the picnic site. If coming from the west, the picnic site is 500 m east of the junction of Highway 5 and Highway 16.

PUT-IN Go 3.6 km east on Highway 16 to the Rearguard Falls pull-off, on the south (right) side of the road. Continue past Rearguard Falls for 5.5 km to a descent in the road. At the bottom of the hill, the river is close to the road.

CAMPING There is developed camping 6.5 km east of the put-in, at Mount Robson.

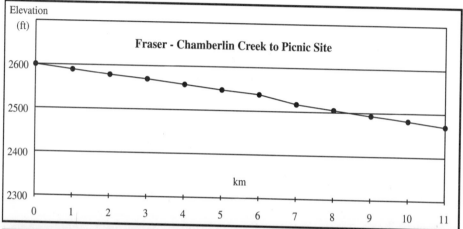

Rearguard Falls at low flow.

GRADE	CLASS	FLOW	TIME	LENGTH
I+	I+–II	Low	1–3 hours	8 km (5 mi)
II	II	High		

Gradient 3.9 m/km (.39%)
20 ft/mi

Max gradient 30 m in 8 km (.39%)
100 ft in 5 mi

Put-in elevation 823 m
2700 ft

Take-out elevation 792 m
2600 ft

Shuttle 7 km (4.3 mi) one way

Season May–October

Maps 83E3 and 83D14

Gauge Yes

Craft Canoes, kayaks and rafts

CHARACTER A scenic run on a medium to large-volume river, with few rapids but incredible views of Mount Robson and the surrounding peaks.

FLOW INFORMATION The river is uncontrolled and fed by snowmelt and glacial runoff. Assess the flow at the put-in.

TRAVEL Access to the run and the shuttle are on paved roads.

DESCRIPTION At the put-in, the river flows swiftly in a single channel until you encounter a couple of islands. Near the confluence with the Robson River (which enters on the right) the valley opens up and the river meanders in a braided channel with wide-open, marshy areas. This continues to near the take-out. Watch for the abundant wildlife in the marshy areas.

GETTING THERE The run is located west of Jasper along Highway 16.

TAKE-OUT From the lights at the junction of Highways 16/93 in Jasper, go west on Highway 16 for 84 km to the gas station at Mount Robson. Continue west for 6.5 km to where the river is close to the road, just before a long ascent. If coming from the west, go 4 km east of the Highways 5/16 junction to the Rearguard Falls pull-off. Continue east for 5.5 km to a descent in the road. At the bottom of the hill the river is close to the road. Park well off the road.

PUT-IN Go 6.5 km east to the gas station at Mount Robson. Turn south (right) and proceed past the campground, for about 250 m, to where a small road leaves on the right, just before you reach the bridge. Turn right and park on the left. A wide trail leads to the river.

CAMPING There is developed camping near the put-in.

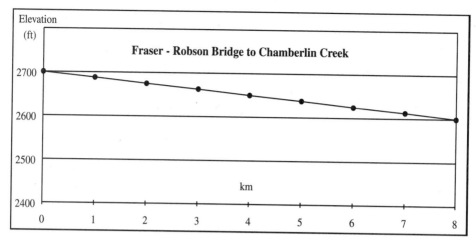

Elevation (ft)

Fraser - Robson Bridge to Chamberlin Creek

km

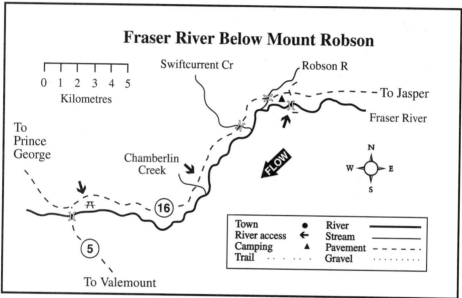

Fraser River Below Mount Robson

Swiftcurrent Cr

Robson R

To Jasper

Fraser River

0 1 2 3 4 5
Kilometres

To
Prince
George

Chamberlin
Creek

FLOW

N
W — E
S

To Valemount

Town	●	River	———
River access	←	Stream	——
Camping	▲	Pavement	– – – –
Trail	· · · · ·	Gravel	· · · · · · · ·

GRADE	CLASS	FLOW	TIME	LENGTH
III⁺	III–V⁺	Low	1–3 hours	4.5 km (2.8 mi)
IV	III–VI	Medium		
V	III⁺–VI	High		

Gradient 14 m/km (1.4%)
73 ft/mi

Max gradient 30 m in 2 km (1.5%)
100 ft in 1.2 mi

Put-in elevation 885 m
2905 ft

Take-out elevation 823 m
2700 ft

Shuttle 4 km (2.5 mi) one way

Season May–October

Maps 83E3

Gauge Yes

Craft Kayaks, canoes and rafts

CHARACTER A spectacular medium to large-volume run through a couple of impressive canyons, with a thundering waterfall and a long constricted section of pushy whitewater at the end. This is an awesome run, with some intense whitewater in magnificent surroundings.

FLOW INFORMATION The river is uncontrolled and fed by snowmelt and glacial runoff. Assess the flow at the bridge described in the take-out section. There is a huge rock outcrop in the middle of the river about 100 m upstream of the bridge. At high flows, this rock creates a massive pourover. At low flows, you will be able to see rock ledges in the river just upstream of the bridge. Walk upstream on the river right shore to scout Terminator, the most difficult rapid, if you are concerned with what the run entails.

TRAVEL Access to the run and the shuttle are on paved roads.

DESCRIPTION The run begins just below The Staircase, which is visible from the road. The river eases to grade II with a couple of easy class III rapids consisting of mainly standing waves. You paddle below the highway at a left turn, and the river leaves the road. You then encounter a bedrock headwall on the left side at a right turn. Look for an eddy on the right shore. The river turns sharply and you are treated to a frightening, misty horizon line, where the river plunges 8–13 m, at Overlander Falls. The portage is on the right, onto the rock outcrop that creates the fall, then down the other side and through the trees to the bowl at the end of the pool below the fall.

The class V⁺–VI waterfall has been paddled numerous times. For those spurred to foolish deeds, but who do not wish to expose themselves to the river's fury,

Looking upstream from the take-out of the Fraser Canyon.
Photo: Hugh Lecky.

there are a couple of seal-launches along the right shore below the fall. These provide the commensurate adrenaline surge, without the hazards associated with the adjacent waterfall.

Below the fall, the river pools and then drops through a narrow slot into a boiling cauldron of water that folds over into the canyon below. At high flows there are few real drops until the walls open up, but at low flows, look for Bank Shot, a class IV fence of offset boulders with three carom-shot slots. The rock walls abate, then the river turns right to a horizon line dotted with massive boulders. This is the class IV–IV⁺ Wondergarden, a riverwide ledge with slots on the left and right, between broken bedrock and huge boulders.

The river is then calm for about 700 m to a sharp left turn at a low rock outcrop from the right shore. At higher flows there is an awesome playhole, Windowshade, with an eddy to get back up on the right. The riverbed then opens up to a sweeping right turn. Just below the right turn, the river accelerates into a riverwide wave/hole and tears off in a boiling fury. The next kilometre is hectic, pushy whitewater in a tight canyon, with a class V drop at the end. Expect awesome, exploding whitewater that eases slightly in a short straight to where the river turns right and drops out of sight. A small eddy on the left, behind a rock outcrop, allows you get out to scout the class IV⁺–V⁺ Terminator, a narrow chute where the river drops into a wicked hole. At low flows the drop is a 3–5-m waterfall, and at high flows, a low-angled ramp into a seething recirculation. You can scramble along the left shore to reach the outcrop that creates the drop. Portaging is best done along the left shore.

Below Terminator, the river erupts with exploding and surging whitewater. It tears off along the right wall to a series of diagonal holes, piles up against a huge midstream rock and plummets into the chute on the left. Below this the river eases. At very high flows look for the incredible surf wave just above the bridge. There is also some great hole-playing at the diagonal hole at the end of the canyon. Take out on the right at the bottom of the big pool, where a trail leads up to your vehicle. The view of Mount Robson coming over the crest as you carry up to the parking lot is simply amazing!

GETTING THERE The run is located west of Jasper along Highway 16. See the map on page 264.

TAKE-OUT From the lights at the junction of Highway 16 and Highway 93 in Jasper, proceed west on Highway 16 for 84 km to the gas station at Mount Robson. If coming from the west, the gas station is 16 km east of the junction of Highways 5/16, just north of Valemount. At the gas station, turn south and go past the campground on the right for about 250 m to a small road on the right, just before you reach the bridge. Turn right, then park on the left where a trail leads down to the river.

PUT-IN Return to Highway 16, then turn east (right) and go 3.1 km to a left bend in the road, where you can look down on The Staircase rapid.

CAMPING There is developed camping near the take-out.

Al Polster, Andrea O'Neill and Hugh Lecky at the take-out, with Mount Robson in the background. Photo: Gilbert Wall.

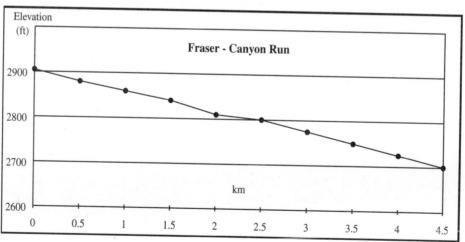

A Day at the Movies

Climbing out of the truck, I inhaled the crisp morning air and stumbled across the parking lot, subconsciously following the familiar aromas wafting from the craft-services unit. The boats were down at the fall by 9:00 a.m. and I was suited in my gear, formally known as "wardrobe". This would not be at all like the other seven times. This was on someone else's schedule, on someone else's command and on someone else's storyboard. At 9:30 a.m. I was above the drop, warming up, stretching and trying to stay loose. The river swept past to the misty horizon line and disappeared into ominous thunder. The details had been finalized moments before: the sacred need for the correct light, the signals, the line I would take and, of course, the emergency response should I fail to execute. Now all there was to do was wait. I repeatedly rehearsed the strokes, played forward in slow motion, then again at high speed, the myriad details crystalized in my mind. I was still ready. At 11:30 a.m., I was stretched out, absorbing heat from the rocks, as the signal guy dozed in the grass, leaving me to my introverted reverie. Then the call came, it was time. "Lunchtime!"

After a long morning I was back above the drop performing my routine of warm-ups, stretching, meditating, and rehearsing. By 2:30 p.m. I was out of gas and just plain snoozing, curled in a fetal ball. Then the call came, "Good light in 15 minutes." I jolted awake, jumped in the boat, breathed deeply and tried to stay focused. "No light for another 30 minutes." Back out of the boat, with more time for warming up, stretching, meditating and rehearsing. Next thing I knew, I jarred awake, my snoring having woken me. The thunder was still below, so it was no dream. Then the call came, "Good light in 6 minutes." Once again in the boat, I was trying to get the peripheral details out of my mind. "15 seconds!" I heaved a few breaths in and out, injecting oxygen to my brain, and at the signal peeled out of the eddy. Then the call came, "Abort! Back to starting position." I almost kept going. Who the hell are those guys?

Back out of the boat, there was more time for stretching, breathing, meditating and rehearsing. When all else failed, I was again nodding off. Then the call came "Good light in 4 minutes." I leapt up and jumped into the boat. A couple of sprints, a few deep breaths, then an agitated signal man was screaming at me, "Go, Go, Go!" I peeled out and paddled toward the brink, each stroke accelerating the boat slightly faster than the last, in a liquid-smooth pulse. Bursting through the hole at the lip, I was suddenly in slow motion and I measured each stroke, placing it easily. I soared in the white chaos, and felt the sudden rush at the bottom as the free fall of gravity gave way to the violent force of the river. I erupted out of the foam, hauling up to daylight. It was over so fast, but the adrenaline surge was faster. I wanted to scream and leap about. But I kept the lid on, while the crew hollered ecstatically. Inside, my elation ran rampant. I had wired it, but now what? A little confusion. The stunt team had agreed to give each of the guys a shot at the fall. But they wanted me again. Perfect(?)! Then suddenly, a lot of confusion. The props guys grabbed the boat, retaping and repainting over the graphics on the deck.

258

Other people carried the boat, as it was being painted, upstream to the top. Then the Assistant Director wanted to renegotiate the fee for the second run. No way! The signal guy was in my face. My mind was racing and I was nauseous from the unused adrenaline. I was struggling to stay focused. Then I was in the boat, and a there was a screaming "Go, Go, Go!"

It was solitary quiet as I paddled toward the mist, abstractly aware of the surrounding mayhem. The move at the top unfolded way too fast, and much too suddenly there was darkness at the bottom, with thunder in my ears. My paddle scraped the rock wall and an erupting boil tore the shaft from one hand. I clawed the cliff and rolled off the rock, releasing the diving blade. None too soon there was daylight and I was safe! A throw bag hit me in the chest as I hand-paddled away from the roar. It was a wrap! Then came the incredible, shuddering release as the pent up exhaustion tore through me. Back at the craft services truck, amid congratulations from the crew, I was unable to struggle when my arms were pinned behind my back. They held me as a fresh pie was plastered into my face, and I laughed, inhaling copious amounts of the filling. And we all laughed. It was just a day at the movies, and Overlander Falls.

Stuart Smith in the mist of Overlander Falls at low flows.
Photo: Arn Terry.

259

GRADE	CLASS	FLOW	TIME	LENGTH
III⁺	III–IV	Low	2–4 hours	8.5 km (5.3 mi)
IV	III⁺–IV⁺	Medium		
V	IV–V	High		

Gradient   13 m/km (1.3%)   **Max gradient**   30 m in 2 km (1.5%)
          68 ft/mi   100 ft in 1.2 mi

Put-in elevation   995 m   **Take-out elevation**   8855 m
                    3265 ft   2905 ft

Shuttle   8 km (5 mi) one way   **Season**   May–October

Maps   83E3   **Gauge**   Yes

Craft   Kayaks, canoes and rafts

CHARACTER   An incredible run on a medium to large-volume river that flows in an obstructed channel of boulders, with bedrock outcrops and spectacular canyons. If you are up to it, this is a must do!

FLOW INFORMATION   The river is uncontrolled and fed by snowmelt and glacial runoff. Assess the flow at the take-out where The Staircase is an example of the rapids above. Go down to the river, so you are not fooled by the road view.

TRAVEL   Access to the run and the shuttle are on paved roads.

DESCRIPTION   The run begins in an open channel, with a few easy rapids in the first kilometre. The river then pools and makes a right turn at a distinct horizon line. This is the class IV–V Outhouse, named for the small structure in the eddy on the left, just above the drop. You can boat-scout the line through the rapid from the river right and scramble down if you want to see more. The first chute thunders into a series of diagonal waves, with the final diagonal funnelling you toward the hole on river right. After this the river erupts in a series of big waves and drops into a boulder garden. There are holes on the left, and a set of boulders in the middle that become holes at higher flows. The river then rushes toward the headwall at the bottom, makes a sharp left turn and drops into the hole against the right shore. The river pools for a short time, then accelerates through a narrow chute into a long straight that ends in a sharp left turn, with a horizon line on the left. This is Eric's Hole, a class IV⁺–V boat muncher that plunges 2–3 m over a bedrock ledge into a ludicrous recirculation on the left. Scouting the left channel means a bush thrash along the steep left shore, which must be undertaken well above the drop. If you descend to the lip of the drop, scouting from the right shore reveals little information about the left channel. Most folks will choose the convoluted passage through the boulder maze on the right. This leads to a couple of tight chutes that drop off the rock ledge, back into the main channel on the left. Rafters will find this drop difficult to negotiate, or portage. Below Eric's Hole, the river opens up and there are some great play features in the next kilometre. A sharp left turn leads to the class IV Boulderdash, a sharp right turn where the river drops off a boulder fence. After Boulderdash, you are treated to more big waves and holes. The river then drops into a long set of exploding waves that ends at a canyon. You can boat-scout from the eddy on river left. In the canyon you will find huge waves and a couple of large holes. Near the end the river is funnelled into a chute on the left by a huge midstream boulder. Watch for a play hole on the left, just below this.

The river then eases until a long, sweeping left turn at Holy Terror, a class IV–V rapid with numerous large holes. The river turns sharply left, then right. At the crux of Holy Terror there are two narrow channels through offset holes. About 400 m of constricted class IV–IV+ leads to a calm section. The river passes a cliff wall on the left, then turns left. Watch for The Regurgitron, a playhole just above a large pool. About 150 m below The Regurgitron the river drops into Toilet Bowl, a class IV–V collection of holes in the narrow bedrock passage. The two-part drop starts with a chute into a diagonal hole off the right. The river then rushes headlong into a set of diagonals off the left shore, which funnel you toward the hole in the centre at the bottom. You can scout the whole thing on the left shore. Immediately below Toilet Bowl, the river turns left and drops off a wicked boulderfield at the class IV–IV+ Otterslide. The left side offers the cleanest route through, with the right side pouring off a steep boulder maze in tight passages. Below Otterslide, the river opens up until you reach a left turn at the base of a steep bank on the right, with the highway at the top. The river turns left and drops into Monster Waves, a class IV–IV+ set of huge waves and holes with some awesome one-shot surfing opportunities. The rapids ease and in about 800 m the river turns right and accelerates toward The Staircase, the class IV–V drop you can look down at from the highway. Take out just below, on river right, before the river turns left. Carry up the steep broken rock slope to your vehicle.

You can paddle the short run just upstream of this one to get a feel for the river. This run is one full grade more difficult than the upper run, and is much more constricted. Check the description on page 263 for details.

GETTING THERE The run is located west of Jasper along Highway 16. See the map on page 264.

TAKE-OUT From the lights at the junction of Highway 16 and Highway 93 in Jasper, proceed west on Highway 16 for about 55 km to where the road runs along Moose Lake. Travel along Moose Lake until the road leaves the lake, then in about 4 km look for a set of gates used to close the highway. From the gates, go west for 11.8 km to where the river is below the road on a sweeping right turn. If coming from the west, go 16 km east of the Highways

5/16 junction just north of Valemount to a gas station at Mount Robson. The take-out is 3 km east of the gas station at a long bend to the left. You can look over the guardrail to see The Staircase.

PUT-IN Go east on Highway 16 for 7.7 km to a long descent with a small road that leaves on the south (right) side at the bottom. There is a yellow gate across the road. Park so as not to block the gate, then carry along the road to just before the third power pole. Watch for the steep trail on the left that leads down to the river.

CAMPING . There is camping 3 km west of the take-out, at Mount Robson.

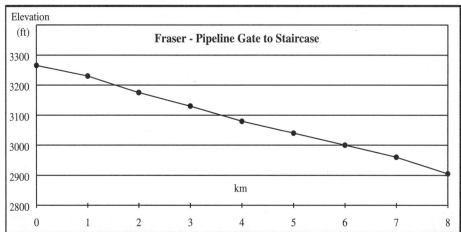

Derek Thomas in Toilet Bowl at low flows.

GRADE	CLASS	FLOW	TIME	LENGTH
II–III	II–III	Low	1–2 hours	5 km (3.1 mi)
III–IV	III–IV	High		

Gradient 5.8 m/km (.58%)   **Max gradient** 30 m in 5 km (.6%)
            31 ft/mi   100 ft in 3.1 mi

Put-in elevation 1024 m   **Take-out elevation** 995 m
                      3360 ft   3265 ft

Shuttle 3 km (1.9 mi) one way   **Season** May–October

Maps 83E3   **Gauge** Yes

Craft Canoes, kayaks and rafts

CHARACTER A medium to large-volume run that has great features at most water levels. The river flows over a boulder-bed with mostly open rapids.

FLOW INFORMATION The river is uncontrolled and fed by snowmelt and glacial runoff. You have to walk 400 m to reach either the put-in or the take-out, so it is difficult to check the flows. You can assess the water level at the take-out for the run described on page 260. At high water the rapids string together into one long section of erupting whitewater.

TRAVEL Access to the run and the shuttle are on paved roads.

DESCRIPTION The run begins in a swift-flowing single channel. About 400 m below the start, you encounter small waves, then a section of class II rapids. Just below is a sharp right turn, with a railroad bridge immediately downstream. The action begins just above the bridge. At most flows the waves under the bridge are huge. Downstream of the bridge is a long section of class II–III before the action picks up at a sweeping left, followed by a sharp right. Expect huge waves and water moving downstream in a hurry. There are some incredible surf waves, though they are mostly one-timers, out in the current. After the sharp right is 1.5 km of excellent exploding waves and holes. The river turns slowly to the right, then heads down a straight to a sharp left turn at an island. Take the right channel around the island to reach the take-out. The exit point is at the base of a short steep hill with a trail that leads up to the pipeline road. Be sure to take the smaller right channel around the island, since you can not see the take-out from the larger left channel!

GETTING THERE The run is located west of Jasper along Highway 16.

TAKE-OUT From the lights at the junction of Highway 16 and Highway 93 in Jasper, proceed west on Highway 16 for approximately 55 km to where the

263

road runs along Moose Lake. Travel along Moose Lake until the road leaves the lake, then in about 4 km look for a set of gates used to close the highway. From the gates, continue west for 4 km to a small road that leaves on the south (left) side of the highway with a yellow gate across it. If coming from the west, the take-out is 11 km east of the gas station at Mount Robson. Watch for a long descent and a small road with a yellow gate on the right at the bottom. Park so as not to block the gate and walk along the road to just before the third power pole. Look for the steep trail on the left that leads down to the river. Mark the take-out at the river.

PUT-IN Go 3 km east on Highway 16 to a long straight at a descent, where the highway has two lanes heading east. At the bottom of the hill, the highway narrows to one lane. Watch for a short section where the shoulder is wide. There is a set of forked railroad tracks on the south (right) side of the highway. Park well off the road and follow the right fork of the tracks to the river.

CAMPING There is camping 11 km west of the take-out, at Mount Robson.

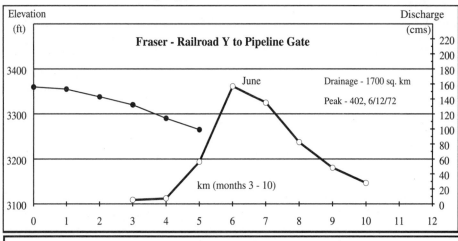

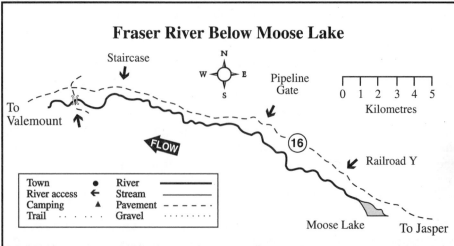

Fraser River Below Moose Lake

FRASER — HIGHWAY 16 TO MOOSE LAKE

GRADE	CLASS	FLOW	TIME	LENGTH
I⁺–II	II	Most Flows	2–4 hours	20 km (12 mi)

Gradient 1 m/km (.1%)
5.2 ft/mi

Max gradient 20 m in 20 km (.1%)
65 ft in 12 mi

Put-in elevation 1052 m
3450 ft

Take-out elevation 1032 m
3385 ft

Shuttle 15 km (9.3 mi) one way

Season May–September

Maps 83D15

Gauge No

Craft Canoes, kayaks and rafts

CHARACTER A medium-volume run through spectacular scenery in an open valley, with towering peaks and cascading waterfalls.

FLOW INFORMATION The river is uncontrolled and fed by snowmelt and glacial runoff. Assess the flow at the put-in.

TRAVEL Access to the run and the shuttle are on paved roads.

DESCRIPTION At the put-in, the river flows in a single channel lined with mud banks. This continues for about 3 km, then the river meanders in large loops, with little current. The river is removed from the highway, though it comes close to the road in a few spots. Expect a couple of class II rapids. Near the middle of the run, and again at the end, the river flows through marshy flats where moose are abundant. When you reach Moose Lake, paddle out into the lake until you can see a boat launch along the north shore, then paddle across the lake to the boat launch.

GETTING THERE The run is located west of Jasper along Highway 16.

TAKE-OUT From the lights at the junction of Highway 16 and Highway 93 in Jasper, proceed west on Highway 16 for approximately 55 km to where the road runs along Moose Lake. At the east end of Moose Lake is a small boat launch where you can park. If coming from the west, the boat launch is about 28 km east of the gas station at Mount Robson.

PUT-IN Go east (right) on Highway 16 and travel approximately 15 km to the first bridge over the Fraser.

CAMPING There is camping 7 km east of the put-in, at Lucerne Campground.

265

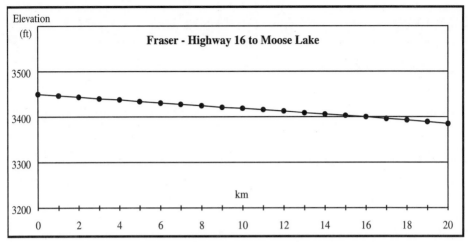

Fraser - Highway 16 to Moose Lake

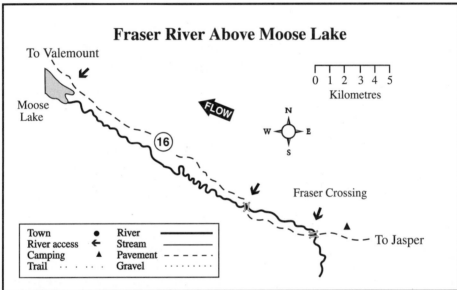

Fraser River Above Moose Lake

To Valemount

Moose
Lake

FLOW

N
W · E
S

0 1 2 3 4 5
Kilometres

16

Fraser Crossing

To Jasper

Town	●	River	────
River access	←	Stream	────
Camping	▲	Pavement	─ ─ ─
Trail	· · · · ·	Gravel	· · · · · ·

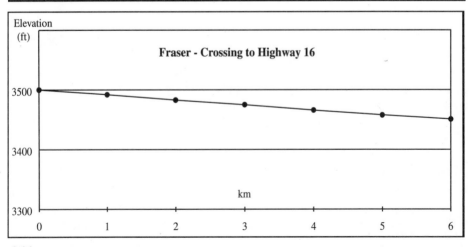

Fraser - Crossing to Highway 16

GRADE	CLASS	FLOW	TIME	LENGTH
II	I⁺–II	Most Flows	1–2 hours	6.5 km (4 mi)

Gradient   2.3 m/km (.23%)   **Max gradient**   15 m in 6.5 km (.23%)
             12 ft/mi   50 ft in 4 mi

Put-in elevation   1067 m   **Take-out elevation**   1052 m
                     3500 ft   3450 ft

Shuttle   5 km (3 mi) one way   **Season**   May–September

Maps   83D15   **Gauge**   No

Craft   Canoes, kayaks and rafts

CHARACTER   A short, medium-volume run through a scenic valley. There are a few rapids where the river is constricted or drops through boulder gardens.

FLOW INFORMATION   The river is uncontrolled and fed by snowmelt and glacial runoff. Assess the flow at the put-in.

TRAVEL   Access to the run and the shuttle are on paved roads.

DESCRIPTION   At the put-in, the river flows in a meandering mud-lined channel. There are a good views of the mountains at the head of the valley. The river twists in the wandering channel and is constricted in a couple of spots. These constrictions produce class II rapids with standing waves, which get bigger at higher flows. There is one long section of class II rapids beside the highway, but for the most part the sections of rapids alternate with calm stretches. Watch for sweepers and log jams along the banks. The gradient profile is on page 266.

GETTING THERE   The run is located west of Jasper along Highway 16. See the map on page 266.

TAKE-OUT   From the lights at the junction of Highway 16 and Highway 93 in Jasper, proceed 37 km west on Highway 16 to the Fraser Crossing Bridge. From there, continue 4.8 km west to another bridge on the Fraser. If coming from the west, the take-out is 43 km east of the gas station at Mount Robson.

PUT-IN   Go east on Highway 16 for 4.8 km to the Fraser Crossing bridge.

CAMPING   There is developed camping 2.2 km east of the put-in, at Lucerne Campground.

SWIFTCURRENT CREEK   TO HIGHWAY 16

GRADE	CLASS	FLOW	TIME	LENGTH
V	IV–V$^+$	Low	4–6 hours	5 km (3 mi)
V$^+$	IV$^+$–VI	Medium		

Gradient   36 m/km (3.6%)
   188 ft/mi

Max gradient   30 m in .5 km (6%)
   100 ft in .3 mi

Put-in elevation   981 m
   3220 ft

Take-out elevation   803 m
   2635 ft

Shuttle   A 4-km (2.5-mi) carry
   and a 2-km drive

Season   May–September

Maps   83E3

Gauge   No

Craft   Kayaks

NOTES   You must push, pull or drag your boat 4 km (2.5 mi) to the put-in.

CHARACTER   A remote, small-volume steep-creek run that pounds down a constricted boulder-bed. You could portage the wild section, but that is a class V$^+$ project in itself. Go to paddle class V$^+$, or don't go at all.

FLOW INFORMATION   The creek is uncontrolled and fed by snowmelt and glacial runoff. Estimate the flow at the Highway 16 bridge as follows: if the water is flowing around the river left bridge support, the flow is medium to high. If water is not flowing around the river left bridge support, the creek is low.

TRAVEL   Access to the run is on paved roads.

DESCRIPTION   At the put-in, the creek is in an open gravel plain, surrounded by towering peaks, with awesome views of the upper valley. The creek is calm for about 800 m, then it drops off the glacial plain into a continuous class IV–IV$^+$ boulderfield of broken rock with a couple of short pinched sections. After 1–2 km of this action, you reach a steep series of class V chutes that lead to Detonator, a constricted four-part class V$^+$ rapid. This begins at a class V boulder garden. The creek then drops 2 m in a tight chute, and hammers off a 2–3-m drop. There is a sharp turn, the creek falls 2 m, goes around a huge boulder and slams into the last 2-m drop. At the end of the whole thing is Firing Pin, the hole on the right at the bottom. The entire section is a class V–VI, 100-m-long torrent. You can portage this bit, but the valley walls are steep and the trees close together, with dense undergrowth. Try the left shore, where a faint trail runs along the edge of the valley.

Below Detonator, the river eases briefly to class IV$^+$–V for about 100 m, then you reach a horizon line where the river drops 5–6 m into Sickle and Hammer, a

Stuart Smith just above Sickle and Hammer. Photo: Peter Stummel.

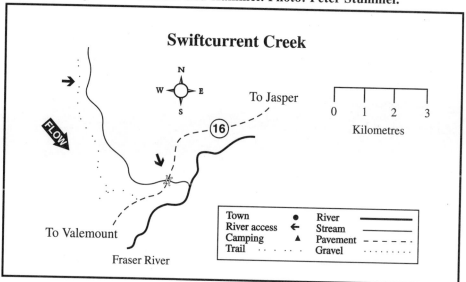

Swiftcurrent Creek

To Jasper

FLOW

16

0 1 2 3
Kilometres

To Valemount

Fraser River

Town	●	River	——
River access	←	Stream	——
Camping	▲	Pavement	– – – –
Trail	· · · · · ·	Gravel	· · · · · · · ·

class V⁺–VI rapid. The 45-degree chute on the left rockets into a 3-m drop against the polished rock wall on the left. The right side hammers onto boulders. Scout or portage on the left. About 70 m below is a class V boulder garden at a sharp left turn. You then reach Split Finger, a large, undercut rock outcrop perpendicular to the current that produces a chute on the left through the slot, and a narrow, boulder-choked passage on the right. Below Split Finger is the old bridge. The river tears over an open, steep and shallow boulder-bed to the highway bridge.

GETTING THERE The run is located west of Jasper along Highway 16.

TAKE-OUT From the lights at the junction of Highway 16 and Highway 93 in Jasper, proceed west on Highway 16 for approximately 84 km to the gas station at Mount Robson. Continue west from the gas station for 3.8 km to the bridge over Swiftcurrent Creek. If coming from the west, the bridge is 12 km east of the junction of Highways 5/16.

PUT-IN Go 400 m west of the Highway 16 bridge, then turn north (right) on Swiftcurrent Creek Road. Go 500 m to just before a sharp left turn. On the right is an overgrown road that leads to the old bridge. You can walk along that road to the creek, then upstream on the river right shore to scout Sickle and Hammer. Continue past the overgrown road to the left turn. Go left for about 500 m to a clearing with a couple of trails on the right side. The most westerly trail, which leads off to the north (right) side, is the one to follow. Carry along the old overgrown road that leads upstream. You will not see the creek until near the put-in. In about 3 km, the road narrows to a trail at a creek bridge. Continue upstream for about 1 km to where you can see the creek on the gravel flats, then cut through the woods to the creek.

CAMPING There is developed camping 3.8 km east of the highway bridge, at Mount Robson.

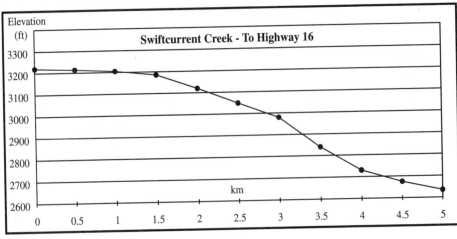

GRADE	CLASS	FLOW	TIME	LENGTH
IV	II⁺–VI⁺	Low	3–5 hours	4.5 km (2.8 mi)
IV⁺	III–VI⁺	Medium		
V	III–VI⁺	High		

Gradient 30 m/km (3%)
157 ft/mi

Max gradient 30 m in .8 km (3.8%)
100 ft in .5 mi

Put-in elevation 985 m
3230 ft

Take-out elevation 850 m
2790 ft

Shuttle A 5 km (3.1 mi) carry

Season May–September

Maps 83E3

Gauge No

Craft Kayaks and canoes

NOTES You must push, pull or drag your boat 5 km (3.1 mi) to the put-in.

CHARACTER A waterfall-studded, small-volume run in a magnificent valley, with spectacular views of Mount Robson. There is a short portage around a gorge. The waterfalls are very difficult, with tight lines.

FLOW INFORMATION The river is uncontrolled and fed by snowmelt and glacial runoff. Assess the flow at the take-out bridge.

TRAVEL Access to the run is on paved roads.

DESCRIPTION At the put-in you are at Kinney Lake, surrounded by the magnificent scenery. Below the lake outlet, the rapids begin as class II⁺–III, and continue that way for about 1–1.5 km. The first fall is a 4–5-m class V⁺–VI drop that is right beside the trail. The fall itself is difficult, but the 2–3-m broken ledge below makes coming out of the fall on a clean line even more important. The left channel below the fall is often jammed with logs, so the tight line on the right around the rock outcrop is often the option of choice. The river then has easy rapids until the next waterfall, which is also right beside the trail. At the class V Photoshot, the river drops 3–4 m in a jagged chute on the left, with a clean line on the right. The riverbed opens up again until you reach a sharp left turn, with a distinct horizon line. This is the class V⁺–VI Double Take, a 4–6-m drop into a wicked recirculation produced by the bedrock ledge 10 m downstream. The second part is a 1–2-m drop off the ledge that backs up the first drop. This has been run, but the stakes are high, with poor spots for safety setups! About 100 m below Double Take is a class V chute through a narrow gap; then the river opens up to more class II–III

Stuart Smith disappearing in Photoshot. Photo: A helpful hiker!

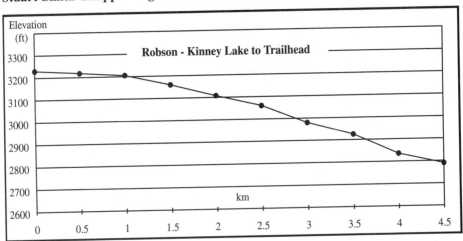

action. Watch closely for an avalanche chute that is followed by a class V drop. This is just above a narrow class VI⁺ gorge that is cluttered with logs. Before you drop down below the avalanche chute, portage on the right up through the dense bush to the trail. Follow the trail downstream for a couple of hundred metres, to where you can descend to the river through an open area, at a left turn. Below this the river runs in a tight channel then opens up a bit until you reach a sharp right turn. Here the river drops off a class V–V⁺ broken ledge with a chute in the centre. There are a few class II⁺–III rapids before you reach the take-out.

GETTING THERE The run is located west of Jasper along Highway 16.

TAKE-OUT From the lights at the junction of Highway 16 and Highway 93 in Jasper, proceed west on Highway 16 for approximately 84 km to the gas station at Mount Robson. If coming from the west, the gas station is 16 km east of the Highways 5/16 junction. At the gas station, turn north and go 2.2 km to the trailhead for Berg Lake.

PUT-IN Grab your boat and carry up the trail to a bridge across the river at Kinney Lake. The trail is an old fire road, so boat buggies will work.

CAMPING There is developed camping near the take-out.

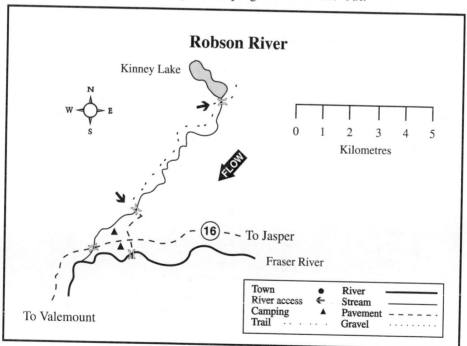

GRADE	CLASS	FLOW	TIME	LENGTH
III	II–IV	Low	1 hour	4 km (2.5 mi)
IV	II–IV$^+$	High		

Gradient 11 m/km (1.1%)
56 ft/mi

Max gradient 30 m in 2.5 km (1.2%)
100 ft in 1.6 mi

Put-in elevation 829 m
2720 ft

Take-out elevation 786 m
2580 ft

Shuttle 11 km (6.8 mi) one way

Season May–September

Maps 83D14

Gauge Yes

Craft Canoes, kayaks and rafts

CHARACTER A great medium-volume run through a short canyon section, with distinct pool-and-drop rapids created by bedrock outcrops. You need to watch for logs in the constricted lower canyon.

FLOW INFORMATION The river is uncontrolled and fed by snowmelt and glacial runoff. Assess the flow at the take-out bridge.

TRAVEL The shuttle is on gravel roads.

DESCRIPTION The run begins with class II rapids, but soon mellows as the river flows swiftly in a wide channel. Watch closely for a glimpse of the overhead powerlines just below a left turn that leads immediately to a right turn. Downstream of the right turn the river drops into Powerline, a class III–III$^+$ riverwide ledge that creates an impressive horizon line. Eddy out on the left below Powerline to scout Headwall, a class III$^+$–IV$^+$ rapid just downstream of the blind left turn below Powerline. Once you start into the left turn there is little chance to stop. At Headwall, the river drops off a diagonal broken ledge with a steep drop on the right. The left side offers the best route through. Below this, the river rips through a constricted section with small ledges and great waves. The rapids then ease and you paddle in the open channel for about 1 km. The river then makes a left turn followed by a right turn and drops into Headwall II, a similar but easier version of the rapid upstream. The river opens up again, then closes in at a sharp left turn. The river drops into Tooth, a class III$^+$–IV drop with a sharp bedrock fin that splits the drop into two channels. Here the river explodes into standing waves, and drops along the right wall into a narrow swirling chute. Not far below this, the river makes a sharp right turn at a calm narrow section, then tears off into Exodus, a class III–III$^+$ boulder garden. The canyon below is incredibly scenic, with a few good surf spots and well-defined features. The canyon opens up at the railroad bridge and the river is open and easy to the finish.

274

Working On The "Chainsaw Gang"

We had to get the log out; it was that simple. The Commercial Rafting inspector was coming to check out the river, and the log was a serious hazard. So we loaded up a raft with chainsaws, ropes, gas, handsaws, and Kelly, a "volunteer" who was Brian's girlfriend. During previous logging operations we had chopped our way down the river, removing logs and sweepers. All that was left was the one tree lodged in the lower canyon. You could climb out from either shore onto the huge log, which rose up into the air in a shallow arch. With a false mask of bravado, I scrambled out on it, gunned the chainsaw and started cutting. I wanted to cut as much as possible while on sure footing, before I tried hacking away from the raft. It was like Russian roulette: standing on the log, trying to estimate how much force the water was putting on it, and how much I could cut before the fibres would snap and I'd be swept into the next rapid, with the log and howling chainsaw. After several moments of terrified cutting, I lost my nerve and clambered off. We then set up a high-line system to lower the raft down to the log. Kelly had one control line, while Brian in the trees on the opposite shore, had the other.

It was Brian's raft and he was a bit nervous as I swayed back and forth in the current, chainsaw in hand, balancing precariously in the stern of his boat. I tried not to let him know that I too was about ready to give up and go paddling. My rational mind was telling me that this was extremely foolish. Eventually I ignored my saner side, got it together and got on with it.

The plan was straight forward: we would lower the raft down to the log and I would hack the partially cut log in two. We hoped the pieces would then flush out. It was the surging waves just above the log that made the process difficult. As the raft swung toward the log, I had to gun the engine and make a lunging jab with the saw, thereby cutting into the log. When the raft swung away, I had to pull the saw out of the deep groove, lest the blade catch during the sideways swing. The irregular waves were making it difficult to start the saw in the boat, so I hauled the raft upstream, tied off my throw bag, then had Brain haul me away to the calmer water, where I started the chainsaw. He was moving the boat back out into the current when it happened. My foot dislodged the quick-release knot in the descent line running to the thwart. I sat there, frozen in horror, with the revving chainsaw in hand, as the line fed out. Twisting around frantically, I gaped at the log. I realized, in terror, that the raft would slip under it, and I would be crushed, then chewed up by the chainsaw. As I was about to jump for it, the stuff sack of my throwbag hit the carabiner that the line ran through, and I came to an abrupt halt, with the back end of the raft surfing under the arched log. I was screaming at Brain, who had no idea what had happened, to get me out of there! When I recovered enough to try again, we finally cut the log out. We never even got around to rafting the run commercially. I sure hope the other folks that do will appreciate what went into cleaning out that river!

GETTING THERE The run is located south of Valemount, off highway 5. See the map on page 278.

TAKE-OUT From the junction of 5th Avenue and Highway 5 in Valemount, go south on Highway 5 for 3.7 km to the Kinbasket Lake turn-off. Continue south for 3.8 km to the bridge over the river.

PUT-IN Go north for 3.8 km to the Kinbasket Lake turn-off. Turn west (left) and follow the gravel road for 1.1 km to a fork. Stay left on the West Ridge Forest Service Road and continue for 4.6 km to a powerline crossing. You go another 1 km to an old bridge site on the left where the river is close to the road.

CAMPING There is developed camping 600 m upstream of the put-in.

Keith Klapstein stroking into Powerline.

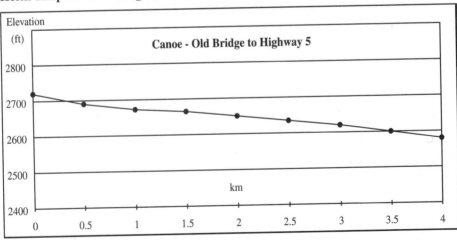

GRADE	CLASS	FLOW	TIME	LENGTH
III⁺	II⁺–III⁺	Low	1–2 hours	7.5 km (4.7 mi)
IV	III–IV	High		

Gradient 18 m/km (1.8%)
  97 ft/mi

Max gradient 30 m in 1.4 km (2.1%)
  100 ft in .9 mi

Put-in elevation 966 m
  3170 ft

Take-out elevation 829 m
  2720 ft

Shuttle 7 km (4.3 mi) one way

Season May–September

Maps 83D11 and 83D14

Gauge Yes

Craft Canoes, kayaks and rafts

CHARACTER A small to medium-volume run that tears down a narrow and shallow boulder-bed with ice-cold whitewater that does not let up. This section is usually combined with the lower canyon for a superb run. There is some good surfing and hole-playing.

FLOW INFORMATION The river is uncontrolled and fed by snowmelt and glacial runoff. Assess the flow at the take-out.

TRAVEL Access to the run and the shuttle are on paved roads.

DESCRIPTION The run begins in a narrow, tree-lined channel with mud banks and sweepers lying off the undercut shore. In a few hundred metres you encounter some class II rapids at a narrow chute. Not far below this, the river makes a left turn and takes off. Expect continuous class III rapids with class III⁺–IV sections. The river is relentless as it drops down the narrow riverbed. At high flows the river is always disappearing around a tight corner or over a horizon line. About 1–2 km into the run you encounter False Teeth, a class IV drop that piles up against the log debris on the right, then drops off a constricted boulder fence on a sharp left turn. You can scout and portage on the right by climbing over and along the log mess, or on the left by eddying out above the drop. The rapid requires a committed move from right to left through one of the slots in the boulder fence. Below this, the river resumes its furious descent, although on a more open channel. This continues until the channel narrows and the river accelerates into tighter quarters, with huge boulders creating the exploding froth that never seems to let up. Expect steady class III with a couple of tougher sections. The river calms down for about the last 1 km of the run.

GETTING THERE The run is located south of Valemount, off Highway 5.

TAKE-OUT From the junction of 5th Avenue and Highway 5 in Valemount, go 3.7 km south on Highway 5 to the Kinbasket Lake turn-off on the west (right) side. If coming from the south, watch for the Kinbasket Lake turn-off on the west (left) side 3.8 km north of the Canoe River bridge. Turn west and follow the gravel road for 1.1 km to a fork. Stay left on the West Ridge Forest Service Road and continue for 4.6 km to a powerline crossing. Go another 1 km to an old bridge site on the left.

PUT-IN Continue upstream for 6.7 km to a tiny, rutted track on the south (left) side that leads 200 m through the trees to the gauging station. If you miss the put-in, you will reach a large sawdust pile on the left side. Turn around and go back downstream for 1.1 km. Trust your odometer and look carefully for the track.

CAMPING There is developed camping at the Upper Canoe Recreation Site which you pass on the way to the put-in.

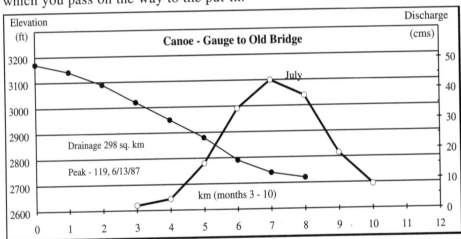

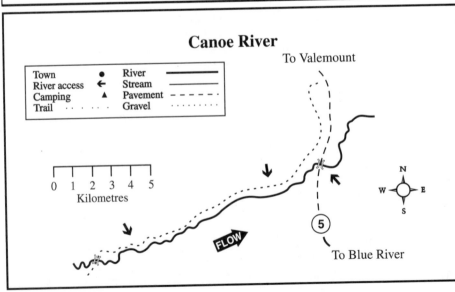

278

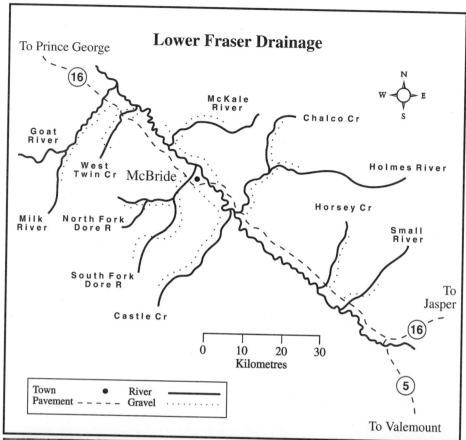

Lower Fraser Drainage

To Prince George

(16)

McKale River

Chalco Cr

Goat River

West Twin Cr

McBride

Holmes River

Milk River

North Fork Dore R

Horsey Cr

Small River

South Fork Dore R

Castle Cr

To Jasper

(16)

0   10   20   30
Kilometres

(5)

| Town | ● | River | ——— |
| Pavement | – – – – | Gravel | ·········· |

To Valemount

Mark Oddy on the North Fork of the Dore upstream of Boreal Creek.

GRADE	CLASS	FLOW	TIME	LENGTH
II–III	II⁺–IV	Low	1-2 hours	9 km (5.6 mi)
III–IV	III–IV⁺	High		

Gradient 10 m/km (1%) 53 ft/mi

Max gradient 30 m in 2.3 km (1.3%) 100 ft in 1.4 mi

Put-in elevation 821 m 2695 ft

Take-out elevation 732 m 2400 ft

Shuttle 13.5 km (8.4 mi) one way

Season May–August

Maps 93H7

Gauge No

Craft Canoes, kayaks and rafts

CHARACTER A medium to large-volume run on an open riverbed in the upper section, with a constricted canyon in the lower part. At higher flows the river has outstanding surf and play opportunities on the well-defined features.

FLOW INFORMATION The river is uncontrolled and fed by snowmelt and glacial runoff. Assess the flow at the take-out. At high flows the constricted canyon squeezes the river into powerful features.

TRAVEL The shuttle is on gravel roads.

DESCRIPTION At the put-in, the river is open with a few rapids where the river encounters boulder gardens. The rapids are class II⁺–III⁺ for the most part, with powerful waves and holes at higher flows. The river changes character at the Slot, a class III–III⁺ drop between rock walls. The narrow 4-m gap through bedrock starts the canyon section and is often jammed with trees, so use caution. Below The Slot the riverbed opens up for about 50–100 m, before you reach a difficult-to-spot diagonal ledge. Below the ledge, the river tears through a section of rapids formed by huge bedrock chunks, then accelerates toward a left turn followed by a drop into a narrow canyon on a right turn. At the class IV–IV⁺ Nozzle, the river drops over broken bedrock ledges, makes a sharp right turn between rock walls and accelerates through a narrow gap. Below The Nozzle, the canyon opens up, though there are a few open rapids not far below. The river is then easier until you reach the take-out.

GETTING THERE The run is located north of McBride, off Highway 16. See the map on page 283.

TAKE-OUT From McBride, go north for 2–3 km to where the highway crosses the rail line at a bridge. From the railroad bridge, continue north for about 37 km to the bridge over the Goat River. There is a paved pull-off on the east (right) side, just north of the bridge. If coming from the north, look for the bridge about 155 km south of Prince George.

PUT-IN Go 3.5 km south from the bridge to a small gravel road on the west (right) side of the highway, just past a left bend. Turn right onto the gravel Goat River Road and go 10 km to the first spot where the river is close to the road. You can add more distance to the run by continuing upstream to the put-in for the run on the Milk. See page 282 for details.

CAMPING There is undeveloped camping along the gravel road to the put-in, or developed camping at the take-out.

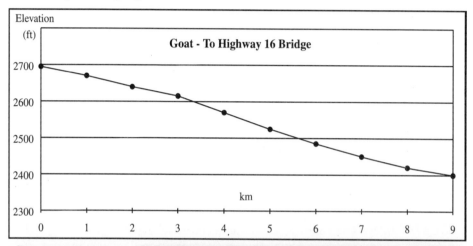

Glen Garrette in The Slot at low flows.

GRADE	CLASS	FLOW	TIME	LENGTH
II⁺	II–IV⁺	Low	1 hour	6 km (3.7 mi)
III	II–V	High		

Gradient 10 m/km (1%)
55 ft/mi

Max gradient 30 m in 2 km (1.5%)
100 ft in 1.2 mi

Put-in elevation 884 m
2900 ft

Take-out elevation 821 m
2695 ft

Shuttle 4.5 km (2.8 mi) one way

Season May–August

Maps 93H7

Gauge No

Craft Canoes, kayaks and rafts

CHARACTER A short, small-volume run over a tight boulder-bed, with one constricted drop in a canyon.

FLOW INFORMATION The river is uncontrolled and fed by snowmelt and glacial runoff. Assess the flow at the put-in.

TRAVEL Access to the run and the shuttle are on gravel roads.

DESCRIPTION The run starts as a small-volume river flowing through a narrow tree-lined channel, with lots of tight corners. There are a couple of class II⁺ rapids where the river is constricted by small bedrock ledges. The river opens up for a short while, until you reach a constricted low-walled canyon. This is Milk Carton, a 2–4-m, class IV⁺–V drop over a bedrock ledge. You can scout and portage on the right side. Below Milk Carton, the river is open, with a few small rapids until you reach the confluence with the Goat River. After the confluence, the Goat is wide and open, with bouncy rapids, standing waves and good surfing at higher flows. Watch for your marker at the take-out.

GETTING THERE The run is located north of McBride, off Highway 16.

TAKE-OUT In McBride, go north for 2–3 km to where Highway 16 crosses the rail line at a bridge. From the bridge, go 26 km north on Highway 16 to the bridge over West Twin Creek. Continue north for another 7.3 km to a small gravel road on the west (left) side of the highway. If coming from the north, look for the gravel road on the west (right) side, just past a left bend approximately 3.5 km south of the highway bridge on the Goat. Turn west and follow the Goat River Road for 10 km to the first spot where the river is close to the road. If you do not like the thought of carrying up the steep bank, continue 2.7 km upstream and take out at the confluence of the Goat and Milk rivers, although this cuts off a lot of the run. Mark the take-out at river level.

PUT-IN Go 4.4 km upstream to where the river is close to the road. Continue for another 500 m to a spot where the river is even closer.

CAMPING There is undeveloped camping along the gravel road to the put-in.

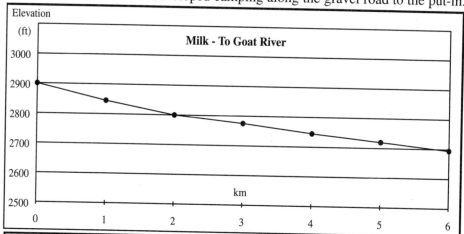

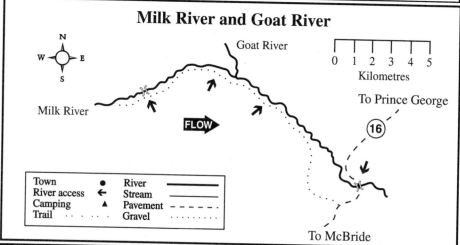

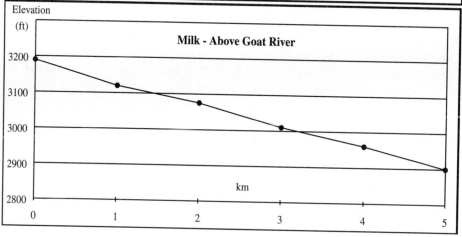

GRADE	CLASS	FLOW	TIME	LENGTH
II⁺	II–III	Low	1 hour	5 km (3.1 mi)
III	II–III	High		

Gradient 18 m/km (1.8%)
   93 ft/mi

Max gradient 30 m in 1.4 km (2.1%)
   100 ft in .87 mi

Put-in elevation 972 m
   3190 ft

Take-out elevation 884 m
   2900 ft

Shuttle 4.6 km (2.9 mi) one way

Season May–August

Maps 93H7

Gauge No

Craft Canoes, kayaks and rafts

CHARACTER A small-volume run in a narrow, tree-lined boulder channel with continuous rapids for most of the run. Watch for sweepers and log jams.

FLOW INFORMATION The river is uncontrolled and fed by snowmelt and glacial runoff. Assess the flow at the take-out.

TRAVEL Access to the run and the shuttle are on gravel roads.

DESCRIPTION The run begins in a narrow channel with continuous class II⁺–III rapids on a boulder-bed. There are a couple of constricted sections where rock outcrops produce well-defined features. The valley is scenic, but the river flows in a narrow channel with few views of the surrounding mountains. Watch for a couple of riverwide sweepers and the occasional log jam. Mark the take-out at the river. See the gradient profile on page 283.

GETTING THERE The run is located north of McBride, off Highway 16. See the map on page 283.

TAKE-OUT From McBride, go north for 2–3 km to a bridge over the rail line. Continue 26 km north of the railroad bridge to the bridge over West Twin Creek. Continue north for another 7.3 km to a gravel road on the west (left) side. If coming from the north, look for the gravel road on the west (right) side, approximately 3.5 km south of the highway bridge on the Goat. Turn west and follow the Goat River Road for 14.4 km to where the river is close to the road. Continue for another 500 m to where the river is closer to the road.

PUT-IN Continue upstream for another 4.5 km to a small gravel road on the north (right) side. Turn right and follow the road for 100 m to the put-in bridge.

CAMPING There is undeveloped camping along the road to the put-in.

GRADE	CLASS	FLOW	TIME	LENGTH
II–III	II–III	Low	1 hour	4 km (2.5 mi)
II+–III+	II+–III+	High		

Gradient 23 m/km (2.3%)
121 ft/mi

Max gradient 30 m in 1.3 km (2.4%)
100 ft in .78 mi

Put-in elevation 823 m
2700 ft

Take-out elevation 738 m
2400 ft

Shuttle 4.4 km (2.7 mi) one way

Season May–August

Maps 93H7 and 93H8

Gauge No

Craft Canoes, kayaks and rafts

CHARACTER A short, small-volume run with the best rapids at the start followed by an open and easier section in the lower part of the run. There are a couple of portages around and over log jams in the middle of the run.

FLOW INFORMATION The creek is uncontrolled and fed by snowmelt and glacial runoff. Assess the flow at the take-out.

TRAVEL The shuttle is on gravel roads.

DESCRIPTION The whitewater begins with a bang directly under the bridge as the creek tears down a narrow, boulder-lined channel. There are a couple of rock-wall remnants before the valley opens up. The rapids ease to class II+ on a fast creekbed, then you begin to encounter a few log jams as the gradient decreases and the creek flows over gravel, with some braiding. In the lower section, the creek flows swiftly through a small, tree-lined channel. The carry down to the creek is quite steep.

GETTING THERE The run is located north of McBride, off Highway 16.

TAKE-OUT From McBride, go north for 2–3 km, to where the highway crosses the rail line at a bridge. Continue 26 km north on Highway 16 to the bridge over West Twin Creek. If coming from the north, the bridge is about 165 km south of Prince George. Go north from the bridge for 600 m to a small unmarked gravel road on the east (right) side of the highway. Turn east (right) and follow the road for 2.6 km to a junction where you stay right. Continue 1.2 km to the bridge over the creek.

PUT-IN Return to the highway bridge and park on the east (left) side, just south of the bridge. Carry down the steep slope to the creek.

CAMPING There is informal camping along the gravel road to the take-out, or developed camping in McBride.

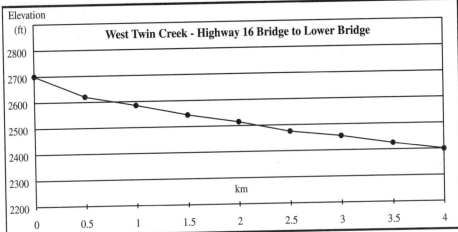

West Twin Creek - Highway 16 Bridge to Lower Bridge

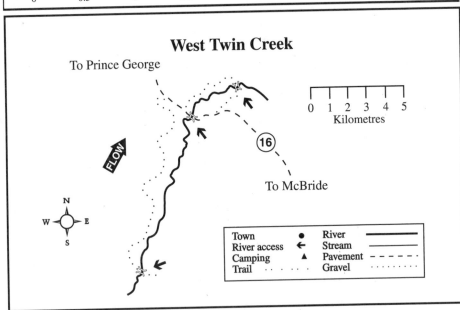

West Twin Creek

To Prince George

To McBride

0 1 2 3 4 5
Kilometres

Town	●	River	————
River access	←	Stream	———
Camping	▲	Pavement	– – – –
Trail	· · · · ·	Gravel	· · · · · ·

WEST TWIN CREEK
BRIDGE TO HIGHWAY 16

GRADE	CLASS	FLOW	TIME	LENGTH
IV⁺	III–VI	Low	2–3 hours	9.5 km (5.9 mi)
V	III–VI	Medium		

Gradient 39 m/km (3.9%)
203 ft/mi

Max gradient 30 m in .7 km (4.3%)
100 ft in .43 mi

Put-in elevation 1189 m
3900 ft

Take-out elevation 823 m
2700 ft

Shuttle 21 km (13 mi) one way

Season May–August

Maps 93H7

Gauge No

Craft Kayaks

CHARACTER A small-volume run that has good whitewater in the top part, and a full-scale grade V canyon in the lower part of the run. The carry up to the highway at the take-out is nothing short of brutal. Consider extending the run to include the section described on page 285.

FLOW INFORMATION The creek is uncontrolled and fed by snowmelt and glacial runoff. Assess the flow at the take-out.

TRAVEL The shuttle is on gravel roads.

DESCRIPTION The run begins in an open valley with continuous class II⁺–III rapids as the river flows over a boulder-bed. There are a couple of class IV drops in the upper part, with quite a few logs in the first kilometre. A second, easier, section has a few more logs and log jams; then you reach a sharp right turn at a bedrock outcrop where the river pounds into the canyon. This section is 1–2 km long and drops through a series of class V–V⁺ bedrock-lined drops that are often cluttered with logs. A couple of the drops are class VI at most flows. The whitewater is constricted and very difficult, with short pools between explosive drops. Portaging is a ridiculous adventure in scaling canyon walls with your boat. The whitewater eases as the river makes a right just above the bridge and is class IV–IV⁺ for the last 700 m.

GETTING THERE The run is located north of McBride, off Highway 16. See the map on page 286.

TAKE-OUT From McBride, go north for 2–3 km, to where Highway 16 crosses the rail line at a bridge. From the railroad bridge, go 26 km north to the take-out bridge. If coming from the north, the bridge is approximately 165 km south of Prince George. The river right bank is probably the easiest carry!

PUT-IN From the bridge, go north for 1.6 km to a gravel road on the west (left) side of the highway. Turn left and go 7.3 km to a fork. Stay left and continue along the road for another 800 m to second fork. Stay left and in 800 m you reach a third fork where you again stay left. Continue for 10.4 km and you will reach the bridge at the put-in. The road up to the put-in is solid, but with many dips and ruts, so travel is slow.

CAMPING There is undeveloped camping along the gravel road near the put-in, or developed camping in McBride.

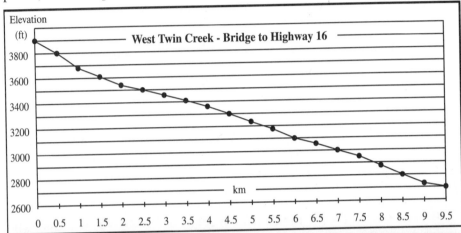

Stuart Smith in the lower canyon. Photo: A helpful fisherman.

Doin' It in the Dark

It looked great on paper: a run with reasonable gradient and contour lines set back from the river enough to suggest it wouldn't be a total canyon. However, this was B.C., where portages mean thrashing through Devils Club on high-angle terrain, and insanely dense bush everywhere. It was about 3 hours until dark so I weighed the options for a while, then made the obvious choice. I dumped my bike at the take-out and raced up to the put-in. I dressed lightly, with one top and a pair of neoprene shorts. That was my first serious mistake.

The first few kilometres had some log jams, but the run was mostly open and lacking in gradient. At the first rock walls, I was out of the boat to scout a blind corner. After a concerted struggle through the bush I saw intense class V, with a few logs. I thrashed back to my boat and leapt into the action. The first rapids were bigger than they had looked, and the water was very fast. But I was still on top of things, so I pressed on, scrambling out to scout at the top of the constricted drops. At the waterfall, I peered into near darkness. A wild move under a log led to a swirling chute that dropped off into the pool. It was class V⁺–VI, but it looked like things eased off below, so I went for it. At the bottom I was pumped, had wired the moves and was feeling cocky, to say the least. So instead of getting out to scout the next wild bit, I glanced down from the eddy, sure I could see a way through. As I dropped the 2 m into the slot, I spotted a log angled across, with one end in the centre of the drop below. I shot out of the gap and toward the log, leaning forward to duck under the upraised end. Just before impact, I was slammed backwards by an unseen branch that caught my dry top and PFD, securely impaling me. I was instantly draped around the tree with my throat held against the log, as my body and boat were torqued underneath. Nearly separated from my boat I made a last-ditch effort to avoid having my airway crushed. Smashing my paddle up against the branch, I threw my body upstream into the current. I heard the rip of my top and PFD as the branch broke and I was swept into the rapid below. Upside down, I hauled my butt back into the boat and rolled just in time to claw my way into the eddy above the rapid below. I could barely make out the channel below. That was it, I was out of there! That is when the real test began.

In the darkness I grovelled up the steep bank, clutching wildly at shadows in order to gain purchase on the steep slope. Several times I clamped onto a spiny Devil's Club in a pathetic attempt to avoiding flailing downhill. In a painful but dictated choice, I held tightly to those hideous handholds. An hour after I left the creek, I could see the bridge high above me, about 400 m away. With grim determination I struggled on, hauling my boat up the steep slopes. Then I reached an impasse, where the trees gave way to a cliff. I repeatedly tried to find a way to get down. In desperation I lowered my boat into the blackness, then looped the rope around the tree and began rappeling into the murk. Several metres down, I was hanging freely below an overhang in the cliff when I reached my boat, tied into the line. I was still some distance off the ground and unable to ascertain how far! I began to swing back and forth, attempting to contact the cliff. After a few tenuous moments of bashing off unseen objects, I clutched some branches and managed to scramble onto a tree and descend to the ground. Climbing back up I retrieved my boat and carried on. The terrain was utter madness. The tortuously steep ground was covered in profusely dense brush that poked, gouged, scraped and clawed at every limb. The footing was slippery twigs and rotting logs, and every few steps I took a peeler, slamming onto the ground, and skidding downhill into unseen objects. Then I lost it. I climbed the loose rock face like a demon possessed with the power of utter lunacy. At the top of the slope I reached gentler terrain, but it was a mixed blessing. The overgrown clear-cut was a mass of tangled trees that blocked every fragment of light. I bumbled along in sensory deprivation, while being simultaneously attacked on all sides by unseen, grasping foes. A dozen times I was poked in the eyes, the nose and lips. My arms were often pinned back, so that even as I fell I was clutched by the bush, coming to rest in painful and horrifying positions.

I gouged my way through the trees for an eternity, until I could hear traffic on the road, then headed for the sound. Staggering out of the undergrowth, I nearly stumbled off the cliff at the road cut. After lowering my boat, I looped a tiny tree and backed off the cliff. At rope's end I was still 3–4 m above the bottom so I untied and started to downclimb, but promptly lost my grip and plummeted to the bottom. Battered but elated, I was on flat terra firma! At 3 a.m. I reached my van and headed to Jasper. Arriving at 6 a.m. I passed out, waking to the wailing of my alarm at 9 a.m.. An hour later, I struggled into work where my boss told me I looked like Hell! The next day my legs scabbed over and the painful truth was revealed. It was months later when I plucked the last festering thorn from my legs. Even now, I occasionally find a small reminder sticking out of my skin. I have since then retrieved my old full-length wetsuit, which I now wear on each and every unknown descent in British Columbia. I am also desperately trying to avoid paddling at night.

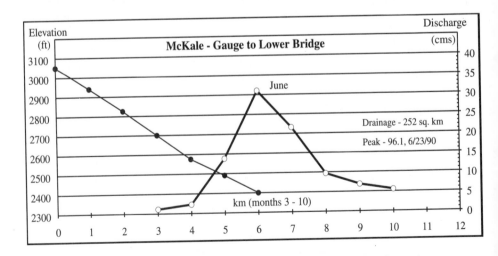

GRADE	CLASS	FLOW	TIME	LENGTH
III+–IV	III–IV+	Low	1–2 hours	6 km (3.7 mi)
IV–IV+	III–V	High		

Gradient 33 m/km (3.3%)
172 ft/mi

Max gradient 30 m in .8 km (3.8%)
100 ft in .5 mi

Put-in elevation 930 m
3050 ft

Take-out elevation 735 m
2410 ft

Shuttle 8 km (5 mi) one way

Season May–August

Maps 93H8

Gauge Yes

Craft Canoes and kayaks

CHARACTER A beautiful small-volume run through a tight and technical riverbed of boulders. The rapids are nonstop and the views excellent.

FLOW INFORMATION The river is uncontrolled and fed by snowmelt and glacial runoff. Assess the flow at the take-out, or on the way up to the put-in, where you can see many of the rapids from the road.

TRAVEL Access to the run and the shuttle are on gravel roads.

DESCRIPTION The run begins at the gauging station where the river flows calmly in an open channel. As you descend the rapids increase in difficulty until a short pool where an avalanche chute descends from the left. This is followed by a long stretch of good whitewater. The next 1–2 km has continuous class II+–III rapids, then you reach a second short pool at another avalanche chute on the left. Below this is a long class III+–IV+ rapid that ends with a log jam on the right at the bottom. This is followed by a long section of class III rapids that contains a few class IV sections. The river then enters a narrow and constricted valley with big boulders and tighter whitewater. A sharp right turn leads to Boulder Pile, a class IV–V drop that twists sharply through the tight channel. Watch for logs here. Below Boulder Pile, the river is easier and the last couple of kilometres below the road bridge are open, with braided channels and more sweepers. The gradient profile is on page 290.

GETTING THERE The run is located near McBride, off Highway 16.

TAKE-OUT From McBride, go about 1.5 km south to the bridge on the Fraser River. Continue south for 150 m to a road on the north (left) side of the highway. Turn left and follow the road for 600 m to a junction with Koeneman Road. Turn left and go north for 19 km, to the bridge on the McKale River.

PUT-IN Go south for 200 m to the McKale River Road, which is on the east (left) side of the road. Turn left and follow the road for 200 m to a fork. Stay left and go upstream for 2.2 km to the bridge over the river. Continue along the river right side for 5.3 km to a turn-off on the right at the gauging station.

CAMPING There is undeveloped camping along the road to the put-in.

Looking upstream at some of the boulder garden rapids.

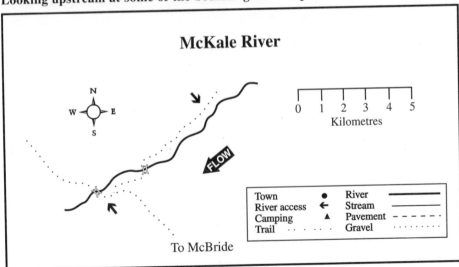

DORE   CONFLUENCE TO HIGHWAY 16

GRADE	CLASS	FLOW	TIME	LENGTH
II–II$^+$	II–III	Low	1–2 hours	9 km (5.6 mi)
II$^+$–III$^+$	II–III$^+$	High		

Gradient   18 m/km (1.8%)   **Max gradient**   30 m in 1 km (3%)
            95 ft/mi   100 ft in .62 mi

Put-in elevation   869 m   **Take-out elevation**   707 m
                     2850 ft   2320 ft

Shuttle   8.5 km (5.3 mi) one way   **Season**   May–August

Maps   93H8   **Gauge**   Yes

Craft   Canoes, kayaks and rafts

CHARACTER   A small to medium-volume run in a scenic valley, with lots of good whitewater as the river flows quickly over a steep boulder-bed. There are some great play spots, with most of the action in the first half of the run.

FLOW INFORMATION   The river is uncontrolled and fed by snowmelt and glacial runoff. Assess the flow at the take-out, or on the way up to the put-in where you can see many of the rapids from the road.

TRAVEL   The shuttle is on gravel roads.

DESCRIPTION   At the confluence the river flows in a constricted, boulder-lined channel. The gradient is nearly constant in the upper part of the run, with a couple of constricted rapids. Watch for log jams where the river spreads out on open gravel sections. Halfway down the run, the road bridge crosses the river. Just below is a sharp left turn that drops into one of the longer class II$^+$–III$^+$ rapids. There are some great surf and play spots as the rapid runs along the road. A couple of kilometres below, is a huge log jam that lines both channels at a sharp right turn, with logs on the island as well. Be wary in this section, as the channel may or may not be open. Below the log jam, the rapids are easier class II–II$^+$, with fewer play spots. Take out on the right, just above the bridge.

GETTING THERE   The run is located off Highway 16, north of McBride. See the map on page 300.

TAKE-OUT   From McBride, go north on Highway 16 for about 2–3 km to where the highway crosses the rail line at a bridge. Continue north for 2 km to the bridge on the Dore. If coming from the north, look for the bridge 24 km south of West Twin Creek. There is a small road on the upstream side, about 200 m south of the bridge. Follow the road to just above the bridge.

PUT-IN Return to Highway 16 and go north to the bridge. Just past the bridge watch for the Dore River Road on the west (left) side of the highway. Turn left and follow the paved road for 1.8 km to the junction with Lamming Pit Road, which is on the right. Stay left on the gravel Dore River Road and go 6.3 km to a fork. To the left is the Dore South Forest Service Road, and to the right is Ozalenka Creek. Stay right and you will cross the south fork of the river in about 100 m. Park well off the road.

CAMPING There is undeveloped camping along the gravel road to the put-in, or developed camping in McBride.

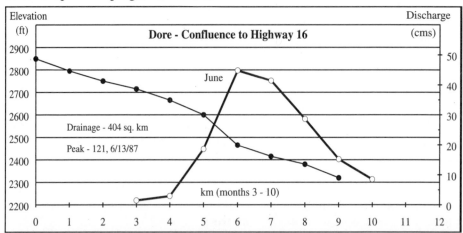

Looking downstream from the road bridge at low–medium flows.

294

NORTH FORK DORE   TO CONFLUENCE

GRADE	CLASS	FLOW	TIME	LENGTH
IV⁺	IV–V	Low	1–2 hours	4 km (2.5 mi)
V	IV–V⁺	High		

Gradient   42 m/km (4.2%)   **Max gradient**   30 m in .4 km (7.5%)
              221 ft/mi   100 ft in .25 mi

Put-in elevation   1036 m   **Take-out elevation**   869 m
                       3400 ft   2850 ft

Shuttle   4 km (2.5 mi) one way   **Season**   May–August

Maps   93H8   **Gauge**   No

Craft   Canoes and kayaks

CHARACTER   An extremely intense, small-volume creek run, tearing down an incessantly steep and narrow boulder-bed. The riverbed is constricted, with many blind corners where logs can be a serious hazard. The whitewater is continuous class IV–IV⁺ with several rapids that are more difficult.

FLOW INFORMATION   The river is uncontrolled and fed by snowmelt and glacial runoff. Assess the flow at the take-out.

TRAVEL   Access to the run and the shuttle are on gravel roads.

DESCRIPTION   The run begins as class II⁺–III rapids, then quickly builds in difficulty to class IV with some class IV⁺–V rapids thrown in. Detailed descriptions are confusing and useless, so use your wits to recognize the nasty parts when you get to them. All the drops are open and runnable, though logs can change that. Expect several class V sections that pound through incredible boulder mazes. The undergrowth along the shore makes scouting and portaging a difficult chore. This is a classic steep-creek run that does not let up.

GETTING THERE   The run is located north of McBride, off Highway 16. See the map on page 300.

TAKE-OUT   From McBride, go north on Highway 16 for about 2–3 km, to where the highway crosses the rail line at a bridge. Continue north for 2 km to the bridge on the Dore. If coming from the north, look for the Dore bridge 24 km south of West Twin Creek. Just north of the bridge is the Dore River Road on the west side. Turn west and follow the paved road for 1.8 km to the junction with Lamming Pit Road, which is on the right. Stay left on the gravel Dore River Road and go 6.3 km to a fork. Stay right to Ozalenka Creek. You will cross a bridge on the South Fork in about 100 m. The take-out is just below the bridge where the North Fork joins the South Fork.

PUT-IN Continue upstream for 500 m to a fork where you stay right. The road starts up a very steep hill, then in 2.4 km crosses a small creek at a bridge. Look for the put-in 1 km past the creek bridge at a small pull-out on the north (right) side where the river is close to the road.

CAMPING There is undeveloped camping along the gravel road to the put-in, or developed camping in McBride.

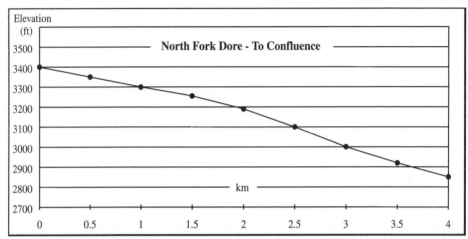

Mark Oddy in one of the easier boulder pitches at low flows.

GRADE	CLASS	FLOW	TIME	LENGTH
IV	III–VI	Low	1–2 hours	4.5 km (2.8 mi)
V	IV–VI	High		

Gradient   34 m/km (3.4%)   **Max gradient**   30 m in .5 km (6 %)
179 ft/mi   100 ft in .31 mi

Put-in elevation   1189 m   **Take-out elevation**   1036 m
3900 ft   3400 ft

Shuttle   3.5 km (2.2 mi) one way   **Season**   May–August

Maps   93H1 and 93H8   **Gauge**   No

Craft   Canoes and kayaks

CHARACTER   An intense, steep-creek run that flows downhill at high speed over a narrow and constricted boulder channel. There are a couple of difficult ledge drops and one possible portage at the Gnasher.

FLOW INFORMATION   The river is uncontrolled and fed by snowmelt and glacial runoff. Assess the flow at the take-out.

TRAVEL   Access to the run and the shuttle are on gravel roads.

DESCRIPTION   The run begins on a narrow boulder-bed that drops through class II⁺–III boulder gardens. Then you begin to encounter bedrock ledges. Watch for a sharp left turn into a short canyon with a constricted class IV–IV⁺ rapid. Below Boreal Creek, which enters from the left, the river picks up. In 1995 there was a riverwide log at a constriction just below the old bridge. The rapids then increase in difficulty to class III–IV and you reach a bedrock canyon with spectacular foaming class IV–IV⁺ whitewater. At the end of the canyon, the river thunders off The Gnasher, a class V⁺–VI broken-bedrock cascade. You can portage on the right from the eddy at the brink; however, you must paddle some tough rapids to make the eddy. Below The Gnasher the river flows through spectacular bedrock outcrops with incredible class IV⁺ whitewater. The rapids then ease and the river mellows to the take-out.

GETTING THERE   The run is located north of McBride, off Highway 16. See the map on page 300.

TAKE-OUT   At McBride, go north on Highway 16 for about 2–3 km, where the highway crosses the rail line at a bridge. Continue north for 2 km to the bridge on the Dore. If coming from the north, look for the Dore bridge 24 km south of West Twin Creek. Just north of the bridge is the Dore River Road on the west side. Turn west and follow the paved road for 1.8 km to the junction with Lamming Pit Road on the right. Stay left on the gravel Dore River Road and go 6.3 km to a fork. Go right to Ozalenka Creek, and you will cross a bridge on the South Fork in about 100 m. Continue upstream for 500 m to a fork where you again stay right. The road starts up a very steep hill, then 2.4 km past the second fork, crosses a small creek at a bridge. Look for the take-out 1 km past the creek bridge at a small pull-out on the north (right) side where the river is close to the road. Mark the take-out.

PUT-IN Continue upstream for 1.4 km to a fork. Stay left and go another 1.9 km to a bridge on the North Fork Dore.

CAMPING There is undeveloped camping along the road to the put-in.

Rob Evans-Davies just below The Gnasher at low flows.

SOUTH FORK DORE — TO CONFLUENCE

GRADE	CLASS	FLOW	TIME	LENGTH
II⁺–III	II–III	Low	1 hour	3 km (1.9 mi)
III–III⁺	II–IV	High		

Gradient 25 m/km (2.5%)
134 ft/mi

Max gradient 30 m in .7 km (4.3%)
100 ft in .43 mi

Put-in elevation 945 m
3100 ft

Take-out elevation 869 m
2850 ft

Shuttle 3.5 km (2.2 mi) one way

Season May–August

Maps 93H1 and 93H8

Gauge No

Craft Canoes, kayaks and rafts

CHARACTER A short, small-volume run with continuous rapids and a couple of more difficult drops.

FLOW INFORMATION The river is uncontrolled and fed by snowmelt and glacial runoff. Assess the flow at the take-out.

TRAVEL Access to the run and the shuttle are on gravel roads.

DESCRIPTION The river in this section is open for most of the run, with a couple of constricted sections where the river flows through boulder gardens. At higher flows expect compression waves and high current speeds in the narrow channel. The river tears over a small boulder-bed, with a few constricted class III–IV boulder-garden rapids, then spreads out in the lower part. The road runs along the river, though the tougher rapids are difficult to see from the road. Watch for logs in the lower part of the run.

GETTING THERE The run is located off Highway 16 near McBride.

TAKE-OUT From McBride, go north on Highway 16 for about 2–3 km, where the highway crosses the rail line at a bridge. Continue north for 2 km to the bridge on the Dore. If coming from the north, look for the Dore bridge 24 km south of West Twin Creek. Just north of the bridge is the Dore River Road on the west side. Turn west and follow the paved road for 1.8 km to the junction with Lamming Pit Road, which is on the right. Stay left on the gravel Dore River Road and go 6.3 km to a fork. To the left is the Dore South Forest Service Road (also signed to Eagle Valley Trail) and to the right is the Ozalenka Creek. Stay right, and you will reach the take-out bridge in 100 m.

PUT-IN Return to the fork and turn right onto the Dore South Road, then follow the road for 3.3 km where the river is close to the road. Park well off the road.

CAMPING There is undeveloped camping along the gravel road to the put-in, or developed camping in McBride.

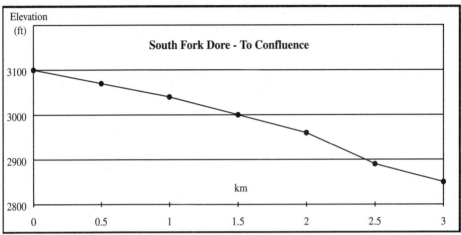

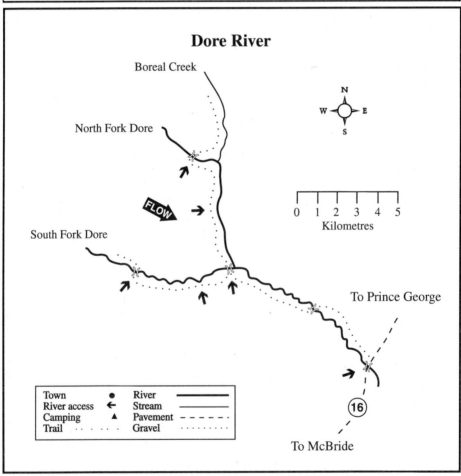

SOUTH FORK DORE   BRIDGE TO ROAD

GRADE	CLASS	FLOW	TIME	LENGTH
IV	III–V	Low	1–2 hours	6.5 km (4 mi)
V	III⁺–V⁺	High		

Gradient 33 m/km (3.3%)   **Max gradient** 30 m in .43 km (7%)
173 ft/mi   100 ft in .26 mi

Put-in elevation   1158 m   **Take-out elevation**   945 m
3800 ft   3100 ft

Shuttle 6.6 km (4.1 mi) one way   **Season** May–August

Maps 93H1   **Gauge** No

Craft Canoes, kayaks and rafts

CHARACTER A short, small-volume run that has lots of tight, constricted rapids in a narrow and steep channel.

FLOW INFORMATION The river is uncontrolled and fed by snowmelt and glacial runoff. Assess the flow at the take-out.

TRAVEL Access to the run and the shuttle are on gravel roads.

DESCRIPTION The river is easy at the put-in. You encounter the first rapids about 200 m below the start, where a short pinched section leads to 350 m of class III–III⁺ rapids. This is followed by a 1-km calm section. Just below an avalanche chute on river left is a constricted class III⁺–IV rapid where the river cuts through a rock outcrop. This is followed 250 m below by a class III–III⁺ boulder mess. About 200 m downstream is a long log-jammed rapid through boulders. This class III⁺–IV⁺ drop is visible from the road on the way up to the put-in. About 250 m below this, the river reaches a short canyon with huge boulders at the start, followed by a class IV–IV⁺ drop in the narrow bedrock channel. Just below this, the river enters another class III⁺–IV boulder jumble that leads to the most difficult rapids on the run. Look for a sharp right turn where the river tears into a class IV⁺–V⁺ rapid, with bedrock ledges and tight, fast features. Scout before you make the right turn, in order to prepare for what lies below. After the river turns right, it enters the long and steep Sucker Punch, a chaotic class V boulder jumble. Below are more rapids, though none as big as Sucker Punch. Look for your flagging on the right bank at the take-out.

GETTING THERE The run is located north of McBride, off Highway 16. See the map on page 300.

TAKE-OUT From McBride, go north on Highway 16 for about 2–3 km, to where it crosses the rail line at a bridge. Continue north for 2 km to the bridge on the Dore. If coming from the north, look for the Dore bridge 24 km south of West Twin Creek. Just north of the bridge is the Dore River Road on the west side. Turn west and follow the paved road for 1.8 km to the junction with Lamming Pit Road, which is on the right. Stay left on the gravel Dore River Road and go 6.3 km to a fork. To the left is the Dore South Forest Service Road (also signed to Eagle Valley Trail) and to the right is the Ozalenka Creek. Stay left and follow the road for 3.3 km to where the river is close to the road. Park well off the road.

PUT-IN Continue upstream for 6.6 km to a bridge over the river.

CAMPING There is undeveloped camping along the gravel road to the put-in, or developed camping in McBride.

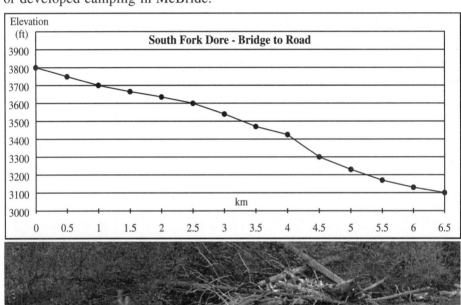

Was that river left, rock left or you go left? Stuart Smith and Donna Bradley on the Holmes River. Photo: Donna Sokolik.

HOLMES   BRIDGE TO HIGHWAY 16

GRADE	CLASS	FLOW	TIME	LENGTH
II–III	II–IV$^+$	Low	1–2 hours	16 km (10 mi)
III–III$^+$	II–V	High		

Gradient   11 m/km (1.1%)   **Max gradient**   30 m in 1.5 km (2%)
              58 ft/mi   100 ft in .93 mi

Put-in elevation   902 m   **Take-out elevation**   725 m
                      2960 ft   2380 ft

Shuttle   15 km (9.3 mi) one way   **Season**   May–August

Maps   83E5 and 93H8   **Gauge**   No

Craft   Canoes, kayaks and rafts

CHARACTER A scenic, medium-volume run that flows over a boulder-bed, with excellent continuous whitewater for most of the upper run. You can skip the one difficult rapid by taking out above Beaver Falls. At most flows there are lots of great places to play.

FLOW INFORMATION The river is uncontrolled and fed by snowmelt and glacial runoff. Assess the flow at the take-out.

TRAVEL The shuttle is on gravel roads.

DESCRIPTION At the put-in, the river is in a narrow boulder-lined channel. Just below the bridge, the river drops off boulders in a rush of exhilarating and exploding whitewater. The water is usually sparkling clean and the scenery is beautiful. There are a couple of more difficult sections, where the river flows through bigger boulders, that make for technical paddling at low flows, or erupting waves and holes at high flows. Watch for the footbridge about 2–3 km below the put-in, where the river is constricted and explodes in a class III–III$^+$ whitewater in a narrow boulder-lined channel. About three-quarters of the way down the whitewater gives way to a long easy section. There are a couple of bedrock outcrops that force the river over ledges and into constricted channels. These produce pool-and-drop rapids, and some good playing. The last couple of kilometres above Beaver Falls are open on a braided channel, with a few log jams on the islands. Watch for the campground on the left, which is just above Beaver Falls, a class IV–V double drop that falls 3–5 m in a low-angled chute through a narrow bedrock outcrop. Scout and portage on river right. The river is then easy to the take-out.

GETTING THERE The run is located near McBride, off Highway 16. See the map on page 306.

TAKE-OUT From McBride, go south on Highway 16 for 11 km to the bridge on the Holmes River. If coming from the south, the bridge is 52 km north of the junction of Highway 16 and Highway 5. About 300 m south of the bridge is a gravel road on the east side. Turn east and follow the road to just above the bridge. If you wish to skip the lower section, and the fall at the bottom, go 5 km upstream along the gravel road to where the river is close to the road.

PUT-IN Continue upstream until you reach a bridge over the river. The bridge is 15 km from the highway.

CAMPING There is developed camping above Beaver Falls, or undeveloped camping along the road to the put-in.

Fred Pfisterer in the left chute of Beaver Falls at medium flows.

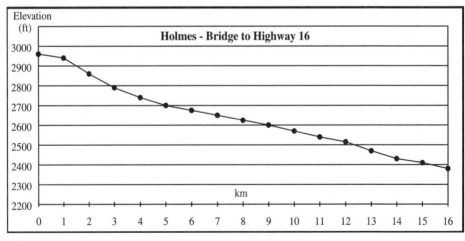

CHALCO CREEK   TO HOLMES RIVER

GRADE	CLASS	FLOW	TIME	LENGTH
II⁺–III⁺	II⁺–IV⁺	Low	1–2 hours	7.5 km (4.7 mi)
III–IV	III–IV⁺	High		

Gradient 19 m/km (1.9%)   **Max gradient** 30 m in 1.5 km (2%)
        99 ft/mi   100 ft in .93 mi

Put-in elevation 1036 m   **Take-out elevation** 896 m
            3400 ft   2940 ft

Shuttle 8.5 km (5.3 mi) one way   **Season** May–August

Maps 83E5   **Gauge** No

Craft Canoes and kayaks

CHARACTER An excellent small-volume creek run with great scenery and lots of tight technical paddling in a narrow boulder-bed.

FLOW INFORMATION The creek is uncontrolled and fed by snowmelt and glacial runoff. Assess the flow at the take-out.

TRAVEL Access to the run and the shuttle are on gravel roads.

DESCRIPTION The action starts just below the put-in at class III–III⁺ boulder gardens. The rapids ease, then you reach a 500-m section of easier water that ends in a right turn at some rock ledges. Here the creek turns sharply, then goes left off Cracker Jacks, a class IV–IV⁺ drop that falls 2–3 m onto bedrock on the left, and has a chute on the right. After Cracker Jacks is 400 m of class II⁺–III⁺ broken ledges and boulder gardens. This leads to a sharp right/left combination at a creekwide log jam. Portage on the left. Below the log jam, the creek is easy for a bit, then a constricted class II⁺–III boulder garden leads to a 1–2-km section of narrow class III⁺–IV rapids. Watch for a couple of logs across the creek in this area. Below the constricted part, the creek opens up and tears over a shallow and spread-out boulder channel until you reach the Holmes River. Proceed about 400 m downstream on the Holmes to the take-out.

GETTING THERE The run is located near McBride, off Highway 16.

TAKE-OUT From McBride, go south on Highway 16 for 11 km to the bridge on the Holmes River. If coming from the south, the bridge is 52 km north of the junction of Highway 16 and Highway 5. About 300 m south of the bridge is a gravel road on the east side. Turn east and follow the road upstream for 15 km to a bridge. From the bridge, backtrack 500 m downstream along the Holmes Road until the river is close to the road. Park well off the road.

PUT-IN Go upstream to the bridge on the Holmes, then go 600 m past the bridge to a fork. Stay left and go 7.4 km upstream on the rutted and rough road. Use your odometer, since the only marker at the put-in is a huge, smooth boulder embedded in the left side of the road at a small opening in the trees. The opening on the left side leads to a rock outcrop that looks down on the valley. You descend the steep bank, then bush-thrash about 60 m to the creek.

CAMPING There is developed camping above Beaver Falls, which you pass on the way to the take-out, or undeveloped camping along the road to the put-in.

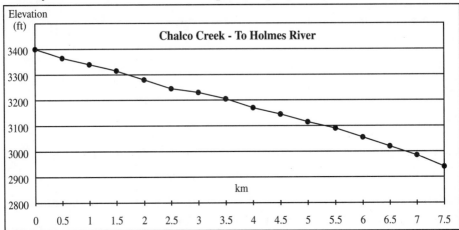

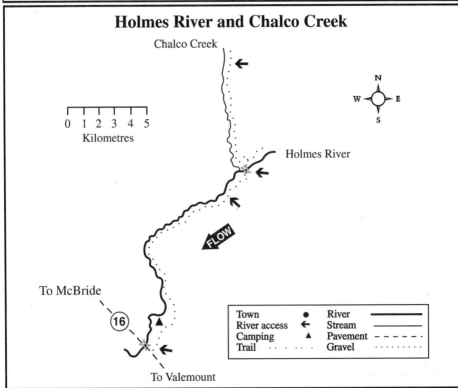

CASTLE CREEK — BRIDGE TO FRASER RIVER

GRADE	CLASS	FLOW	TIME	LENGTH
II–III	II–IV	Medium	1–3 hours	11 km (6.8 mi)
III–III⁺	II⁺–IV⁺	High		

Gradient 8.2 m/km (.82%)
43 ft/mi

Max gradient 30 m in 2 km (1.5%)
100 ft in 1.2 mi

Put-in elevation 800 m
2625 ft

Take-out elevation 710 m
2330 ft

Shuttle 31 km (19 mi) one way

Season May–August

Maps 93H1 and 93H8

Gauge No

Craft Canoes, kayaks and rafts

NOTES There is a 3-km (1.9-mi) paddle on the Fraser to reach the take-out.

CHARACTER A small to medium-volume run that flows over a shallow boulder-bed in the upper section, then enters a short canyon in the lower part.

FLOW INFORMATION The creek is uncontrolled and fed by snowmelt and glacial runoff. Assess the flow at the put-in.

TRAVEL About half of the shuttle is on gravel roads.

DESCRIPTION Below the bridge, the river drops into continuous class II⁺–III rapids. In about 1.5 km is a class III rapid at a left turn, with a log jam on the right at the bottom. About 300 m below this is a sharp right turn with a class III⁺–IV boulder-strewn rapid. The river eases to class II⁺ for the next 1 km, then enters a long, calm section. A series of class II rapids lead to small bedrock ledges, and a sharp right turn. Here the river drops into Entrance Exam, a narrow class III⁺–IV⁺ chute at the mouth of a canyon. Below this, the river runs in a deep narrow canyon to a sharp left turn, dropping into class III–III⁺ rapids at the end of the canyon. There are a couple of short rapids, then the river flows in an open channel. There is a float on the Fraser to reach the take-out.

GETTING THERE The run is located near McBride, off Highway 16.

TAKE-OUT At the Highway 16 bridge on the Fraser, just south of McBride, go 6 km south to Hinkelman Road, which is on the west (right) side. If coming from the south, Hinkelman Road is on the west (left) side, 3.5 km north of the bridge on the Holmes River. Turn west and follow the paved road for 4.3 km to a set of stock corrals on the west (right) side. Turn right and follow the rutted road for 1.6 km to a fork. Go left and in 300 m you reach an old gravel pit. The take-out is 200 m beyond the gravel pit. Mark the take-out at the river.

PUT-IN   Return to Highway 16 and go north (left) to McBride. In McBride, look for Main Street near the north end of town. Turn west (left) on Main Street and go 500 m to Eddy Road, which is on the left. Turn south (left) and follow the road for 9 km to a fork. Stay right on the Castle Creek Forest Service Road, and follow the gravel road for 7.7 km to a fork with a bridge on the left.

CAMPING   There is undeveloped camping along the road to the put-in.

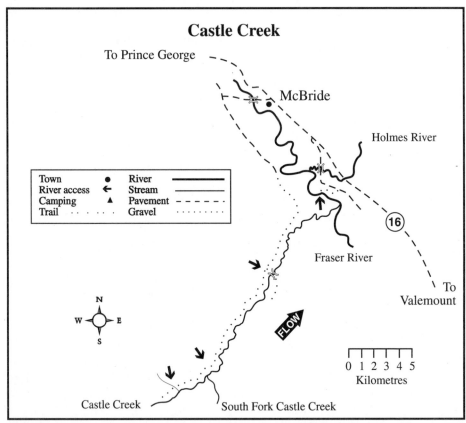

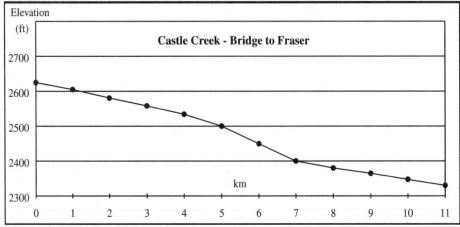

CASTLE CREEK   SOUTH FORK TO BRIDGE

GRADE	CLASS	FLOW	TIME	LENGTH
I+	II	Most Flows	2–3 hours	11 km (6.8 mi)

Gradient 1.6 m/km (.16%)   **Max gradient** 17 m in 11 km (.16%)
8.4 ft/mi   56 ft in 6.8 mi

Put-in elevation   817 m   **Take-out elevation**   800 m
                    2680 ft   2625 ft

Shuttle   9 km (5.6 mi) one way   **Season**   May–August

Maps   93H1   **Gauge**   No

Craft   Canoes, kayaks and rafts

CHARACTER   A scenic, small to medium-volume run in a remote valley. There are few rapids as the river meanders across the flat valley bottom. Watch for sweepers and the odd log in the channel.

FLOW INFORMATION   The creek is uncontrolled and fed by snowmelt and glacial runoff. Assess the flow at the put-in.

TRAVEL   Access to the run and the shuttle are on gravel roads.

DESCRIPTION   The river at the put-in is calm, with slow-flowing current in the meandering channel. The character changes little throughout the run. Enjoy the views of the rock faces on either side of the valley. To avoid the rapids below the bridge, exit on the left and carry up the steep bank.

GETTING THERE   The run is located near McBride, off Highway 16. See the map on page 308.

TAKE-OUT   From the junction of Main Street and Highway 16 in McBride, go west on Main Street for 500 m to the junction with Eddy Road, which is on the left. Turn south (left) and follow the road for 5.5 km to a set of railroad tracks. Continue south for another 3.4 km to a fork. Stay right on the Castle Creek Forest Service Road, and follow the road upstream for 7.7 km to a fork. The bridge on the left is the take-out.

PUT-IN   Go upstream on the right fork. Follow the road for 8.1 km to another fork with an old pulp mill on the left. Stay right and go 1.1 km to where the river is close to the road. Carry through the brush to the river.

CAMPING   There is undeveloped camping along the road to the put-in.

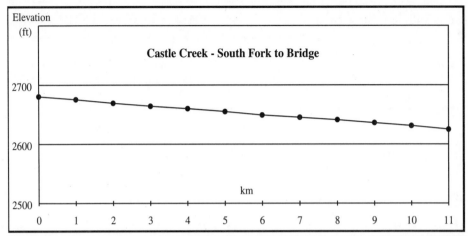

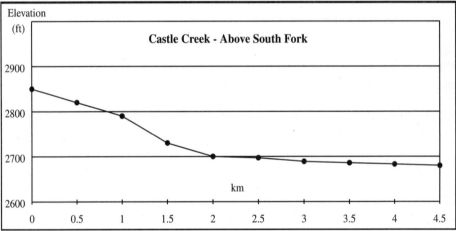

CASTLE CREEK   ABOVE SOUTH FORK

GRADE	CLASS	FLOW	TIME	LENGTH
II⁺–III	II⁺–IV	Low	1 hour	4.5 km (2.8 mi)
III–III⁺	II⁺–IV	High		

Gradient 12 m/km (1.2%)   **Max gradient** 30 m in .75 km (4%)
61 ft/mi   100 ft in .47 mi

Put-in elevation 869 m   **Take-out elevation** 817 m
2850 ft   2680 ft

Shuttle 4 km (2.5 mi) one way   **Season** May–August

Maps 93H1   **Gauge** No

Craft Canoes, kayaks and rafts

CHARACTER A short, small-volume run that tears over a broken bed of sharp rock and boulders. The whitewater is all in the first half of the run.

FLOW INFORMATION The creek is uncontrolled and fed by snowmelt and glacial runoff. Assess the flow at the put-in.

TRAVEL Access to the run and the shuttle are on gravel roads.

DESCRIPTION The run starts with about 500 m of easy water, then picks up to continuous class II–II⁺ whitewater that gives way to class III–IV rapids as the river tears over the shallow boulder-bed. There are a couple of log jams along the river, but there was no wood across the river in 1995. At the confluence with the south fork of the river, there is a short class II–III rapid, then the river is mellow to the take-out. The gradient profile is on page 310.

GETTING THERE The run is located near McBride, off Highway 16. See the map on page 308.

TAKE-OUT From the junction of Main Street and Highway 16 in McBride, go 500 m west on Main Street to the junction with Eddy Road, which is on the south (left). Turn left and follow the road for 9 km to a fork. Stay right on the Castle Creek Forest Service Road and follow the road upstream for 7.7 km to a fork, with a bridge on the left. Stay right and continue upstream for 8.1 km to another fork, with an old pulp mill on the left. Stay right and go 1.1 km to where the river is close to the road. Mark the take-out.

PUT-IN Continue upstream for 4.2 km to where the road crosses a small creek. Carry down the open gravel creekbed to the river.

CAMPING There is undeveloped camping along the road to the put-in.

GRADE	CLASS	FLOW	TIME	LENGTH
III⁺	III–IV	Low	1 hour	4 km (2.5 mi)
IV	III–IV⁺	High		

Gradient   31 m/km (3%)   **Max gradient**   30 m in .8 km (3.8%)
161 ft/mi   100 ft in .5 mi

Put-in elevation   853 m   **Take-out elevation**   732 m
2800 ft   2400 ft

Shuttle   3.7 km (2.3 mi) one way   **Season**   May–August

Maps   83E4   **Gauge**   No

Craft   Kayaks and canoes

CHARACTER   A short, small-volume creek run that tumbles down a steep boulder-bed. The rapids are continuous for most of the upper section.

FLOW INFORMATION   You can estimate the flow as described on page 314. This run can be paddled at much higher flows than the upper run.

TRAVEL   The shuttle is on gravel roads.

DESCRIPTION   At the put-in, the river rips over the boulder-bed in tight technical rapids that continue for the first couple of kilometres. Expect class III–IV boulder-garden whitewater, with a couple of tougher rapids thrown in. You can take out at the old bridge location that you pass at the intersection on the way up, or continue for the extra 500 m down the open lower part. Watch for logs in the more open lower half of the run.

GETTING THERE   The run is located north of the junction of Highway 16 and Highway 5, near the town of Valemount.

TAKE-OUT   At the junction of Highways 5/93 near Valemount, go north on Highway 16 for 23 km to the creek bridge. If you are coming from the north, the bridge is 40 km south of McBride. On the downstream side, just south of the bridge, is a small road that leads under the bridge. Do not block the gate.

PUT-IN   Go 250 m south of the bridge to the junction with Croyden Road. Turn left and follow the gravel road for 500 m to a fork. Stay left and in 200 m you will reach an intersection (with the old bridge on the left). Continue straight through and in about 1.8 km you reach a farm on the left. Go 1.7 km further to a small pull-off on the left that is near the river.

CAMPING   There is informal camping along the road to the put-in.

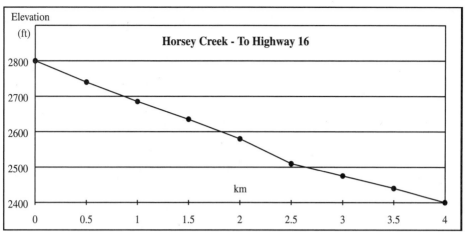

Horsey Creek - To Highway 16

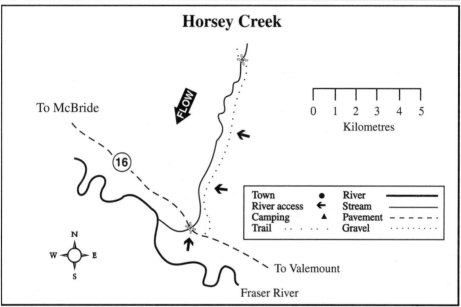

Horsey Creek

To McBride

(16)

FLOW

To Valemount

Fraser River

Town	●	River	——————
River access	←	Stream	————
Camping	▲	Pavement	− − − −
Trail	· · · · · ·	Gravel	· · · · · · ·

0 1 2 3 4 5
Kilometres

N W E S

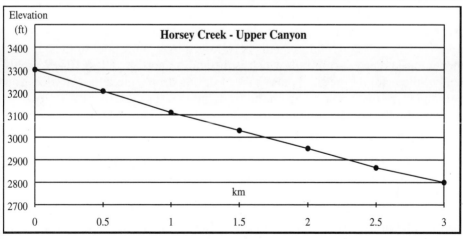

Horsey Creek - Upper Canyon

GRADE	CLASS	FLOW	TIME	LENGTH
V	IV–VI⁺	Low	1–2 hours	3 km (1.9 mi)
V⁺	IV⁺–VI⁺	Medium		

Gradient 51 m/km (5%)
268 ft/mi

Max gradient 30 m in .5 km (6%)
100 ft in .31 mi

Put-in elevation 1006 m
3300 ft

Take-out elevation 853 m
2800 ft

Shuttle 2.6 km (1.6 mi) one way

Season May–August

Maps 83E4

Gauge No

Craft Kayaks

CHARACTER A short, small-volume steep-creek run that pounds down a boulder-bed into a tight canyon with a couple of waterfalls. The terrain around the run is steep bush-covered slopes, so go for the class V⁺ stuff, or stay home.

FLOW INFORMATION The creek is uncontrolled and fed by snowmelt and glacial runoff. Estimate the flow as follows; on the downstream side of the highway bridge is an old bridge piling on river left. There are three columns of timbers lying perpendicular to the shoreline, each with 5 timbers. Use the middle column. If the bottom timber (perpendicular to the shoreline) is covered the creek is medium to high. If the bottom timber is about half-covered, the creek is medium. At high flows the run is a howling waterslide.

TRAVEL Access to the run and the shuttle are on gravel roads.

DESCRIPTION The run starts in a narrow boulder-lined channel that quickly drops into steep class IV, then class V, boulder-strewn drops. You can boat-scout most of the drops if you can stop. A left turn with a rock wall on the right, precedes the canyon. The action starts at Pressure Cooker, a 3–5-m, class V⁺–VI drop into a wild recirculation. This is followed by a short pool in the canyon, then a log-jammed 4–6-m fall, which is difficult to portage. Class III–IV rapids lead to the brink of the final class V–V⁺ fall that drops into a narrow slot. You could portage the whole thing on the right but that looks desperate. Below the canyon, the creek tears along the boulder-bed with many excellent drops until the take-out. See the gradient profile on page 313.

GETTING THERE The run is located north of Valemount, off Highway 16. The map is on page 313.

TAKE-OUT From the junction of Highways 5 and 93 near Valemount, go north on Highway 16 for approximately 23 km to the bridge over the creek. If you are coming from the north, the bridge is about 40 km south of McBride. Go 250 m south of the bridge to Croyden Road. Turn east (left) and follow the gravel road for 500 m to a fork. Stay left and in 200 m you will reach an intersection. Continue straight through and in about 1.8 km you reach a farm on the left. Go 1.7 km further to a small pull-off on the left that is near the river.

PUT-IN   Go upstream for 1.4 km to a gate across the road. About 1.2 km past the gate you will reach a spot where the river is close to the road.

CAMPING   There is undeveloped camping along the road to the put-in.

Looking upstream at the rapids just above the take-out at low flow.

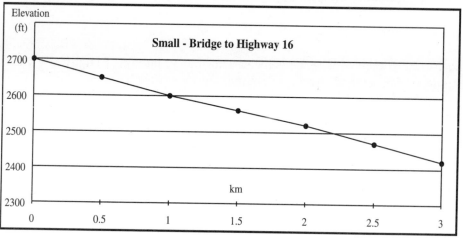

GRADE	CLASS	FLOW	TIME	LENGTH
III⁺–IV	III–IV⁺	Medium	1 hour	3 km (1.9 mi)
IV–IV⁺	III–V	High		

Gradient 28 m/km (2.8%)   **Max gradient** 30 m in 1 km (3%)
150 ft/mi   100 ft in .62 mi

Put-in elevation 823 m   **Take-out elevation** 738 m
2700 ft   2420 ft

Shuttle 3.5 km (2.2 mi) one way   **Season** May–August

Maps 83E4   **Gauge** No

Craft Canoes and kayaks

CHARACTER A short, small-volume run that starts with a bang, then screams down a narrow, obstructed boulder-bed with a few pieces of wood in the river.

FLOW INFORMATION The creek is uncontrolled and fed by snowmelt and glacial runoff. Assess the flow at the take-out, or look at the put-in where you can see exactly what you will be paddling.

TRAVEL The shuttle is on gravel roads.

DESCRIPTION The river is calm just above the put-in bridge, then shoots into Mr. Big, a class IV⁺–V boulder jumble that is about 100-m long. Things ease to class IV for about another 300 m, then the river runs in fast and shallow class II⁺–III for the remainder of the run. Watch for a riverwide log jam about 450 m below Mr. Big, with a channel on the right. There are a couple of log jumps/ducks, not far below. In the lower section, there are a few features you can play on. Take out at the parking lot above the bridge, on river right. The gradient profile is on page 315.

GETTING THERE The run is located north the junction of Highway 16 and Highway 5, near the town of Valemount.

TAKE-OUT At the junction of Highways 5/93 near Valemount, go north on Highway 16 for 16 km to the bridge over the river. If coming from the north, the bridge is 47 km south of McBride. Just north of the bridge, turn east onto the Small River Road, and park in the parking area near the river.

PUT-IN Continue upstream on the Small River Road for 3.2 km to a bridge over the river.

CAMPING There is informal camping along the gravel road, near the put-in, or developed camping near Valemount.

Mark Oddy in Mr. Big.

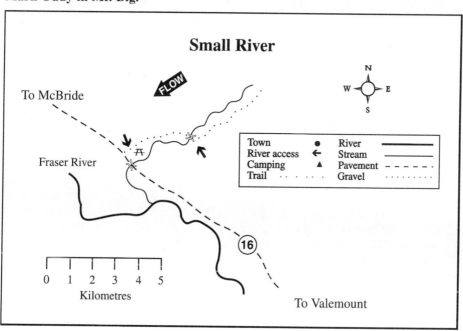

Active Environment Canada Water Gauging Stations for Runs in this Book

River	Location	Number
Athabasca River	Near Hinton	07DA002**
Athabasca River	At Entrance	07AD001
Athabasca River	Near Jasper	07AA002
Brazeau River	Below Cardinal River	05DD007**
Cardinal River	Near the mouth	05DD008
Clearwater River	Near Rocky Mountain House	05DB001**
Clearwater River	Near Dovercourt	05BD006
Clearwater River	Above Limestone Creek	05DB003
Gregg River	Near the mouth	07AF015
Maligne River	Near Jasper	07AA004
McLeod River	Above Embarras River	07AF002**
McLeod River	Near Cadomin	07AF013
Miette River	Near Jasper	07AA001
Mistaya River	Near Saskatchewan River Crossing	05DA007
N Saskatchewan River	Near Rocky Mountain House	05DC001**
N Saskatchewan River	Below Bighorn Plant	05DC010**
N Saskatchewan River	At Whirlpool Point	05DA009**
North Ram River	At the Forestry Trunk Road	05DC011
Ram River	Near the mouth	05DC008**
Red Deer River	Below Burnt Timber Creek	05CA009**
Red Deer River	Above Panther River	05CA004
Siffleur River	Near the mouth	05DA002
Snake Indian River	Near the mouth	07AB002
Sunwapta River	At Athabasca Glacier	07AA007
Whirlpool River	Near the mouth	07AA009
Wildhay River	Near Hinton	07AC001**
Beaver River	Near the mouth	08NB019•••
Blaeberry River	Near Golden	08NB001
Blaeberry River	Above Willowbank Creek	08NB012
Blaeberry River	Below Ensign Creek	08NB015
Canoe River	Below Kimmel Creek	08NC004
Dore River	Near McBride	08KA001
Fraser River	At Red Pass	08KA007
Gold River	Above Palmer Creek	08NB014
Gold River	Above Bachelor Creek	08NB013
McKale River	Near 940 m contour	08KA009

** – Listed on Alberta Environmental Protection's River Report Recording. Call (403) 422-0072 or (403) 422-0073. In Alberta call toll free through the RITE Operator at 310-0000.

••• – Real-time flow checks are available by calling (604) 664-9360. The remaining gauges offer historical flow data.

Conversions

Distance

1 mile = 1.6 kilometres	1 foot = .3 metres
1 kilometre = .6214 miles	1 metre = 3.28 feet

Volume

1 cubic foot per second = .0283 cubic metres per second

1 cubic metre per second = 35.3 cubic feet per second

Index to Runs by Grade

Clearwater	Cutoff Bridge to Seven Mile	most flows	34	C,K,R
Clearwater	Elk Creek to Cutoff Bridge	most flows	36	C,K,R
Clearwater	Seven Mile to 940 Bridge	most flows	33	C,K,R
Dore	Confluence to Highway 16	low–medium	293	C,K,R
Fiddle	Above Hot Springs	low	135	C,K
Fraser	Chamberlin Creek to Picnic Site	most flows	250	C,K,R
Fraser	Crossing to Highway 16	most flows	267	C,K,R
Fraser	Railroad Y to Pipeline Gate	low	263	C,K,R
Goat	To Highway 16 Bridge	low	280	C,K,R
Gold	Below Bachelor Creek	low	219	C,K,R
Gregg	40 Bridge to Teepee Creek	most flows	125	C,K,R
Gregg	Teepee Creek to McLeod River	most flows	123	C,K,R
Holmes	Bridge to Highway 16	low–medium	303	C,K,R
Hummingbird Cr	To South Ram	most flows	47	C,K
Jacques Creek	Jacques Lake to Rocky River	most flows	147	C,K
Maligne	5th to 6th Bridges	most flows	157	C,K,R
Maligne	Maligne Lake to Picnic Site	most flows	173	C,K,R
Maligne	Picnic Site to Picnic Site	most flows	170	C,K,R
Miette	Geikie Siding to Picnic Site	most flows	179	C,K
Miette	Picnic Site to 16 Bridge	most flows	178	C,K
Milk	Above Goat River	most flows	284	C,K,R
Milk	To Goat River	most flows	282	C,K,R
Mistaya	Above the Canyon	low–medium	83	C,K,R
Mistaya	Canyon Run	low	79	C,K
North Ram	940 to South Ram	most flows	49	C,K,R
N Saskatchewan	Below Weeping Wall	most flows	59	C,K,R
N Saskatchewan	Horburg to Rail Bridge	most flows	22	C,K,R
N Saskatchewan	Rampart Creek to 93	most flows	54	C,K,R
N Saskatchewan	Saunders to Horburg	most flows	24	C,K,R
N Saskatchewan	To Rampart Creek	most flows	56	C,K,R
N Saskatchewan	Upper Canyon	low	58	C,K
Panther	Sheep Cr to Red Deer River	most flows	17	C,K,R
Red Deer	Cache Hill to Williams Cr	high	4	C,K,R
Red Deer	Deer Creek to Cache Hill	most flows	6	C,K,R
Red Deer	Gooseberry Ledge to Deer Cr	most flows	8	C,K,R
Red Deer	Williams Creek to Coal Camp	most flows	2	C,K,R
Rocky	Medicine Tent to Jacques Cr	most flows	144	C,K,R
Snake Indian	Willow Creek to Bridge	most flows	137	C,K,R
South Fork Dore	To Confluence	low–medium	299	C,K,R
South Ram	940 to North Fork Road	low	38	C,K,R
South Ram	Upper Canyon	most flows	45	C,K,R
Sunwapta	Below Falls to Athabasca	most flows	203	C,K,R
Sunwapta	Raft Put-in to Above Falls	most flows	205	C,K,R
West Twin Creek	16 Bridge to Lower Bridge	low	285	C,K,R
Whirlpool	Above Corrals	most flows	201	C,K,R
Whirlpool	Corrals to S-Bend	most flows	198	C,K,R
Wildhay	Old Bridge to Group Camp	most flows	128	C,K,R

Grade III–IV	**C = Canoe**	**K = Kayak**	**R = Raft**	
Astoria	93A to Athabasca River	low–medium	181	C,K
Beaver	Beaver Glacier to Bear Creek	low–medium	232	C,K
Bighorn	Crescent Falls to Highway 11	most flows	63	C,K
Blackstone	Gap to Old Bridge	high	106	C,K

Blaeberry	Split Creek to Blaeberry Falls	high	241	C,K,R
Brazeau	Nigel Pass to Ford	high	93	C,K,R
Canoe	Old Bridge to Highway 5	most flows	274	C,K,R
Canoe	Gauge to Old Bridge	most flows	277	C,K,R
Castle Creek	Above South Fork	medium–high	311	C,K,R
Castle Creek	Bridge to Fraser River	medium–high	307	C,K,R
Chalco Creek	To Holmes River	high	305	C,K
Cline	Pinto Lake to Coral Creek	medium	71	C,K
Fiddle	Above Hot Springs	high	135	C,K
Fraser	Canyon Run	low–medium	254	C,K,R
Fraser	Pipeline Gate to The Staircase	low–medium	260	C,K,R
Fraser	Railroad Y to Pipeline Gate	high	263	C,K,R
Goat	To Highway 16 Bridge	high	280	C,K,R
Gold	Lower Canyon	low–medium	216	C,K
Gold	Below Bachelor Creek	high	219	C,K,R
Holmes	Bridge to Highway 16	medium–high	303	C,K,R
Horsey Creek	To Highway 16	most flows	312	C,K
Maligne	Behind the Mountain	most flows	166	C,K,R
Maligne	Canyon Run	low–medium	159	C,K
McKale	Gauge to Lower Bridge	low	291	C,K
McLeod	Above Whitehorse Creek	low–medium	119	C,K
Mistaya	Above the Canyon	high	83	C,K,R
Mistaya	Canyon Run	high	79	C,K
Nigel Creek	93 to North Saskatchewan	most flows	61	C,K
N Saskatchewan	Upper Canyon	high	58	C,K
Rocky	Jacques Creek to Highway 16	most flows	140	C,K
Small	Bridge to Highway 16	low–medium	316	C,K
South Fork Dore	To Confluence	medium–high	299	C,K,R
South Ram	940 to North Fork Road	high	38	C,K,R
West Twin Creek	16 Bridge to Lower Bridge	high	285	C,K,R

Grade IV–V	C = Canoe	K = Kayak	R = Raft	
Astoria	93A to Athabasca River	high	181	C,K
Astoria	Cavell Creek to 93A	low–medium	183	C,K
Blaeberry	Bridge to Ensign Creek	low	246	C,K
Cline	Pinto Lake to Coral Creek	high	71	C,K
Coral Creek/Cline	To Highway 11	most flows	68	C,K
Fiddle	Villeneuve Creek to Highway 16	low	130	K
Fraser	Canyon Run	medium–high	254	C,K,R
Fraser	Pipeline Gate to The Staircase	medium–high	260	C,K,R
Gold	Above Bachelor Creek	low	221	C,K
Gold	Lower Canyon	medium–high	216	C,K
Maligne	Canyon	high	159	C,K
Maligne	Excalibur Run	medium	162	C,K
McKale	Gauge to Lower Bridge	high	291	C,K
McLeod	Above Whitehorse Creek	high	119	C,K
North Fork Dore	Above Boreal Creek	most flows	297	C,K
North Fork Dore	To Confluence	most flows	295	C,K
Poboktan Creek	Above Highway 93	most flows	209	C,K
Robson	Kinney Lake to Trailhead	low–medium	271	C,K
Siffleur	To North Saskatchewan	most flows	76	C,K
Small	Bridge to Highway 16	high	316	C,K
Swiftcurrent Cr	To Highway 16	low	268	K

| South Fork Dore | Bridge to Road | most flows | 301 | C,K,R |
| West Twin Creek | Bridge to Highway 16 | low–medium | 287 | K |

Grade V–VI	**C = Canoe**	**K = Kayak**	**R = Raft**	
Astoria	Cavell Creek to 93A	high	183	C,K
Bachelor Creek	Above Gold River	most flows	223	C,K
Beauty Creek	Above Highway 93	most flows	212	K
Blaeberry	Bridge to Ensign Creek	medium	246	C,K
Fiddle	Villeneuve Cr to Highway 16	medium	130	K
Gold	Above Bachelor Creek	medium	221	K
Horsey Creek	Upper Canyon	low–medium	314	K
Maligne	Excalibur Run	high	162	C,K
Robson	Kinney Lake to Trailhead	high	271	K
Swiftcurrent Cr	To Highway 16	low–medium	268	K
West Twin Creek	Bridge to Highway 16	medium–high	287	K

My Favourites—By Category

River	Run	Grade	Page
Scenic Floats in the Mountains			
Athabasca	16 Bridge to Brule Lake	I–II	116
Athabasca	Fort Point to 16 Bridge	I–II	150
Beaver	Bear Creek to Cuppola Creek	I–II	230
Blaeberry	Redburn Creek to Bridge	I–II	239
Castle Creek	South Fork to Bridge	I–II	309
Fraser	Highway 16 to Moose Lake	I–II	265
Fraser	Robson Bridge to Chamberlin Cr	I–II	252
Miette	16 Bridge to 93A Bridge	I–II	176
N Saskatchewan	Rampart Creek to 93	II	54
N Saskatchewan	Below Weeping Wall	II	59
Red Deer	Bighorn Creek to 940	II	13
Sunwapta	Grizzly Creek to Raft Put-in	II	207
Overnight Trips			
Brazeau	Nigel Pass to Ford	II–IV	93
Rocky	Jacques Creek to Highway 16	III–IV	140
Snake Indian	Willow Creek to Bridge	II–III	137
South Ram	940 to North Fork Road	II–IV	38
The Best Moderate Whitewater			
Bluewater Creek	Bridge to Blackwater Creek	II–III	237
Canoe	Gauge to Old Bridge	III–IV	277
Canoe	Old Bridge to Highway 5	III–IV	274
Chalco Creek	To Holmes River	III–IV	305
Dore	Confluence to Highway 16	II–III	293
Holmes	Bridge to Highway 16	II–III	303
Fraser	Railroad Y to Pipeline Gate	II–IV	263
Maligne	Behind the Mountain	III–IV	166
Maligne	Maligne Lake to Picnic Site	II–III	173
McKale	Gauge to Lower Bridge	III–IV	291
Mistaya	Above the Canyon	II–III	83
South Fork Dore	To Confluence	III–IV	299
Sunwapta	Raft Put-in to Above Falls	II–III	205

River	Run	Grade	Page
Fun Stuff for Playing			
Athabasca	Mile 5 Bridge to Fort Point	II	152
Blackstone	Recreation Site to 940 Bridge	II–III	102
Bluewater Creek	Bridge to Blackwater Creek	II–III	237
Brazeau	Smallboy Camp to Ford	II–III	91
Dore	Confluence to Highway 16	II–III	293
Fraser	Railroad Y to Pipeline Gate	II–IV	263
Fraser	Pipeline Gate to The Staircase	III–V	260
Goat	To Highway 16 Bridge	III–IV	280
Holmes	Bridge to Highway 16	II–III	303
Maligne	Maligne Lake to Picnic Site	II–III	173
Maligne	Picnic Site to Picnic Site	II–III	170
North Saskatchewan	Rail Bridge to Brierley's	II	20
Red Deer	Gooseberry Ledge to Deer Creek	II–III	8
Red Deer	Williams Creek to Coal Camp	II–III	2
Whirlpool	Corrals to S-Bend	II–III	198
Difficult to Extreme Whitewater			
Astoria	Cavell Creek to 93A	IV–V	183
Bachelor Creek	Above Gold River	V–VI	223
Blaeberry	Bridge to Ensign Creek	V–VI	246
Fraser	Canyon Run	IV–V	254
Fraser	Pipeline Gate to The Staircase	IV–V	260
Gold	Above Bachelor Creek	V–VI	221
Horsey Creek	Upper Canyon	V–VI	314
Maligne	Canyon	IV–V	159
Maligne	Excalibur Run	V–VI	162
North Fork Dore	Above Boreal Creek	IV–V	297
North Fork Dore	To Confluence	IV–V	295
South Fork Dore	Bridge to Road	IV–V	301
Swiftcurrent Creek	To Highway 16	V–VI	268
West Twin Creek	Bridge to Highway 16	V–VI	287
Vertical Whitewater Adventures			
Beauty Creek	Above Highway 93	V–VI	212
Bighorn	Crescent Falls to Highway 11	III–IV	63
McLeod	Above Whitehorse Creek	III–V	119
Robson	Kinney Lake to Trailhead	IV–V	271
Canyon Escapades			
Coral Creek/Cline	To Highway 11	IV–V	68
Fiddle	Villeneuve Creek to Highway 16	V–VI	130
Maligne	Canyon	IV–V	159
Mistaya	Canyon Run	III–IV	79
Rocky	Jacques Creek to Highway 16	III–IV	140
Siffleur	To North Saskatchewan	III–V	76

Outdoor Program Centre

Kayak Lessons
Introduction to Kayaking
-2 Lectures
-Pool Sessions
-River Progressions
Offered year-round
Choice of evening modules or weekend clinics

Intermediate Kayak Clinics
Throughout the summer

Off-Season Pool Sessions
from September to April

Phone 220-5038 for details or registration information

Canoe Schools
Basic Stillwater Lessons
-evenings or weekends
from May - September

Introductory River Canoeing
-7 hour progression of fundamental river skills

Wilderness Canoe Schools
-Week-long Skills Camps on:
 -The Oldman River
 -The Red Deer River
 -The Kootenay River
 -The Nahanni River
-Ocean Canoe Schools
-Canoe Instructor Certification

Raft Instruction
Raft Rental Primer
Introductory Paddle Rafting
Instructional Raft Trips
-Red Deer River
-Kootenay River

Sea Kayaking
Introductory Lectures
Deep-Water Rescue Clinics
Basic Paddling Instruction
Week-long Instructional Tours
-around Vancouver Island
-the Queen Charlotte Islands
-Baja, Mexico & Lake Powell, Utah

Outdoor Equipment Rentals

River Kayaks
-Over 40 kayaks available
Dagger Response & Crossfire
Perception Danger & Reflex
Wavesport Lazer & Excel

Tandem Whitewater Kayak
All kayak acessories

Sea Kayaks
Single Kayaks
Double Kayaks
"Folding" kayaks
-over 40 boats available

Wetsuits etc
Paddling Drysuits
Farmer John Wetsuits
Paddling Jackets
Booties & Pogies
Dry Bags & Packs

Canoes
Tripping Canoes
Old Town & Dagger

Whitewater Tandem Playboats
Dagger Dimension & Caper

Whitewater Solo Playboats
Dagger Genesis & Ocoee

C-1 Closed Canoe

-all boats completely outfitted
Canoe/Kayak trailers available

Rafts
Professional Whitewater Rafts
4-Person (10'-11')
6-Person (13')
8-Person (14'-15')
with heavy duty "wrap" floors

Self Bailing Professional Rafts
6-Person (12'-14')
8-Person (15'8")
10-Person (17'-18')

Easy Floater Rafts
5-9 person sizes available

BOOK AHEAD
All gear can be reserved in advance by phone or in person
Phone: (403) 220-5038, Location: Phys. Ed. B-180, The University of Calgary
Hours: Mon-Thurs: 8am - 7pm • Friday: 8am - 9pm • Weekends: Noon - 9 pm
Closed Statutory Holidays

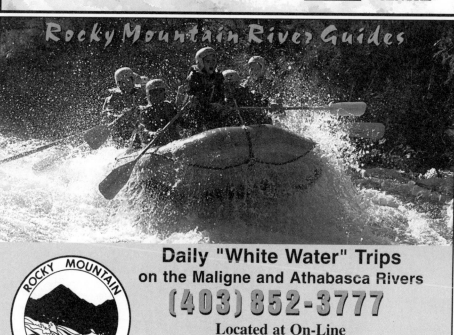

328

*Special Thanks
to the*

Jasper River
Runners

*Canoe And Kayak
Club*

*for supporting
this project*

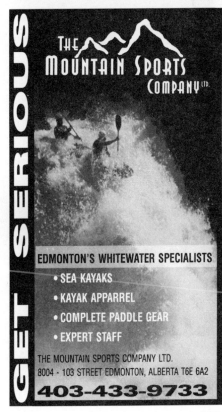

330

Organizations and Clubs

Alberta Recreational Canoe Association (ARCA)

ARCA is the provincial umbrella organization for recreational canoeing and canoe clubs in Alberta. ARCA speaks for the canoeing community to the federal and provincial governments on environment and recreation issues. ARCA sets standards for open canoe courses, instructors and instructor trainers and registers instructors and instructor trainers in Alberta.

    1111 Memorial Drive NW   Phone: (403) 270-2262
    Calgary, Alberta T2N 3E4

Alberta Whitewater Association (AWA)

The AWA is the sport governing body for whitewater closed canoe and kayak recreation and competition. The AWA sets standards for closed boat instruction, instructor and leader development and river safety and rescue courses. The AWA provides funding through the Alberta Provincial Slalom and Wildwater Team and provincial kayak polo teams. The AWA runs education, coaching, recreational and competitive events throughout the summer.

    11759 - Groat Road   Phone: (403) 453-8585
    Edmonton, Alberta T5M 3K6

Whitewater Kayaking Association of B.C. (WKABC)

The WKABC is the provincial sport governing body and is involved in all aspects of river paddling in closed boats. With assistance from the Government Sports Branch and the Gaming Commission, support is provided to clubs for recreational and racing activities, as well as liability insurance for sanctioned events. The WKABC instructors association has been active for over 30 years and information is available for visitors paddling in British Columbia.

    1367 W Broadway   Phone/Fax: (604) 275-6651
    Vancouver, B.C. V6H 4A9

Clubs in the Area

Bow Waters Canoe Club

A recreational canoeing club offering: educational programs for novice and intermediate paddlers, rentals, safe and environmentally friendly lake and river canoe tours and social activities.

    P.O. Box 697, Postal Station J   Phone: (403) 235-2922
    Calgary, Alberta T2A 4X8

Ceyana Canoe Club

A recreational canoe club offering: day, weekend and group camping trips on lakes and rivers in a safe environment. Trips for novice to expert canoe paddlers and their families. Education program, river rescue clinics, stroke improvement sessions, socials, monthly newsletter, meetings and equipment rentals.

    Box 72023 Ottewell Postal Outlet   Contact: Mark Lund
    Edmonton, Alberta T6B 0J1   Phone: (403) 436-4252

Edmonton Whitewater Paddlers
A mixed recreational and racing club for open and closed boat paddlers offering: river tripping, newsletters, kayak polo competitions, slalom and wildwater racing and winter and summer social activities.

1817 - 65 Street
Edmonton, Alberta T6L 1H1

Phone: (403) 434-9192

Friends of the River Recreation Association
A recreational club offering lake and whitewater trips for intermediate paddlers in a relaxed and fun atmosphere. New members welcome.

9726 - 158 Street
Edmonton, Alberta T5P 2X1

Contact: Bob Sylvester
Phone: (403) 489-8244

Hinton Strokers
A recreational club offering: canoe and kayak lessons, river trips for beginners to experts and their families, equipment rentals for club members and safe and fun paddling experiences.

Box 5124
Hinton, Alberta T7V 1X3

Phone: (403) 865-5743

Jasper River Runners
A recreational club offering: canoe and kayak lessons, roll clinics, Wednesday evening club trips during paddling season, winter pool sessions, equipment rentals to members, newsletters, a leader development program and river trips for beginners to experts.

Box 2443
Jasper, Alberta T0E 1E0

Northwest Voyageurs Canoe and Kayak Club
A recreational club offering: canoe and kayak trips during the summer, monthly newsletter, kayak polo tournaments, summer picnics, monthly meetings with guest speakers, lessons for beginners to intermediates in canoes or kayaks and leader/instructor courses.

Box 1341
Edmonton, Alberta T5J 2N2

Contact: Kurt Sejr
Phone: (403) 922-6200

University of Alberta Paddling Society
A recreational club offering: kayak lessons for beginners to intermediates, stroke improvement clinics, social activities, summer paddling trips, instructor/ leader courses, equipment rentals, newsletters and lots of fun.

Box 132 Students Union Building
University of Alberta
Edmonton, Alberta T6G 2G7

Phone: (403) 492-9908

Glossary of Terms

access - place to reach the riverside

bedrock - the parent rock material underlying the river

boat entrapment - broaching, pinning, or otherwise lodging the boat in the river where the paddler(s) cannot exit or get free from the craft

bony - a particularly rocky section of river

boulder garden - a rapid or section of river where boulders produce many channels, with convoluted passages

boulder-bed - a river bottom composed of large rocks or boulders

boulderfield - a particularly large or complex boulder garden

braided - a section of river with many islands and different channels

broach - lodging a boat sideways against an obstruction

C-1 - a closed (decked) single whitewater canoe

canoe - a traditional open topped boat

canoeist - a paddler of an open or closed canoe

canyon - a steep-sided, rock-walled section of river

carry - to carry one's boat, usually as a portage

cascade - a low-angled, steep section of river, usually a waterfall

cataract - a very steep section of river with extremely constricted passages

choked - a very constricted section of river, usually with many boulders or logs

chute - a constricted passage where the river drops and is compressed

class - technical rating of a particular rapid or short section of river

clean - a river passage with no rocks in the way on the specific line

closed boat - decked canoes or kayaks

confluence - the meeting of two streams

constriction - a narrowing of the river channel

controlled - a section of river with an upstream dam or other flow control structures

creeking - technical paddling on low-volume streams

crux - the most difficult passage or rapid on a particular section of river or the most difficult move in a rapid

curtain fall - a clean fall with the water falling vertically into the pool, usually with a 90 degree drop off the lip

dam - a flow control structure with a pool created upstream of a blockage in the river

discharge - the river flow volume in cubic feet per second (cfs), or in cubic metres per second (cms)

downstream - the river below a certain point

drop - a particularly steep but short section of river or a single short rapid

eddy - a slowing or reversal of the rivers flow caused by an obstruction in the current

fall - a particularly steep section of river where the river drops freely. The difference between a drop and a fall is the distance the water drops, although this is often an arbitrary difference

333

ferry - crossing the river at an angle to the current to reach the other side

first complete descent - the first time all the rapids on a particular run are paddled

first descent - the first time a section of river is paddled

flatwater - on the river this is a section of calm water with no rapids

flow - the volume of water in the river

foot entrapment - lodging one or both feet in the riverbed such that the person is unable to escape

gauge - a device for measuring the rivers flow

glacial melt - rivers fed by melting of glaciers

gorge - a particularly narrow or deep canyon

grade - the rating for a section of river

gradient - the vertical drop per unit of horizontal distance travelled

gravel-bed - a river bottom composed of small rocks and gravel

gravelbar - gravel deposited in the river channel

grippy - difficult to escape, usually refers to a hole

hairball - a pariculary daring or extreme manoeuvre or section of river

haystack - an exploding wave produced in fast moving deep water where the river is constricted

headwall - a rock outcrop where the river runs directly at the obstruction before turning sharply

hole - the vertical depression formed behind obstructions in the river

hole riding - playing in holes, usually sideways to the current

hydraulic - a particularly strong recirculation in a hole

hydrograph - the discharge of the river plotted over a period of time

ledge - a rock outcrop that produces a short vertical or near vertical drop in the river

line - the path through a rapid

log jam - a pile of logs trapped in the current

log pile - a pile of logs deposited at high flows

logs - dead trees in the river

low-angled - a ramp like drop

mean instantaneous discharge - the average river flow at any given instant

meander - a looping bend in the river

outcrop - exposure of the bedrock

outlet - the point at which a river flows out of a lake

pin - to lodge a boat parallel to the current, usually at a steep drop

pinch - a short, narrow section where the river is constricted

playing - purposefully utilizing features on the river to practice

pool - a calmer section of river backed up by a downstream obstruction

pool-and-drop - a type of river that has sharp drops alternating with calm pools

portage - to carry around a rapid or other feature on the river

pourover - the river backing up against an obstruction, then falling vertically on the downstream side

put-in - the point of entry for a river run

raft - a large stable craft usually built of inflatable chambers

ramp - a low-angled section of river

rapid - a distinct section of constricted or obstructed river where whitewater forms

recirculation - the surface flow that moves upstream below a hole

river left - the left bank when facing downstream

river right - the right bank when facing downstream

riverwide - a feature or obstruction across the entire river

run - a section of river or to paddle a section of river

runoff - surface water flow feeding the river: rain, snowmelt, or glacial melt

scout - to look downstream to determine the best route through a rapid

shoal - a very shallow section of river usually found on the inside of bends

shovey - surging whitewater that is flowing downstream so fast that it pushes the paddler around

shuttle - to move vehicles between the put-in and take-out

snowmelt - river flow fed by melting snow

spillway - the overflow that channels flow over a dam

squirrelly - boiling unpredictable water

stage - the vertical height measurement of the rivers flow

standing waves - exploding waves formed below constrictions or where the gradient decreases

surf - to ride on a wave or hole, lined up more or less parallel to the current

sweeper - an object low to the water which can knock paddlers over

take-out - the point of exit for a river run

technical - convoluted rivers or rapids requiring precise moves around the numerous obstructions

topo map - abbreviation for topographic map

topographic map - a map showing the vertical relief of the area

uncontrolled - a river with no flow control structures upstream

undercut - a rock, bank, or cliff along the river that has a pocket or crevice below the waters surface

unrunnable - a rapid where the height of the drop or a combination of features makes running the rapid impossible

upstream - the river above a certain point

vee - a vee shaped feature when viewed from above

volume - the three dimensional amount of water in the river, expressed per unit of time (e.g.: cubic metres per second)

waterfall - a particularly steep section of river where the river drops freely. The difference between a drop and a fall is the distance the water drops, although this is an arbitrary difference

weir - a river flow control structure, with a very strong recirculation

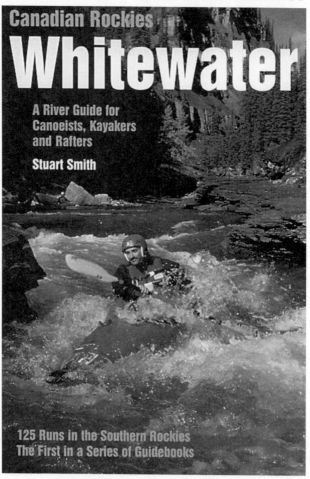
336